**On the City's Rim:
Politics and Policy
in Suburbia**

On the City's Rim: Politics and Policy in Suburbia

Frederick M. Wirt
University of California, Berkeley

Benjamin Walter
Vanderbilt University

Francine F. Rabinovitz
Deborah R. Hensler
University of California,
Los Angeles

D. C. HEATH AND COMPANY
Lexington, Massachusetts • Toronto • London

Clothbound edition published by Lexington Books.

International Standard Book Number: clothbound: 0-669-81976-X
                                    paperbound: 0-669-81968-9

Library of Congress Catalog Card Number: 70-185325

Contents

List of Figures

List of Tables

Foreword

In the recurrent rise and fall of America's urban crisis, as our metropolitan areas struggle to stay on the national agenda, suburbia vies with the central city as the appropriate target for attention. All through the 1950s, the exodus of the World War II veteran from the city produced a spate of commentary on the nature of the mass-produced suburb and the character of the Americans who moved there. In the 1960s, the nation's attention shifted back to the slum, the central city, the ghetto, with the problems made more urgent and more complex by the fact that the majority of urban newcomers were black.

Now it's the suburbs' time again, helped along as new consciousness about the use and misuse of physical space, and by the issue of metropolitan interdependence raised in the ugly politics of school bussing. If we are to deal more effectively with the process of suburban development and the conduct of suburban affairs in the 1970s than we did in the 1950s, we need to have all the knowledge and wisdom we can muster about life just outside the central city.

On the City's Rim takes a giant step beyond the facile, erroneous first assumptions that devalued much of the early suburban analyses. Part solid empirical social science, part explicit policy recommendations, the book explains how our suburbs came to be, why two centuries of changing waves of immigration made a crucial difference in the American urban structure, as compared to that of Europe and Asia, and the high private and public costs we pay now for our heritage. Some of the most cherished myths about subdivision social behavior and tract life style are exploded. The "self-evident" assumption about suburban life that guided so many experts of the 1950s an expectation of a homogeneity of values, mostly middle class, white and business-oriented—is systematically dissected.

Other pieces of folklore disappear too, such as the belief that sharp social and economic differences set central city and suburbs apart. Simultaneously, the popular notion of look-alike suburbs—if you've seen one, you've seen them all—is overturned. The common urge of city neighborhood and suburban town to find community, and the differences that result from the common impulse, is a force that was scarcely identified twenty years ago. The authors' treatment of the black suburb is an especially valuable contribution.

But the major emphasis of the pages that follow is political, and here the contribution is to take us beyond the slender base of evidence on which earlier analyses of suburban attitudes and voting behavior depended. Some of us in the 1950s tried to dispose of the Republican-suburban correlation and discount the "conversion" theory of suburban politics. But of necessity, we relied on scraps of data tied together by heroic logic. Now, in the age of social scientists seasoned in the use of the computer, the data base is comprehensive, the analysis deft and rigorous, and the conclusions substantial. Treating eleven key states, in Presidential elections from 1948 to 1964, the authors dispose first of the impact of suburban location in the Eisenhower years. They examine outcomes in lesser elections and restore the importance of party organization and party competition. They make plain the crucial force of racism and establish the greater tolerance in central city and older suburb. They explore the importance of class differences within a suburban locale in affecting attitude and trust in government.

Most of all, the authors begin the serious treatment of what we called "destiny politics" ten years ago—that is, the suburban decisions governing the use of the land: how zoning, parking, and public housing policies vary predicably according to the type of suburban polity involved.

Introducing complexity in analysis sweeps out the litter of mythology and fallacy. It complicates prescription as well. Here the authors provide a singular service in tracing the steps and missteps of a generation. As one who participated in some of those efforts in effective urban policymaking, I am perhaps more conscious of constraints and more ready to settle for several steps forward rather than abstract recommendations.

But for the first time Professor Francine Rabinovitz makes clear the relation between national party politics and national urban policy, highlights the new importance of black big-city majorities, and calls for differentiation in policy approaches to match differences in suburbs.

That's a difficult assignment for governmental institutions, elected officials, and civil servants. But it is a necessary one if there is to be some prospect for *whole* American cities. Building metropolitan unity from an appreciation of suburban diversity is the theme of this book. Hopefully, it is a course of action this country can recognize, appreciate and undertake to pursue.

Robert Wood

Preface

Following the end of the Second World War, social critics and novelists stumbled upon the American suburb.[a] They saw little to applaud, much to condemn. Their first, and most provocative, charge was to brand the suburbanite a copy-cat. Uprooted from a familiar urban setting and not knowing how to behave in his new social environment, the newcomer mimicked the consumption and leisure patterns of the people next door. Since each new arrival followed the same cues, the alleged result was a stifling homogenization of tastes, activities, and attitudes.

Other critics saw in suburban life the devastation of the family. Because suburban men spent their days working in the city, women were left alone most of the time. Freed from domestic chores by the gadgets that came with affluence, suburban women shed their function as homemakers. In the critical view, the household was made up of a father tangled in rush-hour traffic and a nagging mother perennially harassed by her 2.7 children. Other essayists fumed at the architectural poverty of the mass-produced suburb. Intent on turning a quick profit, the enterprising builder set standardized bungalows on top of concrete slabs, pocketed his fee, and left to commit the same architectural outrage in another tract development ten miles away.

Most disturbing of all to the critics who looked at the census returns, suburban life stood a good chance of becoming universal. For one thing, each census found more people living in suburban belts. What is more, young men and women in their childbearing years accounted for a large proportion of net suburban population growth. With these data in mind, pessimistic critics looked grimly forward to the day when all of the United States would be suburbanized.

In the eyes of many commentators, the shift of population to the suburbs also spelled the end of the Democratic ascendancy. As families abandoned the tenements and row houses of the core city for a new split-level in the suburbs, they also turned away from the Democratic party and began voting for Republican candidates. Moreover, much was said about the conduct of local affairs in these suburbs, which emphasized nonpartisanship and disinterested rationalism as the solvent for all community problems.

[a]E.g., Frederick Allen, "The Big Change in Suburbia," *Harper's Magazine* (June 1954); Hal Burton, "Trouble in the Suburbs," *Saturday Evening Post* (Sept. 1955); R. Gordon, K. Gordon, and M. Gunther, "The Homogeneized Children of the New Suburbia," *New York Times Magazine* (Sept. 19, 1954); Harry Henderson, "The Mass Produced Suburbs," *Harper's Magazine* (November, December 1953); T. James, "Crackups in the Suburbs," *Cosmopolitan* (October 1961); John Keats, *The Crack in the Picture Window* (Boston: Houghton Mifflin, 1956); Alice Miel, *The Shortchanged Children of Suburbia* (New York: Institute of Human Relations, American Jewish Committee, 1968); A.C. Spectorsky, *The Exurbanites* (Phila.: Lippincott, 1955); William H. Whyte, *The Organization Man* (New York: Simon and Schuster, 1956); Peter Wyden, *Suburbia's Coddled Kids* (Garden City, N.Y.: Doubleday, 1960).

This book is about the political consequences of massive suburbanization. Throughout we use the Census Bureau definition of "suburb," although alternative definitions change the results very little, as we will show. In Part One, Wirt and Walter present an historical and demographic sketch of American suburbs, with a special chapter on the phenomenon of the black suburb. In Part Two, they examine the behavior of the suburban electorate since the end of World War II. In Part Three, Hensler explores attitudinal differences between city and suburb on a variety of public issues. Parts Four and Five consider public policies affecting life in the suburbs. In Part Four, Walter and Wirt explore local conflicts over slating and electing candidates for local office, forms of government, and issues involving money, zoning, and schooling. In Part Five, Rabinovitz examines the nature of and need for national policy towards suburbia in the last few decades.

At one time, commentators feared that the mere fact of suburban residence would inevitably produce a sort of suburban "mass man." On our journey beyond the city's rim, we will show the rich diversity of living styles, the remarkable sensitivity of suburbanites to national election moods, the attitudinal linkages of status which span the jurisdictional lines dividing city from suburb, how the domestic politics of suburban communities have responded to massive immigration, and the first fumbling efforts of the national government to realize what the suburban diffusion implies for public policy.

FMW
BW
FFR
DRH

Acknowledgments

No work of this scope can proceed without the support and encouragement of many agencies and colleagues. Some provided financing, others data from private collections, and still others helpful criticism of early drafts.

Frederick Wirt offers especial note of the support of the Institute of Governmental Studies, University of California, Berkeley, and its director, Eugene C. Lee. He also received support from the Denison University Research Foundation and the International City Managers Association. Critical assistance was provided by Aaron Wildavsky and Victor Jones.

Benjamin Walter acknowledges financial support from the Vanderbilt University Research Council and the ICMA. Ben W. Bolch, Neidhard Fuchs, Timothy Schiltz, Marian Wambley, and Joseph Zikmund II provided searching criticism and other help. He and Wirt acknowledge research assistance for the case studies in chapters 10-12 prepared by students at Denison University (Julia Everitt, Diane Downs, Barry Roseman, Karen Asselta, Thomas Stege, Richard Carson) and at the University of California, Berkeley (Alan Greenwald, Neil Naliboff, Lauren LeRoy). Virginia Kennedy's MA work at Vanderbilt University is acknowledged in chapter 9.

Francine Rabinovitz's initial investigation of the impact of national policy on suburbs was conducted with support from the Housing Subcommittee, U.S. House Committee on Banking And Currency, in 1970-71; the Committee claims no responsibility for ideas expressed here. She also notes appreciation for assistance from reviews and ideas provided by Steve Erie, Paul Halpern, John Kirlin, Gary Schwartz, and Robert Wood.

Deborah R. Hensler gratefully acknowledges the support of the UCLA Survey Research Center in providing her with the opportunity to field questions in the Los Angeles metropolitan area survey, computer time, and general staff support. In particular, she would like to thank her husband, Carl P. Hensler, for his critical and methodological assistance, encouragement and endurance.

All of us appreciate the training and skills brought to the task of preparing our index by Diane Baerwald.

**Part 1
History and Social
Demography**

1 Suburban Origins

The trek to the suburbs that began after World War II has turned into one of the largest population movements in our history. Commentators gloomily forecast that this development would produce a "mass man," as if both the movers and their life in suburbia were churned into a homogeneous pulp. This book explores how accurate this analysis was over the quarter-century since 1945, and how suburbia stands today, both demographically and politically, on the rim of the city. Most centrally, we are concerned with the degree of difference between the political and policy worlds of city and suburb.

First, a caution as to definitions. Nowhere does the Bureau of the Census specify any firm criteria that can be uniformly used in delimiting suburbs. Consequently, the term wobbles from one tacit usage to another. Some scholars identify suburbs with the portion of the *SMSA* (Standard Metropolitan Statistical Area) that lies outside the political boundaries of the core city. Others equate them with the densely settled *urbanized area* that spreads away from the core city, a residue that is generally called the "urban fringe." Briefly, the SMSA assembles the core city and the predominantly nonagricultural *counties* it borders into one unit; the urbanized area contains the core city and the *closely settled area* outside it. The urban fringe generally covers a smaller area than the non-core city residue of the SMSA, which takes in entire counties.[1] (One SMSA spreads across a mass of land larger than four New England states.)

It is not known how shifting from one classification to another will alter empirical research, although the possibility worries many scholars. Despite all the fretting, there are firm grounds for concluding that variations would be negligible. For one thing, only a small fraction of the entire population of the SMSA lives outside the urban fringe. Even more substantial conclusions may be inferred from the efforts of Hadden and Borgatta, who showed high correlation between SMSAs and urbanized areas on a wide variety of measures, taken one at a time and statistically aggregated into various factors.[2] The only really large disparities occurred on measures relating to area and population density. That is to be logically expected, as the authors note. For once the population in the SMSA builds up to the density specified by the Census Bureau, it will automatically become part of the urban fringe.

To be circumspect, we will distinguish among the usages. When we say SMSA, we mean SMSA. When we deal with social and political characteristics of particular suburban municipalities, we will be talking about communities that fall within the urban fringe and, of course, the more inclusive SMSA. Where the data are

LANE LIBRARY
RIPON COLLEGE
RIPON WISCONSIN 54971

available, we will take care to distinguish urban fringe from the more thinly populated segment. Our references to suburbs in western civilization deal with places—sometimes quite small—just outside the city walls; our guides here are set not by the Census Bureau but by scholars of the era. The term is traced from the Latin *suburbium* through Old French *surburbe* to Middle English *suburb* and directly on into the modern era. In all eras, the meaning corresponds to the original—near the city—and the term's historical ubiquity marks also the continuing presence of such places in urban life.

It is important, then, to begin this study within a historical framework, because much of the post-World War II suburban critique hastily assumed suburbs were an entirely new and distinctive pattern of human settlement. But they appeared alongside the first cities in world history and have always been present, if not always prominent, in the social ecology of urban America. To gain a clearer perspective on the contemporary American scene, then, it is well to keep the broad sweep of urban history firmly in mind.

Early Suburbs

Suburbs cropped up around the rim of core cities many centuries before the birth of Jesus. In Mesopotamia, men of wealth and high social rank dwelt within city walls. Workers and farmers lived in suburbs outside the battlements that guarded treasure and grain from marauders. Riches and status piled up in the protected city while the poor hazarded life outside, an inversion of the pattern popularly associated with American suburbs. In those early times, as Hoffer has urged, suburbs sheltered dropouts from the vital life of the city, the basic force shaping early civilizations. Later on, the city began to assume a characteristically modern form. As the Roman army was able to guarantee the peace of the countryside, the rich could break away from the city, leaving behind its noise and odor. Some lived more or less regularly on manorial estates; others summered in hillside villas. But only a small proportion of city dwellers could afford such a move, and many of those who could still spent much of their time in the city for residence, entertainment, politicking, and commerce. For it was here that the managerial skills and political decisions that formed the essence of the Roman way of life were developed and carried out.[3]

With the dismantling of the Roman Empire came the destruction of cities that once had prospered under the protection of Roman legions. As a consequence, the urban organization of social life declined. Although approximately 10 percent of the population could be called urban, most of the cities sheltered no more than 6,000 permanent inhabitants.[4] Even so, suburbs began to cluster around these tiny medieval settlements. Merchants seeking access to local markets and protection from bandits set up bazaars and workshops in untilled fields ringing the towns. During the eleventh and twelfth centuries, self-governing asso-

ciations of wealthier merchants hired masons to erect fortified walls around these open suburbs. As one suburb after another shut itself off from the open country, temporary shops and factories became permanent. Thus protected, merchants were no longer compelled to seek the safety of the old enclosed city when night fell. Finally, walled suburbs were splayed out all around the circumference of the old city, engulfing it. The slender spires of old episcopal cathedrals that once rose majestically over the old city were now lost in a jumbled heap of shops, factories, warehouses, and masonry. No longer needed for protection, the original city walls were torn down or left to decay.[5]

Suburbs in Colonial America

When the Old World invaded the New, the men carried across the seas by the British merchant companies were primarily farmers, not villagers. This was no accident, for the land did not produce a surplus generous enough to feed large numbers of city dwellers. Later, as farm yields increased, small villages did grow up here and there amidst a predominantly rural terrain. At first, these urban sites were used less for commerce than for important way stations and ports of entry for new immigrants headed towards the open interior. For example, most of the goods traded with England and the continent never moved through the larger colonial ports. They were shipped directly from plantation wharves in the Tidewater South and from deep coves further up the shore.[6]

Of all the colonial cities, only Boston was able to dominate its hinterlands. Towns in Maine, upper Massachusetts, Rhode Island, and Connecticut established regular commercial relationships with Boston, which by 1690 was a city of some 7,000 people. From these towns, cattle and sheep were driven overland to Boston; the first American cowboy was a New Englander. Trappers in upper New England traded beaver pelts in Boston, while farmers brought grain, fresh vegetables, and other produce to sell or barter. On their return trip they carried dry goods, whiskey, ammunition, and a few luxury goods to moderate the harsh life of the up-country. Little towns which now are Boston neighborhoods were independent suburbs three hundred years ago. Even at that time their welfare was tightly knit to the commercial development of Boston. Ipswich supplied Boston with the beef its citizens consumed. From Malden, Hingham, and Weymouth came timber used in building houses and mansions for Bostonians.[7]

The suburbs of colonial Boston supplied more than commodities for city consumption; some provided recreation. The suburban resort town is not a product of later affluence. Increase Mather and his son Cotton went to the "noated" Red Spring at Lynn, reputed to have remarkable therapeutic properties for easing the miseries of ague.[8] Prosperous colonial townsmen reached out into the countryside in their quest for comfortable living space. In Newport, an aristocracy emerged as sons and daughters of the wealthy intermarried. First these families built town houses within the city limits, finally resplendent manors and mansions in the open country. By 1675, a third of all Newport's houses sat outside the city.[9]

As the seventeenth century ended, suburbs outside New England cities had already been functionally differentiated, each specializing in the goods and services it offered for sale. Some gave the gentry the opportunity to display its fortunes; some were vacation spots; and others exported commodities to the metropolitan core. Seventeenth century suburban developments began to trace a pattern that was more sharply etched during the century that followed. The prosperous suburban town is often seen as a relatively modern invention, but Bridenbaugh's careful examination of colonial population movements showed that people who could shoulder the expense were leaving the city as early as 1700. As the center of Philadelphia became congested with tanneries and choked by dust, many drifted away to nearby suburbs. Benjamin Franklin, for one, found that he could not live an urbane life in urban surroundings, complaining that the din made him "say some things twice over."[10] An earlier "flight to the suburbs" created such towns as Moyamensing, Passyunk, Northern Liberties, Chevy Chase, Kensington, and Southwark. In Southwark, a syndicate of speculators carved up a big parcel of property into small lots for residential construction. They also persuaded the city fathers to provide the neighborhood with a market, helping, as Bridenbaugh notes, to "move their real estate."[11] All this occurred in 1745, exactly two centuries before the Levitt brothers began building suburban communities on farmed-out potato fields and fallow pasturelands.

In New York, population slowly ebbed away from the areas of densest concentration. It would have moved faster had the land not been held as a monopoly by a government which sold parcels only when revenue was needed. By 1750, what is now mid-Manhattan was dotted by country estates, which were later razed for tenements, boarding houses, and apartment buildings.[12]

As suburbs developed a political and communal life of their own, some of their inhabitants came to resent the political control exerted by the big city they bordered. As early as 1735, the outlying communities around Boston sought unsuccessfully to detach themselves from the county government. A similar effort occurred seven years later in Newport; freeholders "from the woods part of Newport" sought to rid themselves of domination by the established oligarchy in "the compact part of town." They enjoyed little success. The town meeting, whose jurisdiction extended to the suburbs, was run by prosperous men from the big city. The wealthy seized the offices, retained them, and used their authority to frustrate nearby country folk.[13] Men living outside the old city thought they were paying too much for too little. They chafed at prices charged by governments for municipal services and grumbled at the lack of adequate market space. Thus, early in American urban life may be seen the mutual suspicion between city core and suburban ring.

As conditions of the colonial market economy heightened the interdependence of city and suburb, the consequences of public and private decisions spread across the whole network of purposeful action. There were, to use the economist's language, "external effects" or "externalities" rolled up in the decisions of city fathers to charge suburban merchants fees for city services. Cutting into the merchants' profit margins, fees adversely affected their welfare, but charging suburban merchants more meant that the city fathers could charge urban residents less. Today, of course, the network of dense causal connections is far more pronounced and inclusive, but their origins may be traced to the colonial era.

Other harbingers of the twentieth century are to be seen in the suburban life of the eighteenth. In 1727, businessmen built an iron furnace in Durham, a suburb of Bucks County, the first intimation of an industrial suburb. Philadelphia eventually dominated a local market economy that tied together counties in Maryland, Delaware, and western New Jersey. The stern city fathers of Philadelphia deplored the lax moral standards of some of its suburbs. Society Hill, just south of the city, became a suburban sin spot as early as 1712, when youngbloods enjoyed the illicit pleasures of wagering on horses and baiting bulls.[14] In much the same way, people today in Cincinnati bridle at the suburbs of Newport and Covington across the Ohio River in Kentucky.

Although each major American city had suburban settlements, only a very small proportion of the nation's population lived there. Suburbs presuppose cities, but at that time very few people lived in cities. In 1790, only twenty-four cities housed more than 2,500 people, and only one had more than 40,000. Altogether, cities accounted for just about 5 percent of the entire American population. Furthermore, the rhythm and pace of population movement to the suburbs were tethered by the tight ratio of space to time. Suburban spread was held to the distance one could comfortably travel. Not only were coach and horse slow and undependable, they were so expensive that only a few could regularly afford them. In this era population dribbled out to the suburbs. Even so, certain themes which were to be repeated again and again in every portion of the country were already visible: the suburbanite's distaste for the crush and hubbub of the city, his fear of metropolitan political control, and, most important, functional differentiation between city and suburb. Those who had no other options stayed in the city; men who could bear the cost settled on the land beyond.

Suburbs in the New Nation

In the nineteenth century, the city became more important in the life of the nation. By 1820, thirteen cities numbered at least 8,000 inhabitants. Although the pressure of growth was most intense downtown, it was indirectly reflected in the dispersion of homesites to the periphery of the old city. As commercial and industrial enterprises bid frenetically for land at the center of the city, it became much too expensive to accommodate land-extensive residential uses. Landowners sold their homes on the fringe of the old business district and used the proceeds to build new houses on the outskirt of the city, where land was cheaper. By and large, suburban diffusion of this era selected the middle class, leaving the very poor and the very rich behind. Because fierce competition for real estate drove up the price of land, apartments and houses originally designed for one or two families were cut up to provide housing for many. As this occurred, the core of the old city became daily more congested, and the poor were compelled to live their lives amidst great squalor. The rich, who could afford to hold on to their town houses and mansions, chose to live in downtown neighborhoods far enough away from the factory and the railhead to be insulated from grime, smoke, and noise, yet close enough to enjoy the cultural facilities they patronized.[15]

We can see all of this as early as 1819 when advertisements in New York newspapers lured families to Brooklyn, "a select neighborhood, for a summer's residence or a whole year's." A steam ferry that plied the East River between Manhattan Island and Queens did much to stimulate the growth of this suburban village. Thus a man was encouraged to live in Brooklyn and work in Manhattan. It was a seller's market, possibly because of such alluring advertisements as this one, printed in 1823:

... being the nearest country retreat, and easiest of access from the centre of business that now remains unoccupied; the distance not exceeding an average of fifteen to twenty-five minutes' walk, including the passage of the river; the ground elevated and perfectly healthy at all seasons; views of water and landscape both extensive and beautiful; as a place of residence. . . [it has] . . . all the advantages of the country with most of the conveniences of the city.[16]

Modernize the language, and you have something that a contemporary entrepreneur pushing "Edge-o'-Woods Manor" might place in a metropolitan newspaper. All the familiar themes are there: the rustic appeal of living close to nature, a short trip from homesite to workplace, and a picturesque view that puts a worried man at his ease.

Further up the Atlantic shore, the growth of central Boston opened suburban lands to residential settlement. In 1804 forests south of Boston were optimistically felled for construction of cheap housing. The effort was premature, for the cleared land stood largely idle for three decades. But as competition for space increased the price of land in downtown Boston, lower suburban rentals eventually offset the discomfort of a longer walk to and from work. Many little towns around Boston, some by now a full century old, began to fill up and grow—Charlestown, Cambridge, East Boston, Roxbury.

These suburbs were not all bedroom cities for a swelling and prosperous middle class seeking relief from discomforts of a crowded city. Their class composition was heterogeneous. Some residents did commute to work at respectable jobs downtown. But other suburbs housed manual workers, who accompanied industry and manufacturing that had been driven out to the fringes of Boston Harbor as land downtown became more expensive.[17] These were among the earliest industrial suburbs, whose importance in the fabric of American life has been obscured by the attention given wealthier residential suburbs.

Suburbs also popped up around cities newly founded across the Appalachian range. In 1806 a traveler to Lexington could write that the "country [around it] had insensibly assumed the appearance of an approach to a city."[18] So much urban growth had spilled over into its suburbs that almost half the entire population of Pittsburgh lived in such little surrounding villages as Alleghany and East Liberty. Two thousand of Cincinnati's population lived in neighboring settlements, and suburbs grew up along axial roads converging on St. Louis.

In only a few river cities was the territorial demarcation between city and suburbs so clear as it was in Pittsburgh, where the Alleghany and Monongahela held the downtown area to river flats, while suburbs hugged both sides of surrounding hills. From the brow of one of these hills, a traveler wrote of the "city [that] lay beneath . . . enveloped in smoke—the clang of hammers resounded from numerous manufactories . . . churches, courts, hotels, and markets and all the 'pomp and circumstance' of busy life were presented in one panoramic view. [Yet on the other side of the hills] were all the silent soft attractions of rural living."[19] Overcome by the panoramic view, this traveler failed to write about Pittsburgh's industrial suburbs, with their cotton mills, iron works, and glass factories.

Wade's *The Urban Frontier* notes the ubiquity of suburbs in the Old Northwest.[20] Covington and Newport on the Kentucky side of the Ohio River laid out their streets as continuations of those in Cincinnati, as if no river came between. Writing about Cincinnati in the mid-nineteenth century, an observer noted the existence of different kinds of suburbs. There were industrial suburbs for entrepreneurs seeking "cheap rents and ample space" for factories and warehouses near the city and the river. Some suburbs offered inexpensive lots for families who wanted to leave the city, and some families moved out to benefit from lower suburban taxes.

The rise of Louisville may also be measured by the growth of its suburbs. By 1810 it was already a transportation and market hub for the entire region. Indeed, so strained were its harbor and warehouse facilities that overflow traffic had to be accommodated at Shippingport and Portland, suburbs two miles away, while across the river in Indiana, Jeffersonville and New Albany were also increasingly drawn in. In time, political boundaries began to honor economic interdependence. Shippingport and Portland lost their separate identities and were absorbed by Louisville, just as Pittsburgh annexed Alleghany and St. Louis swallowed St. Genevieve.

Occasionally, relationships between the central city and the suburbs became strained, even bitter. Some city dwellers accused suburban residents of freeloading on the city. For their part, many suburbanites could detect no benefits from city expenditures. In 1813, Lexington officials encountered resistance in collecting taxes from suburbanites who "alleged that no benefit resulted to them from either the Watch, Lamps, fire-buckets or fire companies." Officials in Cincinnati muttered that residents on the edge of town did not yield up "their quantum of taxes." In 1829, a desperate St. Louis council petitioned the Missouri legislature to consent to the incorporation of some outlying areas because they revelled in "all the benefits of City residence without any of its burdens . . . although the evil is now in its infancy it promises to increase greatly in the next few years and produce much evil."

By mid-nineteenth century, suburban dispersion was a characteristic by-product of urban growth. Wherever cities had developed, suburbs had grown up around them. In 1850, Chicago had more than sixty, most of them residential, with firm economic ties to the city from the very beginning as homesites for part of the city's labor supply. Overall, however, the size of the population living in the suburbs was still not large, as transportation costs were still restrictive. Only a few could afford the daily fare for commuting to Chicago.

The Late Nineteenth Century

If this process reads like current events, it is well to recall that we are now describing conditions of a century ago. Flight from the eighteenth century city had been spurred by a rural ideal which from the first had attracted Americans. It was that the citizen could somehow reclaim the placid amenities of the countryside if he were able to spend some of his time there. Even though his work bound him to pavement and factory loft from eight to six every day but Sunday, he could still spend the rest of his time with his family in a semi-rural environment "far from the madding crowd" of the city. True, the suburbanite needed the city to earn his livelihood, but in his private life with family and neighbors he could enjoy surroundings untouched by the industry and commerce that provided his income.

Movement to the suburbs was furthered by a mode of transportation less tiring than walking but cheaper and more adaptable than the railroad. Warner has painstakingly traced the impact of new transportation systems on the growth of Boston suburbs.[21] Until 1850, people employed in downtown Boston or any city had to walk to work. In this pedestrian city, the row houses and triple-deckers of less well-to-do Bostonians extended about 2.5 miles out from City Hall, no more than a forty minute walk for a man in his prime. However, between 1850 and 1870 horse-drawn trolley cars added another mile or so to the commutation radius, which almost doubled the area available for home construction. As the electric streetcar gradually replaced the horse-drawn trolley, public transportation lines probed still further into the thinly populated country, again doubling the area for building sites.

The expansion of Boston was in large measure due to the new mode of transportation. Early Boston was a compact city, with only the prosperous able to afford suburban homesites. Next, in the era of the steam train affluent settlements clustered around railroad stops at intervals of five miles or so, for it was impractical for the steam-driven train to stop more frequently. In this way the rich suburbs that hugged the rails were spaced out like pearls on a knotted cord. Then, the streetcar lines that spread away from central Boston like spokes of a wheel encouraged a much denser pattern of settlement. Since streetcars normally stopped at every other corner, buildings were put up on either side of the tracks in a continuous strip. After a time, real estate operators built a second row of houses and stores behind the first. Finally, as land close to the lines filled up with detached houses, churches, playgrounds, and stores, streets and blocks crisscrossed much of the area between spokes.

The new suburbanites formed a swelling middle class propelled outwards by what was happening to the city they once had inhabited. By 1900, Greater Boston was a divided city with its concentric social geography resembling a dart board. In town lived low-income families jammed together in dreary railroad flats or rotting three-deckers, an area gripped by decay and blight. It was also a Balkan patchwork of ethnic neighborhoods. Where one enclave touched another, street gangs fought for control of the border, a social process James T. Farrell has recorded for Chicago in the *Studs Lonigan* trilogy. Next out, in a band surrounding the old central city, lived middle-class families in detached housing. Even in this band, areas were differentiated by social class. Just beyond the inner core were modest homes of the lower-middle class; beyond that, the suburbs inhabited by a more secure middle class.

In the green ring furthest away from the tumult of central city lived the patricians. Counterparts of Boston's Brookline were to be found pitched out on the far rim of many American cities—Chicago's Lake Forest, Philadelphia's Chestnut Hill, San Francisco's Burlingame, and New York's Tuxedo Park and Old Greenwich, Connecticut. One community symbol of social identity that differentiated these outlying suburbs from their neighbors further in was the country club where the rich met weekends and holidays to gossip, dine, and play golf.[22] The pattern was not uniform. Some of the wealthy were hesitant to desert the central city their forebears were thought to have founded. So long as the opera and theatre were downtown, many found suburban life tranquil but enervating. Because slum areas were compact and relatively localized, the patricians could remain aloof by sequestering themselves in such prim downtown neighborhoods as Beacon Hill in Boston, Murray Hill in New York City, and Rittenhouse Square in Philadelphia.

But, overall, the procession to the suburbs reflected a pervasive social mobility. Sons and daughters began to infiltrate the suburbs a little more than a generation after their impoverished parents emerged from steerage. By 1900 in Boston, and in other urban centers as well, there had emerged features of urban life that are familiar to the mid-twentieth century American. They are all chronicled in the development of Boston: the dormitory suburbs segregated by income and occupation; the speed with which entire downtown neighborhoods complete the round of birth, growth, and senescence; and a bursting of the metropolis that devastates inherited boundaries.

Along with the commuter colony, there developed another type of suburb in the last quarter of the century. It was called a "Milltown" long before a public relations man hit upon calling it an "Industrial Park." For reasons of economy, large-scale industry sought to concentrate all the physical facilities of production and distribution in one central place. Slowly it was forced to leave the old downtown, whose harbors, warehouses, cramped factory lofts, and congested streets could no longer accommodate sharply increased demands for space. Outside the city, manufacturing plants cropped up near a wharfside or new rail spur. Vacant land in Brooklyn was used as a site for light industry. Once a well-to-do and pleasant suburb, Brooklyn was invaded by dock and factory workers who wanted to live close to their places of work. The residential suburb separated family from workplace; the industrial suburb spliced them together.

In other places, where a new social structure was not rudely and suddenly superimposed upon an existing pattern, the industrial suburb was more homogeneous. Workers lived in suburban "company towns," bought staples from company stores on company credit and at company prices. The population was set in a grid around the focus of community existence, the factory whose smokestacks dominated the landscape, at times threatening to conceal it entirely. Thus, in 1881, Andrew Carnegie moved his Bessemer steel plant to Homestead, just outside Pittsburgh. Mills and factories that fabricated steel and other semi-finished goods popped up all around the city rim in Duquesne, McKeesport, Aliquippa, and Ambridge. Further west, Granite City, Alton, and East St. Louis all bordered St. Louis; Cudahy became an industrial satellite of Milwaukee; Gary and East Chicago adjoined Chicago; and Barberton became a manufacturing suburb for Akron, itself already heavily industrialized.

The millworker lived a depressing existence in these suburban slagheaps which were possibly the first planned communities in the United States. The grinding monotony of working ten to twelve hours a day, six days a week, left little time to enjoy the libraries Carnegie erected in more favored settings. The houses were all alike, their unremitting monotony of style a mute testimonial to the economies of standardization. We are inclined to see labor-management strife as a characteristically urban phenomenon, but some of the bloodier pages of American industrial history have been written in such industrial suburbs as Homestead, Pennsylvania; Pullman, Illinois; and Gastonia, North Carolina.[23]

Conclusion

In this chapter we have tried to sketch briefly the role which suburbs have played in the social ecology of the American metropolitan region up to the twentieth century. At the minimum, it is important to recognize that suburbs are not a twentieth century innovation. What is novel about suburbs is the concern they have evoked over the past two decades. After all, our social history has been told as a biography of American cities, a narrative of urban places undergoing convulsive changes of technology and population composition. Because cities have loomed so large in the writing of American social history, their shadow has tended to blur the development that has always taken place on the fringe.

Initially, suburbs produced goods and services for inhabitants of the neighboring city to consume, and provided solitude and elbow room for the well-to-do, men who had time of their own and the money to enjoy it. Later, immigrants and new modes of transportation decreased the attractiveness of aging urban centers for people whose ancestors had been raised in the city. As railroad and trolley lines opened up suburban land for the commuter trade, a greater variety of socially distinguishable suburbs appeared. Each suburb that sat astride new facilities of public transportation housed a somewhat different mix of people—all, however, seeking permanent relief from urban congestion and disarray. The price of housing segregated the suburban population, with each income class settling in the suburb it could best afford. The wealthiest, for whom constraints of time and money mattered the least, lived furthest away from the city. Somewhat closer lived the solid and secure middle class, cordoned off from exclusive suburbs by the high price of land. Suburbs in the ring just outside the old city line were filled by those who had just made it into the middle class, some of whom occupied housing recently surrendered by men who had made enough money to afford something better.

There were industrial suburbs as well. Unable to assemble large parcels of cleared land in the crowded city core, manufacturers began to seek vacant suburban land along a rail spur or near a dockside. A portion of the industrial labor force joined the drift of industry to the suburbs. Lacking the income for a better house and more pleasant surroundings, employees lived in dreary slums backed up right to the factory gates.

Suburban growth, as everyone knows, has been accelerating over the first seven decades of the twentieth century, and there is no reason to predict that it will soon stop. It would be a mistake, however, to conclude that decentralization of jobs and homesites is unique to this century. There has been no sharp break with the past, but simply a continuation and accentuation of patterns that were forming over a century ago.

2

**Growth in Twentieth
Century Suburbs**

Sources of Urban Growth

The Foreign Immigrants

Great movements of people have helped shape the social structure of the United States. One of these was the arrival of European immigrants. Some became sod-busters on open prairies; others farmed rich bottomlands threading into the Mississippi River basin. But many more settled in aging sections of established seaboard cities, or added to the growing population of raw urban centers in the North Central states.

The immigrants were not greeted with any great warmth by the old settlers; no Welcome Wagon met them at the tenement door in Little Italy, Paddyville, or the ghettos.[1] The natives resented and feared these aliens who swamped core city neighborhoods. Coming to the city in massive numbers, immigrants strained public facilities and services designed for another era. Knowing nothing of refuse collection, they dumped their rubbish in any convenient open space, and their pushcarts choked streets built barely wide enough to accommodate a pair of horse-drawn wagons. As the city's population increased, aldermen had to wrestle with old problems quickly built up to a new and formidable scale by the pressure exerted by sheer numbers of people: how to finance enough policemen, firemen, jails, schools, hospitals, law courts, and reservoirs to absorb increased demands for public services.

Worse, the newcomers' conduct seemed to disregard conventional distinctions separating private place and public thoroughfare. Leaning out of tenement windows, mothers scolded their rowdy children playing outside, and old-clothes dealers, scissors-grinders and icemen noisily hawked their wares in the streets. Around pushcarts lining the curbstones, peddlers higgled and chaffered with their customers, transforming the street into an open-air bazaar. The cultural and moral standards of the host society made no room for the life-styles aliens favored. For people living in neighborhoods that backed up into rapidly developing immigrant enclaves, the arrival of the newcomers was unsettling.

Not all of this symbolized conflict *between* ethnic groups; some of it reflected differences *within* the same group. Thus the earlier wave of genteel German Jews were scandalized by the new immigrants coming from Russia and Poland. They wore outlandish clothes; their manners were outrageous; and they were suspected of dark socialistic plots. The German Jews in New York City

15

financed settlement houses so that the shabby immigrants might be reshaped "along what the Germans considered 'acceptable' German lines—to clean the immigrants up, dust them off, and get them to behave and look as much like Americans as possible," according to Birmingham.

As the immigrants came, the natives left. The second half of the nineteenth century brought enormous changes in urban patterns. As impoverished immigrants crowded into the city, older citizens became alarmed by the physical disarray that seemed to accompany their arrival. Feeling that their old, familiar city was being vandalized by immigrant hordes, many older citizens surrendered their aging flats and left the city for the suburb. Those who could stand the greater time and money costs of living in more distant suburbs settled there. Others less well off moved to the inner ring of suburbs on the rim of the city. Here at least there were yards and trees. Seeking to recreate an accustomed pattern of life in another city neighborhood, they traded a longer streetcar trip to and from work for more space and comfort.

The inner city they left behind had dissolved into a patchwork of crowded ethnic enclaves, the end of one lapping against the beginning of another. The spacious apartments and brownstones they vacated were sliced up by real estate operators into small flats. Even unventilated cellars and attics, once used only for storage, were converted into seamy living quarters for families fresh off the boat. Each ragged square in the patchwork developed its own network of community facilities which proclaimed its distinct ethnic identity: restaurants, saloons, burial societies, shops and pushcarts, churches and synagogues, settlement houses, charities, and workingmen's associations. Now that these sections have been domesticated, visitors tour them and admire their quaintness. When they were first established, many contemporaries viewed them as catastrophes.

Scholars have recorded the profound impact transatlantic migrations registered on the size and social composition of the American city. From 1880 to 1890, Chicago doubled in size, going from 500,000 people to over a million. Further north, the population of the twin cities of St. Paul and Minneapolis experienced a threefold increase in the same decade, and the number of people living in Detroit, Milwaukee, Columbus, and Cleveland grew by 80 percent. As immigrants poured in, the 1890 urban population surged to almost one-third the total. In that year, every fifth person living in an American city had been born abroad. In some older cities, the proportion of foreign-born inched even higher, reaching a fourth in Philadelphia and a third in Boston. Only Berlin and Hamburg housed more Germans than Chicago, and for every Irishman in Dublin two more lived in New York City. Jews crammed into tenements of New York's Lower East Side were half as numerous as the Jews of Warsaw.[2]

The Native Migrants

Internal migrations have also increased the size and diversity of the American city. Throughout our history, streams of people have deserted farms and moribund rural trading centers for the city. The clue to the swelling migration from farm to city lies in the increasing interdependence of farm and city. Exported from industrial cities to the countryside, farm mechanization made much manual labor redundant and expensive. It also profoundly altered the pattern of land tenure by encouraging the amalgamation of many small farms into large landholdings, for mechanization requires land-extensive farming. As they were displaced, hired help and tenant farmers left for the city. Then, too, both World Wars produced serious urban labor shortages, helping to draw surplus agricultural labor into the cities. Such forces in the four decades between 1920 and 1960 increased the *net* migration from farm to city to nearly 27 million, helping to swell the city population and deplete the rural.

For native migrants, as for alien immigrants, misery, privation, and discrimination often accompanied the transition from soil to asphalt. Since the migrant's skin was so often black, his coming stimulated deep racial antagonisms. The longer view is often the ironic view. Grandchildren of the tenement generation whose arrival alarmed the old settlers are now restless about the blacks who threaten to invade their neighborhoods. A "neighborhood going downhill" is a neighborhood going black. As one generation has given way to another, yesterday's greenhorns have evolved into today's old settlers. Those who can afford the option, as we shall later see, join the suburban drift, repeating the same social process their forefathers set in motion two generations earlier.

The Metropolis and the Suburb

Fed by tributary streams of immigrants and migrants, the share of the nation's population living in or near cities has grown geometrically, doubling itself every fifty or sixty years.[3] Looking only at the last half century of this progression, we find that only about a third of the population at the turn of the century lived in metropolitan areas (see Table 2-1). Sixty years later, more than three Amer-

Table 2-1

Distribution of the Population in Metropolitan Areas, 1910-1966

Year	Population in Millions	Percentage of U.S. Population	Percentage of Metropolitan Population in Central Cities
1900	24.1	32	67
1910	34.5	38	66
1920	46.1	44	66
1930	61.0	50	64
1940	67.1	51	62
1950	85.6	57	58
1960	111.9	62	51
1966	123.8	63	47

icans in every five lived somewhere in one of the nation's metropolitan complexes, which concentrated a large proportion of the nation's population on a small fraction of its vast land mass. Despite all the anguished chatter about "metropolitan sprawl" engirdling what it is unable to devastate, there is actually more woodland east of the Mississippi River today than there was a century ago.[4]

Dramatic as has been this metropolitan growth, another population shift has been occurring *within* the metropolis. People from both core cities and rural areas have poured into suburban rings, shrinking the city's share of metropolitan population. Large cities reached their peak populations before the Great Depression; they have been declining ever since. In the first three decades of the century, core cities had a population almost twice as large as their suburban rings. At first they were able to hold their own because their growth rates outpaced population increases in the hinterlands. But between 1920 and 1930, growth rates of the suburban belt first equalled and then overtook those in the core cities narrowing the difference in absolute size between the two segments of the metropolitan population.

From then on, the gap in growth rates has progressively widened in favor of suburbs. From 1940 to 1950, suburbs grew at twice the annual rate of central cities. In the next decade, the ratio doubled again, and between 1960 and 1966, yearly suburban growth rates averaged 3.1 percent in contrast to an annual core city increase of 0.5 percent, a ratio slightly in excess of 6 to 1.[5] By 1960, the central core's edge in size had almost vanished, and, by the end of 1966, more people lived in the suburban belt than in the core.

Furthermore, only a very small proportion of total metropolitan growth can be chalked up to the largest cities. Most of the increase has occurred in smaller complexes. In 1930, the twelve largest metropolitan aggregations accounted for 24.4 percent of the nation's population. Growth over the next three decades pushed this figure up an additional 1.9 percent, much smaller than the overall metropolitan growth increment of 12 percent during the same period.[6] In 1960, 159 of the 212 Standard Metropolitan Statistical Areas had fewer than a half-million people. All but five ringed cities numbering fewer than 250,000; of these, almost two-thirds (101 of 154) had no more than 100,000. Of 282 American cities in the 50,000 to 250,000 population range, only 164 were counted by the Census Bureau as core cities. Most of the rest were themselves suburbs lying outside a metropolitan core.[7]

Demographers and ecologists confidently expect continued suburban growth as the spokes and arcs of cobwebbing highways constantly expand the supply of land within reach of the core city. One projection concludes that over 113 million Americans will live in the suburbs by 1985, a sum greater than the entire population of the United States in 1920.[8]

Housing and Business

*Growth in Transportation and
Housing*

In the last quarter of the nineteenth century, the streetcar made suburban homesites available along the rim of the old city. Those who could afford higher costs
of railroad commutation lived somewhat further away in settlements that clustered around train stations. The twentieth century saw automobiles, trucks and a
spreading network of roads and highways combine to open up new areas for
homes and factories in the metropolitan region.

Although metropolitan areas as a whole experienced population growth during the first two decades of the century, suburbs grew less rapidly than cities
they bordered. As we earlier noted, new suburban construction was confined to
narrow strips on either side of the railroad or trolley line. At the edges of these
corridors, residential development thinned out, quickly giving way to field,
swamp or woodland.

But new modes of transportation overcame the locational disadvantages of
land beyond walking distance of a train or trolley station. As the automobile
became popular during the twenties, suburbs silted in the vacant land between
major arterial spokes. Wherever it was possible to lay down a hard-surfaced road,
a commuter settlement could be situated close by. Once too distant from rail or
trolley lines to be profitably developed, land lying midway between transportation lines filled up with new homes. In some older inlying suburbs, bus lines
supplemented private vehicles in ferrying passengers from home to station. In
such towns, much new construction took the form of land-intensive, multi-
family, apartment buildings, which increased residential densities. They may still
be seen in such places as Yonkers and Mount Vernon outside New York, as well
as in Evanston, Illinois. Further away, where land was still cheap enough to
encourage land-extensive settlement, suburban residential areas began to peel
away from the older transportation arteries.[9] Each year they conquered more
land that an earlier pattern of settlement had left vacant. Here, a large share of
all new construction was in single-family dwellings and duplexes, resulting in
lower ratios of man to land than those prevailing in the inner band.

These housing opportunities pulled people out of the city. In the twenties,
for the first time in the history of the United States, suburban growth rates surpassed those of the inner city. Although the depression retarded metropolitan
growth generally, its effects were more sharply felt in the city than in suburbs.
During the thirties, core cities grew at an average annual rate of 0.6 percent,
compared with 2.2 percent during the previous decade. By contrast, the suburban yearly average declined less drastically, from 2.8 to 1.4 percent.

Part of the explanation may be found in federal housing policies, a matter to be treated more fully later. But we note now that the Federal Housing Administration insured mortgage loans for purchase of *new* houses. Since most vacant land for such houses was located outside central cities, the FHA became a silent partner helping to promote suburban growth. Fueled by the wartime prosperity of the early forties, the appetite for new housing outstripped supply. To help absorb the demand, the Veterans Administration joined the FHA after the war in guaranteeing money for new houses. This time they accommodated many new families formed just after the war, as well as those forced to double up during it. Constantly adding to the flow of mortgage money to the outskirts were policies of savings and loan associations. Their deposits guaranteed by the Federal Home Loan Bank System, these associations were legally bound to plow most of their investment capital into home construction.

Since the supply of new land available in the cities was no more plentiful after the war than before, by far the greater fraction of all postwar housing was put up in expanding suburbs. New families could have chosen to remain in the cities, using their income to update older structures, but high labor costs made extensive renovation prohibitive. For example, to provide enough plumbing and hot water for a washing machine and two bathrooms meant ripping through walls in order to tear out old plumbing caked with the sediment of decades. Installing the same plumbing in a new home cost less money.[10] So couples skipped over dilapidated inner neighborhoods to settle somewhere in the commuter belt, which was constantly widening as the highway system expanded and as the automobile became as commonplace as the electric toaster.

Increases in the volume of land available for residential construction, in wage and salary levels, and in a generous credit structure coaxed the tradition-bound home construction industry to experiment with new mass production techniques. Until the end of World War II, the industry was dominated by small operators. Would-be homeowners purchased land and then hired a contractor to erect a house on the site. The result was a rampant variety of architectural styles built to suit the taste and income of the customer and the capabilities of the contractor. To shave labor costs and exploit economies of scale, suburban developers in the postwar era bought up vast stretches of land. There they put up many homes in a few basic floor plans, whenever possible using units prefabricated far from the actual building site.

These economies were not uniformly available, however. In the older suburbs, owners held land in small, fragmented parcels. This pattern of land tenure impeded the entrepreneur who wanted to assemble the large spreads of contiguous land the new construction technology demanded. Lacking the means to compel *all* the owners to sell their holdings, developers shifted their operations to the outer reaches of the metropolitan fringe. These considerations often led to a dispersed pattern of suburban settlement; the metropolitan area does not always expand by accretion at its margins, with the population pulsing outward in a steady surge. Developers moved to remote areas where land was available, often leaving vacant land behind them.[11]

Commercial and Professional Jobs

The ubiquity of the automobile, rising affluence and the inadvertent consequences of mortgage guarantee programs produced a mix of inducements that sent people scurrying to the suburbs in a search for new homesites. In turn, the sheer magnitude of suburban residential growth has stimulated a parallel diffusion of job opportunities. The suburban resident is also a consumer of goods and services. Once built, the home draws the marketplace to a location nearby. Suburban shopping centers provide a good example of these locational pressures. In the city, storefronts line the wider streets and avenues of the established neighborhoods. Laid out in a continuous strip, they are accessible to shoppers who come and go on foot. (Given the shortage of curbside parking, there frequently is no other way.) In these stores, housewives purchase their everyday staples. Downtown, in the area where the mass transit lines converge, are located the big department and specialty stores which sell infrequently purchased, "high-ticket" items.

The suburban shopping centers congregate all these activities around an acre or so of pavement, offering a free outdoor garage for the shoppers who motor in from their homes. These centers bring together a wide variety of stores selling goods produced in workshops and factories all over the world. The income levels and dominant lifestyles of neighboring communities produce discernible variations in the mix of goods offered for sale. Centers near the more exclusive suburbs have stores specializing in expensive imported items; others offer goods to satisfy an outdoors work-and-leisure style.

Taken altogether, these suburban retail outlets bid for the services of a great many employees: salesgirls, stockboys, bookkeepers, and checkout clerks. In the stores that specialize in highly individual personal services, many of them small proprietary businesses, are found barbers, beauticians, restauranteurs, and travel agents. One step behind them in the overall pattern are the warehouses and distributors who have to deliver small quantities of goods to large numbers of retail outlets a day or two after the order is received. These enterprises have also moved out of the city to central points in the commuter belt in order to be close to the shops they supply.[12] In short, then, since retail demand is best expressed as a function of population density weighted by ease of access, many jobs in trade, wholesaling and distributing have drifted out to the suburbs, where the people are.[13]

Other jobs have been swept up in the shift from inner core to outer zone. Suburban governments and special districts require the services of teachers, principals, meter readers, pipe layers, streetsweepers, firemen, policemen, sanitarians—the whole gamut of occupations that make up the community housekeeping staff. Then, too, there are lawyers, accountants and other practitioners operating on a fee-for-service basis. Caught up in the same calculus that propelled retailers to suburbs, they too have flowed outward, making up another component of the suburban drift. Doctors have also joined in the suburban flow. Internists and pediatricians offering "first-line" medical care often join in a group practice close to the suburban shopping center. Not only do they benefit from the traffic flow, but they offer their patients the minor convenience of being able to fill a prescription on the way home and the major one of auxiliary medical facilities (such as a laboratory) too expensive and infrequently used for any single physician to afford.

Thus has a pervasive suburban residential movement generated tides of demand that displaced consumer service jobs from the core of the metropolitan region to its suburban arcs. Since supply chases demand, population dispersion led to job diffusion. For a somewhat different pattern of causes, many manufacturers have also transferred part of their operations to the outskirts.

Manufacturing

One reason for the relocation of manufacturing has been the extension of electrical power lines, water mains, and other public utilities to the suburbs. So long as machines were powered by steam, manufacturers were directly dependent on fossil fuels as a source of energy. Coal cost least where it was delivered, at the dockside or at the tip of the rail spur. Hauling it overland rapidly boosted transportation—and hence total production—costs. Consequently, the large plants of the era clung to the shores of rivers, inlets, and canals; somewhat later they filtered out to more distant locations outfitted with rail spurs. Just as the advent of the automobile decisively reduced the comparative advantage of land close to public transit lines, so did electrical power wipe out the competitive edge enjoyed by manufacturers located on land close to the metropolitan heart. Produced by water or coal at central generating facilities, electrical power could be delivered wherever a transmission line could be installed. The networks that furnished homeowners in suburban towns with electricity for their appliances also provided manufacturers with a source of power.

More than electrical power is involved in accounting for the propensity of plants to locate in suburban zones rather than in the central city. Electricity may have been a necessary condition for suburbanization of manufacturing; it was not a sufficient one. One clue in unravelling other causes is to be found in the advent of trucks. So long as train and barge were used to haul bulky goods over long distances, plants needed a big city location for access to remote markets. But with the truck, manufacturers became increasingly less dependent on trains and timetables. Goods could be loaded on a truck as fast as they could be produced. Furthermore, scheduling was considerably more flexible once trucks came into widespread use. Goods could depart for their destination as soon as they filled the cargo space; it was no longer necessary to wait until the yard-master assembled a long-enough string of cars to warrant a locomotive.[14] The transportation revolution begun in the twenties considerably weakened the hold of the central city on manufacturing industries.

A third reason for the relocation of manufacturing stems from the perennial quest for space. There was space in the city, but it was chopped up into cramped factory lofts stacked atop one another in the city's congested areas. New factories demanded much more floor space per worker, since their assembly lines were laid out in continuous moving strips, and this layout placed a premium on the *horizontal* movement of materials. The limited floor space of an urban factory loft meant that materials had to be carried *vertically*, from floor to floor, once the required output passed a certain limit. For this reason, space in the city failed to meet new technological requirements.[15]

The result has been a pronounced tendency for manufacturers to seek sub-urban locations for their factories. This tendency is reflected in the buoyant rate of increase in manufacturing jobs in suburban zones engirdling core cities.[16] When we add jobs in suburban service employment to those in manufacturing, we can begin to appreciate the magnitude of the outward shift of employment opportunities. By the late sixties, almost half the labor force of Nassau County, outside New York, commuted to jobs in Nassau or in Suffolk County, further east on Long Island.[17] Almost 60 percent of Westchester County's labor force was employed in Westchester County itself, or in Fairfield County, Connecticut.

Few observers can foresee any developments that will arrest the outward swing of jobs. As strips of concrete continue to link suburb to suburb and one metropolitan area to another, the hold of the city on manufacturing employment will steadily weaken. Short of confiscating thousands of parcels of private property on many contiguous city blocks and relaxing zoning requirements, there is no way to provide factories with the uninterrupted ground space required by modern industrial layouts. Even this would not suffice, for traffic would have to be diverted underground to make way for the rigs that carry goods from loading dock to marketplace. Add the additional considerations that holders of well-paying manufacturing employment in the city would further strain traffic circulation systems, and it becomes even more difficult to see how central cities will be able to seize a robust share of the new jobs created each year.

The Demography of Suburbia

We noted earlier that post-World War II growth of suburbs generated the popular notion that suburbs were new. This we found to be untrue. In this chapter we explore a related notion that the middle class and wealthy have everywhere deserted the city for surrounding suburbs, leaving behind a poorly educated lower class to stagnate in the inner core. As we will find here, too, the evidence just does not support that belief.

City-Suburb Status Patterns

If there is anything to the belief, however, it would require us as an absolute minimum to find suburban residents uniformly better off than city dwellers. Data to apply to this proposition are found in a massive compendium by Hadden and Borgatta, who calculated the means for a number of variables commonly used to differentiate social class.[1] Many of the comparisons do bear out the pervasive stereotype, but even so, the *magnitude* of differences was scarcely overwhelming. Income is an example. Although almost a fifth (18.9 percent) of families in central cities had an annual income of less than $3,000, almost 11 percent of all suburban families also had to make do on the same meager income. Despite the familiar image which sees only affluence in suburbs, more than a tenth of all suburban families in 1960 lived beneath the poverty line. At the upper end of the income distribution, the margin between suburban and urban families with incomes of more than $10,000 a year came to less than 10 percent (24.0 versus 14.9 percent), while median incomes were little more than a thousand dollars apart ($7,161 vs. $5,695).

Turning to education, we perceive a roughly similar profile. Fewer than eight percent of all central city adults in 1960 failed to complete five years of formal schooling, a figure not much larger than the five percent for suburban adults. Slightly more than a tenth of all suburbanites possessed a college degree, about two percentage points greater than for central city residents; two more college graduates for each 100 adult residents is a difference, but not a substantial one. Similarly, even though 49.7 percent of the suburban labor force worked at white-collar jobs, so did 44.3 percent of city workers. Although these differences all run in the expected direction, their relatively small size shows that status characteristics of the two locales are not as widely divergent as conventional wisdom would have it.

25

There are more refined ways of presenting the same comparisons than using the mean, which fails to take variations into account. Though the means show that suburbs generally possess a higher socioeconomic composition than cities they skirt, the disparity is not at all constant from one urbanized area to the next. Schnore has shown how stratifying urbanized areas by size and age of central cities makes status measures fall into an arresting and predictable pattern.[2]

By Size and Age of Locale

Let us look at size first (see Table 3-1). In every one of 38 urbanized areas with 1960 populations in excess of 500,000, suburbs led their respective core cities in median income and in the percentage of high school graduates. In more than 85 percent, suburbs also had a greater proportion of white-collar workers in the labor force. But it was only in this relatively small group that status differences were so pronounced in favor of suburbs. They leveled off considerably in medium-sized urbanized areas, and were actually reversed in the smallest, where cities outstripped suburbs in educational level and occupational standing. In only 80 of 109 urbanized areas having between 100,000 and 500,000 inhabitants was income greater in suburbs than in the central city. In the smallest urbanized areas (50,000-100,000), suburban income exceeded that of city families in only 56.6 percent of the 53 urbanized areas in this category.

Roughly the same progression can be traced for education and occupation measures. Only two-thirds of suburban zones in the medium-sized group had a higher proportion of high school graduates than the core city, and, in the smallest urbanized areas, the chances were only fifty-fifty that suburbs would have a higher proportion of adults with a high school education. Correspondingly, in a little less than half (52 of 109) of all areas in the medium-sized group, core cities

Table 3-1
Distribution of City-Suburban Differences by Size of Urbanized Area, 1960

Total Population of Urbanized Areas, 1960	Number of Areas	Number of Urbanized Areas Whose Suburbs Are Higher In:		
		Median Annual Family Income	Percentage of High School Graduates	Percentage of White Collar Workers
500,000+	38	38	38	33
100,000-500,000	109	80	73	52
50,000-100,000	53	30	26	16

Source: Calculated from data presented by Schnore, "The Socio-Economic Status of Cities and Suburbs," *American Sociological Review*, 28 (1963), 78, who divided urbanized areas into six groups. For simplicity's sake, we have collapsed them into three. Since the indices followed the same gradient throughout, no harm is done by combining adjacent groups.

housed a higher proportion of white-collar workers than the suburbs that en-circled them. The smallest urbanized areas displayed the most dramatic inver-sions of all. Here, only about a third had a higher proportion of white-collar workers in their suburban bands.

Thus, Schnore's analysis shows how sheer size of the urbanized area exerts a powerful effect on the distribution of status characteristics. Status variations correlate with a size gradient; the smaller the area, the greater the tendency of the core city to equal or outrank its suburban band on any of three analytically separable dimensions of social class.

Schnore further found that *age* of the central city took on even greater im-portance than size in predicting status differences between city and suburb, as may be seen in Table 3-2.[a] A quick glance at two extremes of the distribution permits the sharpest comparison. In every one of 31 urbanized areas whose cen-tral city had attained a population of 50,000 by 1880, suburbs surpassed their respective central cities on all three indexes. However, of 85 central cities which have reached the same population size since the depression, only 58.8 percent of their suburban zones had a higher median income than their central cities; 50.5 percent had a higher proportion of high school graduates; and only 27.1 percent had a higher concentration of white-collar workers in the labor force. The inter-mediate cases pursue the same pattern. In general, then, the more mature the urbanized area, the greater the status advantage of its suburban residents.

Table 3-2
Distribution of City-Suburban Differences by Age of Urbanized Area, 1960

Census Year in Which Central City First Attained 50,000 Population	Number of Areas	No. of Urbanized Areas Whose Suburbs Are Higher In:		
		Median Annual Family Income	Percentage of High School Graduates	Percentage of White-Collar Workers
1800-1860	14	14	14	14
1870-1880	17	17	17	17
1890-1900	36	31	27	21
1910-1920	48	36	36	26
1930-1940	32	23	18	10
1950-1960	53	27	25	13

Source: Schnore "The Socio-Economic Status of Cities and Suburbs," *American Sociological Review*, 28 (1963), 80.

[a]As one might expect, size and age of urbanized areas correlate positively. However, the correlation is far from perfect. In Schnore's collection of 200 urbanized areas, the zero-order correlation coefficient was +.50, i.e., only 25 percent of the total variance was shared by these two variables. Partial correlation analysis showed that age, not sheer size, was the best single predictor of status differences.

By Region

By digging a little deeper, we can identify some complex factors which have combined to produce these results. One preliminary step is to glance at some regional variations in urban-suburban status differentials. The oldest and most heavily populated metropolitan complexes are to be found in the northeast. Accordingly, one would expect that polarization of status between city and suburb should follow a regional pattern. We should find the sharpest difference of all in northeastern states, followed closely by those in the north central region.[3] One good measure of status is income; Table 3-3 presents a cross-sectional distribution of urban and suburban family income in 1960 in the four major geographical divisions. By comparison with the rest of the country, metropolitan areas in the northeastern states simultaneously display the greatest excesses of urban poverty and suburban affluence, but the percentage differences are not overwhelming. Once outside the Northeast, differences dwindle. Next in historical order, north central states present a less extreme version of disparities found in the Northeast. Although the percentage of very poor urban families is still greater than for suburban belts, the absolute difference has shrunk from seven to two percent. Furthermore, there is virtually no difference in respective proportions of *prosperous* families living in the two places. In the West, on the other hand, suburbs have proportionately *more* poor and *fewer* wealthy families than the central cities they border.[4]

As might be expected from generally high correlations between income and occupational standing, these differentials translate rather readily into occupa-

Table 3-3

Distribution of Annual Family Income by Metropolitan Status and Region, 1960 (Percent)

| | Families by Income Category | | | | | | | |
| Region | Under $4000 | | $4000-$7999 | | $8000-$14,999 | | $15,000+ | |
	Core City %	Suburb %	Core City %	Suburb %	Core City %	Suburb %	Core City %	Suburb %
North East	27	20	48	48	21	26	4	6
North Central	23	21	48	48	25	26	4	4
South	37	35	39	43	18	18	4	3
West	23	24	44	46	27	25	6	5
U.S.	29	26	44	46	22	23	4	4

Source: Advisory Commission on Intergovernmental Relations (Report A-25), *Metropolitan Social and Economic Disparities: Implications for Intergovernmental Relations in Central Cities and Suburbs* (Washington, D.C.: United States Government Printing Office, 1965), 15-16. Hereafter referred to as ACIR.

Note: It is to be noted that the designation "suburb" refers to the portion of the SMSA that lies outside the core city. Therefore, the data are subject to the biases specified earlier.

tional disparities. In north central, southern and western states, the residential concentration of elite white-collar occupations (managerial, technical, and professional workers) is greater in the city than in the outlying suburban zones, with the most extreme disparities of all again found in the South and the West. Distributions in the northeastern states cling to the "expected" pattern, with proportionately more suburbanites in elite occupations. One urban-suburban difference, however, turns up in every section of the country—household and service workers tend to live within the city. Since these categories make up the poorest paid segment of the nonagricultural labor force, they help depress the income level of the core city. In light of this consideration, the higher income of inner city residents living in western states is all the more noteworthy.[5]

As with income and occupation, so with education. Only in the larger and older northeast metropolises were suburbanites conspicuously better educated than city residents. In 30 of 41 urbanized areas in the New England and Middle Atlantic states, those with no better than a grade school education congregated in core cities. Another seven revealed a somewhat modified pattern. Both the very lowest and very highest educational classes were over-represented in the city, with their suburbs having a disproportionately high share of people who had spent some time in high school. Thus, the distribution in the core cities resembled an hourglass, wide at top and bottom but pinched in at the center. The north central states showed a somewhat larger proportion of the hourglass distribution, but the largest single category of all still assigned the least educated to the city and the best educated to suburban belts. Moving further west, there were sharp inversions in such places as Albuquerque and Tucson, where city dwellers led their suburban neighbors in the number of years of formal education completed.[6]

While we could carry these cross-sectional comparisons much further to show regional variations in urban-suburban status differences,[7] this would still add up to nothing more than the first stage of a more discerning analysis. After all, the concept of a "region" is far too clumsy to promise much in the way of explanatory power. What is most important about a region is not its location or topography but its history and demography.[8]

The West as an Alternative
Suburban Model

In every comparison, urban cores in the Mountain and Pacific states come off much better than their hinterlands. Because they present the most arresting case of all, they require special explanation. We have referred to the role of a changing transportation technology in allocating land among alternative uses. Because new transportation technologies have sharply reduced costs of locating industry outside the city, factories have been free to prospect for work sites on the periphery. As noted, the propensity for new industry to bypass the core city has had a double-barreled impact on land-use patterns in the West. First, competition between residential and nonresidential uses for central city land supply has become less fierce than it had been in older metropolitan areas. Hence the expanding middle class has been able to find housing in the city at a reasonable cost. And, because newer core cities have never experienced much industrialization, residential areas are not interrupted by vast stretches of dilapidated neighborhoods left behind from an earlier day, as has happened in the northeast and north central states.

To complete the picture, manufacturers have been able to hold down costs of acquiring land by choosing a peripheral location. Since prime housing areas are for the most part located in the city, market forces work to their advantage. Although details can be expected to vary from one locale to another, suburban industrial uses by and large do not have to bid against developers who want to put up exclusive residential compounds. In combination with the play of market forces, transportation technology has worked toward a sharper segregation of land-use patterns. Land-extensive industrial uses drift out to the periphery, at the same time that land-intensive residential uses tend to stay within the city.

In turn, there occurs a relatively straightforward relation between job and residence concentrations, leading to suburban dispersion of blue-collar workers. Once, low-income groups rushed into the center of the city to stay close to their restricted employment opportunities; now that the automobile and truck have made it advantageous for industry to locate on land outside the city, factory hands keep pace with the demand by moving to the outskirts, sometimes living in suburban shanty towns.[9] As industry has dispersed, so has its labor supply.

Moreover, inferences from available data support the notion that dispersion of low-status people to suburban bands is more a function of new technology than of sheer size alone. In 1960, there were 24 SMSAs of at least one million. On the whole, the proportion of people in higher education, income, and occupation brackets was greater in suburban rings than in the central city. But for Dallas, Houston, Los Angeles-Long Beach, San Diego, and Seattle, the status of people living in suburban belts was either lower than or equal to those living in the central city. All these SMSAs, of course, have had their largest growth spurts since the development of new transportation technology.[10]

Intra-Suburbia Patterns

So far, our discussion has shown how people living in core cities tend to differ from their neighbors in suburban bands. We have demonstrated the fragility of conventional imagery which divides metropolis into an impoverished city and its affluent suburbs. In making these coarse-grained comparisons, however, we have treated suburbs as if they were an undifferentiated aggregate. Though this procedure is indispensable in contrasting city with hinterland, it is completely insensitive to any possible diversity *among* individual suburbs. For as we saw in the first chapter, American suburbs even in an earlier day diverged noticeably in their social composition and economic function. At one end of the spectrum, there were bedroom suburbs inhabited by fairly affluent white-collar workers who traded the convenience of living close to their jobs for the greater space and luxury of a home in a remote suburb. At the other were the dismal industrial suburbs that cropped up throughout the nineteenth century.

Building on this distinction, Schnore divided 300 American suburbs into three categories based primarily on journey-to-work patterns. Residential suburbs comprised the first group, having at least twice as many employed trade and manufacturing workers as there were jobs available locally. By inference, they had to spread their resident labor force among opportunities throughout the metropolitan region. Employing suburbs constituted the second major category; they had more jobs in trade and manufacturing than workers to fill them. These suburbs must draw at least part of their labor supply from other communities. The "intermediate" suburbs fell somewhere in the range between these two.[11]

In totting up the number of suburbs contained in each of these three groups, Schnore upset the common notion of the American suburb as specializing in the provision of residential amenities. These stereotypical suburbs accounted for only a third of all suburbs tabulated; the remainder were almost evenly divided between the other two types. Jobs in employing suburbs were sharply concentrated in manufacturing, so much so that "employing" and "manufacturing" were virtually interchangeable terms. By contrast, the internal economy of the residential suburb revolved around retailing, the most frequently encountered activity. Sorting out the strands, we may say that a residential suburb exports labor and imports goods, while an employing suburb imports labor and exports goods.

As also might be anticipated, residential suburbs scored highest on status measures, with employing suburbs footing the ladder. Residential suburbs had the highest proportions of high school graduates and white-collar workers, the largest median family income, and the fewest aged people, nonwhites, and foreign-born. These differentials predictably translated into variations in housing characteristics. Having the highest income levels, residential suburbanites were better able to satisfy a stubborn American preference for owning new, one-family homes. Renters occupying older multifamily-housing predominated in employing suburbs. Thus, the economic function of a particular suburb corresponded closely to status characteristics of its resident population.

Schnore's painstaking analyses point up the futility of concluding simplistically that all suburbs adhere to a common pattern. The nicknames assigned cities by novelists and feature writers for the Sunday magazine section celebrate their individuality. We have "Baghdad-on-the-Subway," "The City of Brotherly Love," "Athens of the South," and the like. Within each city, cabdrivers can show visitors the Gilded Ghetto, black slum, "Hippie-Heaven," silk-stocking ward, financial district, and office-building section. By contrast, "suburbia" is commonly lumped together as an aggregate, each suburb supposedly differing only in its location and housing cost. But nationwide surveys of suburbs discover that they differ from one another as much as cities they skirt.

The variety sketched above rubs against a stereotype that pervades the pop sociology of middlebrow monthlies as well as the popular mind. According to this image, suburbs are standardized commuter colonies populated by families stubbornly middle class in occupation, income, education, and outlook. Close analysis reveals a much different picture. Although none of the bands encircling our cities is *perfectly* homogeneous, they can be readily distinguished from one another by the dominant type of housing and economic activity.

In the inner ring of suburbs spreading away from the city line, one sees high-rise apartment buildings lining major thoroughfares and mass transit lines burrowing into the big city. Some of these apartment houses are quite new, charging high rentals; others, more moderately priced, are left over from an earlier day, having been vacated by the upward-bound who have found more space and comfort in newer suburbs built further away from the city core. Because there are very few large apartments, many adult occupants are either childless or have small families. The buildings they inhabit tower over the private houses, duplexes, and small Tudor-style apartment houses that date back to the era when the inner suburban ring consisted of isolated commuter villages. Because so much housing stock is in multi-family units, inner-suburb densities tend to approach those of central city.

The occupational mix of the congested portion of inner suburbia reflects its location halfway between the city core and more distant suburbs. Some are members of the lower white-collar cadre—secretaries, sales clerks, and office workers—who commute daily to city jobs. Others work at skilled or semi-skilled industrial jobs located in the inner band or suburban areas somewhat further away from the city. Interspersed throughout the inner ring are pockets of low-income housing, occupied by people who have spilled out of city slums into industrial satellites which still retain the indelible imprint of their nineteenth century origins.

Nor is this all. Adding to the diversity of the inner band are exclusive suburbs which, as we will later illustrate, have preserved their character by ingeniously manipulating zoning and other land-use controls. Commonly these suburbs were built to exploit some natural features, e.g., a beachfront or a calm inlet that serves admirably as a yacht basin. In short, although the inner band of suburbs houses mainly those of modest means, there are upper- and lower-class compounds dimpled throughout.

As we penetrate the outer ring of the bull's-eye target, we find that some of the suburbs are filled with low-priced tract housing. From the air, the traveler can see these subdivisions winding monotonously over vast acres of hillside and flatland. Here we find people who earn stable but moderate incomes from better-paying office jobs in the city or a new suburb or from growing suburban service and retail establishments. Some of these tract suburbs, constructed for returning veterans, are already showing signs of unmistakable decay, pointing to the possibility, explored in a later chapter, that someday soon we may perceive the need for a program of suburban renewal to salvage them. As the original occupants of postwar tract housing left for more expensive suburbs, their homes were snapped up by low-income groups. Often, the heads of families living in second-hand housing found employment in aircraft and other land-extensive industries built close to spreading expressways, thus splicing residence to homesite like older satellite suburbs a half-century before.

Somewhat further out from suburban industry and retailing centers we find a wide array of more comfortable suburbs. Compared with tract suburbs, these houses sit on larger lots and have deeper front yards. They are obviously occupied by those with higher incomes—skilled industrial workers and the upper echelon of the white-collar corps. A notch above them in the social scale and further out in the country are suburban reservations fencing in the downright wealthy. These ripe villages, a century or more in the aging, are so far away from the city that "exurbia" seems more an appropriate label than suburbia.[12] There are also older prestige suburbs which have become strange amalgams, with a recent tide of *arrivistes* from the city or from another suburb, now in the process of being downgraded. For the most part, those living in the outer ring have traded accessibility to work for greater space and comfort. To be sure, doctors and other professionals live in the same community where they work, but many more executives and professionals accept a relatively long time spent in traveling to and from work as a fair price for ample living space and neighborhood homogeneity.

In short, then, both inner and outer bands present a wide array of occupational profiles and income levels. Generally speaking, there is more prosperity further away from the core city, but even so we have noted clusters of high-income people in suburbs close to the city and lower-income groups further out. So far, we have been dealing with residential distributions of rich and not-so-rich.[13] In this highly simplified model, the people have no racial and ethnic attributes. It is time to say a few words about those qualities of suburbs.

The Black Suburb

If there is one abiding notion in the popular conception of suburbia, it is its whiteness. Suburbs are the white man's tribal reservation, isolated from the growing blackness of the core city. As a matter of fact, the demographic evidence is closely congruent with the popular notion, as far as black-white distinctions go. Nonetheless, there is unsuspected ethnic variety on the city's rim.

Thus, Los Angeles reveals ethnic shifts to suburbia which cannot be totally absent elsewhere.[1] Of that area's 75 suburbs, ten have proportionately more Mexican-Americans than the national or county average. One has proportionately more Oriental-Americans, one has a large fraction of black and Oriental-Americans, and a third is heavily saturated with citizens of Oriental and Mexican origins. Pico Rivera and Montebello have become heavily flavored with Spanish-speaking suburbanites, while Monterey Park and Gardena contain sizable minorities of Japanese-Americans.

Across the continent as late as 1960, there were other suburbs where the foreign stock population confounded those who saw suburbia as a WASP abode. Some suburbs are heavily Jewish; Long Beach, New York, and University Heights, Ohio, have a relatively large population able to speak Yiddish. Or, one notes outside Pittsburgh the large Italian enclaves in Norristown and Aliquippa, and outside Boston the Irish in Brookline. Then there is the ethnic stew of South San Francisco with its large contingents of Chinese, Mexicans, and Italians.

There is no more stark evidence of this ethnic variety than the presence of suburbs where the proportion of blacks is as large, or larger, than in the nation. Despite these few black suburbs, not enough blacks live in suburban bands, however, to demolish the popular notion, and, as we shall see, there are severe constraints working against a future increase. But there are enough blacks in suburbs and enough black suburbs to justify focusing upon them. Their patterns of geographical mobility, their status distinctions, and the discrimination and economic displacement they suffer add an important dimension to the variety of suburban life.

Patterns of Geographical Mobility

Although southern blacks have always flowed into northern cities in search of better housing and employment, their migration crested only after World War II. As late as 1940, more than three-quarters of all American blacks still lived in the South, and about 70 percent were rural. However, because of subsequent black migration elsewhere, a much smaller percentage of all blacks now live in southern states.[2] Moreover, they moved from farms to cities. Between 1940 and 1950, the total population of the 14 largest SMSAs shot up by almost a fifth, much of it traceable to the arrival of blacks, particularly those in their childbearing years. In the forties, the growth rate of the black metropolitan population soared to 65 percent, more than four times the white increase of 16 percent.[3] Meanwhile, young white families were pouring out of the city into the suburbs. As whites moved out and blacks moved in, the ghetto expanded and the rate of black increase within core cities shot up to 67.8 percent, overwhelming a white inner city growth rate of only 3.7 percent. Many migrant blacks had to settle in the dilapidated housing of inner cities because it was within reach of low-paying, casual jobs for the men. In any case, it was all they could afford. The housing was also accessible to the inner ring of suburbs where black women could find jobs as domestics.

During the fifties, even more blacks left the rural South for the urban North at the same time as young white couples flocked to the suburbs. Central cities of the twelve largest SMSAs gained 4.5 million nonwhites and exported 3.6 million whites elsewhere.[4] Nor was the black influx confined only to the biggest cities. Kain and Persky estimate that there were about 2.5 million southern-born blacks in non-southern cities in the 250,000-1,000,000 size range.[5]

Since dominant patterns of migration have concentrated blacks within core cities, it should come as no great surprise to hear that they still account for only a sliver of the suburban population. Figure 4-1 shows the precipitate decline in the southern black suburban population since 1900 while holding remarkably stable elsewhere. The southern decline stems from white migration into formerly rural—and black—areas outside central cities. But in both the North and South, blacks have for over seven decades been more urban than suburban migrants. As shown in Table 4-1, seven out of ten blacks resided in a SMSA by 1970, but only about 16 percent of the entire black population lived in suburbs. Whites also were mostly metropolitan by then, too, but almost 40 percent lived in suburbs. Everywhere but in non-SMSA areas, blacks exceeded whites in the intercensal proportion of growth. But, regardless of region or size of SMSA, relatively few blacks lived in suburbia, as shown in Table 4-2. Nonetheless, the proportion of black suburbanites had increased by 1970 in all regions except the South, whether in big or small SMSAs. The largest proportion of these was outside any SMSAs (9.4 percent non-SMSA vs. 4.9 percent all SMSAs) in small southern and large northern (particularly western) SMSAs. But in all metropolises during the sixties, blacks raised only a small wave in the white suburban tide, increasing marginally from 4.5 to 4.9 percent.

Where did these black suburbanites go when they fled the ghetto? Black suburbs can be traced back for many decades, as Farley has shown. Kinlock, outside St. Louis, was a subdivision where building lots were sold to blacks before 1900, while Robbins, near Chicago, emerged as a black suburb before World

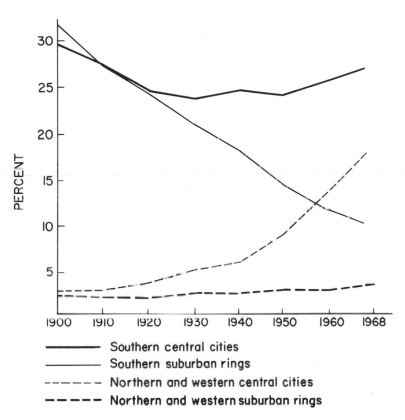

PERCENT

| | 1900 | 1910 | 1920 | 1930 | 1940 | 1950 | 1960 | 1968 |

——————— Southern central cities

——————— Southern suburban rings

– – – – – – Northern and western central cities

━ ━ ━ ━ ━ Northern and western suburban rings

Figure 1-1. Metropolitan Black Population, 1900–1968. Source: Reynolds Farley, "The Changing Distribution of Negroes within Metropolitan Areas: The Emergence of Black Suburbs," *American Journal of Sociology*, 75 (1970), 514.

War I; so did Lincoln Heights near Cincinnati in the twenties, Richmond Heights, a suburb of Miami, after World War II, and North Shreveport, Louisiana, in the fifties.[6] Some blacks during the sixties not only filtered across the city line into the inner band of these aging suburbs but also found brand new sites. This black increase appeared in three kinds of suburbs: older and densely settled suburbs with, or near, job opportunities (Yonkers, New York, or East Cleveland, Ohio); new suburban developments, some of which are integrated (Richmond Heights, Florida, or Hollydale near Cincinnati); and very poor enclaves with inadequate municipal facilities, dilapidated homes, and sometimes public housing (Robbins or East Chicago Heights outside Chicago).

In the New York area, for example, blacks have moved into such "old line" suburbs as Mount Vernon and New Rochelle, occupying decrepit housing in dilapidated corners of the city once inhabited by first- and second-generation

Table 4-1
Percentage Distribution of Population by Place and Race, 1960 and 1970

	1960	1970	% Change[a]
White:			
SMSA:	62.7%	64.0%	14.3%
Core	30.0	25.4	−5.4
Suburban	32.6	38.6	32.3
Non-SMSA	37.3	36.0	7.7
Total (thousands)	158,698	177,429	11.8%
Black:			
SMSA:	64.8%	70.7%	35.4
Core	51.5	55.2	32.8
Suburban	13.2	15.5	45.5
Non-SMSA	35.2	29.3	3.1
Total (thousands)	18,391	22,807	24.0%

[a]Percentage does not represent difference between 1960 and 1970 percentages to the left. It is product of the difference between 1960 and 1970 absolute data as a proportion of 1960 data.

Source: U.S. Bureau of the Census, *Social and Economic Characteristics of the Population in Metropolitan and Nonmetropolitan Areas: 1970 and 1960* (Washington, D.C.: Government Printing Office, 1971), Current Population Reports No. 37, Table A at 1.

Table 4-2
Suburban Black Percentage by Size and Region of SMSA, 1960 and 1970

	Northeast	North Central	South	West	Total
1970					
SMSA:					
All	3.7	2.7	10.9	2.7	4.9
Over 1,000,000	4.5	4.7	3.5	6.9	4.5
Under 1,000,000	1.6	1.4	12.8	0.6	5.2
Non-SMSA	2.9	1.2	19.8	1.9	9.4
1960					
SMSA:					
All	3.0	2.3	11.8	2.1	4.5
Over 1,000,000	4.0	2.9	7.8	2.9	3.9
Under 1,000,000	0.9	1.3	13.7	0.7	5.2
Non-SMSA	1.2	1.2	21.4	0.7	9.8

Source: U.S. Bureau of the Census, *Social and Economic Characteristics of the Population in Metropolitan and Nonmetropolitan Areas: 1970 and 1960* (Washington, D.C.: Government Printing Office, 1971), Current Population Reports No. 37, Table 2 at 19.

Jews. Blacks moving from Chicago's South Side have discovered similar caches of worn-out housing in Evanston, just north of Chicago. Much the same concentration of poor suburban housing can be found around the automobile factories in Detroit suburbs. To be sure, a trickle of well-to-do blacks have used their high incomes to acquire better housing in more prosperous suburbs further out toward the rim of the metropolis. For black and white alike, greater income obviously confers greater choice; the move out is often a step up.

During the sixties, about 85,000 blacks, many of them young couples with children, annually found housing somewhere in a suburban belt; these constitute only about six percent of the 1.4 million whites who moved to suburbs each year in the same decade. Because the racial mix of the suburban migrants closely matches that of the population already there, the general pattern has tended towards great stability. However, the shift in black proportions is hardly dramatic.[a]

The diffusion of blacks into suburbia has not drawn them into white residential neighborhoods, as surveys and field studies clearly show. In 1960, there were some 800 suburbs having more than 10,000 people. Of these, 313, or 39 percent, had no more than one black for every 500 residents; another 390, or 49 percent, had 1-10 percent black. Thus, almost 90 percent of all suburbs had fewer blacks than their proportion of the nation's population would warrant. Of the remaining 97 suburbs, 52 were more than 15 percent black, as can be seen in Table 4-3.[b] There were thus many suburbs with a few blacks and a few suburbs with many blacks, a pattern resembling the distribution of blacks among core city neighborhoods. In 1960, these heavily black suburbs were concentrated in the older metropolitan areas of the East and in the smaller suburbs of southern cities, generally impoverished shacktowns on the fringe.

Chicago illustrates this sorting out pattern. There, blacks made up 23.6 percent of the 1960 city population and 3.1 percent of the suburban. Of the 147

---

[a]We should caution that high growth rates calculated on a small population base can be very deceiving. Because there are so few suburban blacks, each new increment will turn up as a relatively robust percentage increase. Conversely, even a substantial addition to the white suburban population stock will be reflected in a low growth rate. For this reason, we stress net population composition rather than growth rates.

The 1970 census shows, for example, a black increase in suburbs over the decade of 45.5 percent while whites increased 32.3 percent (see sources in note 9 for this chapter). But the black increase in suburbs did little to alter the total proportion of blacks there, and according to Farley (see note 6), the blackness of city cores will not increase substantially over the next two decades.

In addition, owing to the mathematics of such processes, even though the racial composition of suburbs may stay constant, the absolute gap between the number of suburban blacks and whites will widen as suburbs get more populous. Even a considerable increase in the suburban growth rate for blacks will only chip away at the disparity in numbers. For these reasons, it is wise to be skeptical about statements emphasizing growth rates.

[b]The data on which these computations are based have been drawn from source of Table 4-3.

Table 4-3

Distribution of Suburbs by Region and Percentage Nonwhite

Percentage Nonwhite	Region				
	New England & Middle Atlantic	North Central	Pacific & Mountain	South	Total
11.0-15.0	11	10	2	22	45
15.1-20.0	6	4	2	3	15
21 +	14	7	4	12	37
Total	31	21	8	37	97

Source: Victor Jones, Richard Forstall, and Andrew Collver, "Economic and Social Characteristics of Urban Places," *National Municipal Yearbook, 1963* (Chicago: International City Managers Association, 1963), 117-56.

Note: Note that "nonwhites" includes Orientals and American Indians as well as blacks, in accordance with Census Bureau practice. Since there are so few Orientals and Indians in the population, lumping them with blacks produces only minor distortions; only for Mountain states are the data even marginally suspect. Overall, it makes little difference if one joins blacks and Orientals into a nonwhite category, or whites, Indians, and Orientals into a nonblack aggregate.

suburbs with over 2500 people, only 19 (almost 13 percent) had not a single black living within their borders. Another 97 suburbs contained no more than one black in a hundred, and an additional 21 had 1-11 percent blacks. That is, all but 7 percent of Chicago suburbs had fewer blacks than the national average. Of the remaining ten suburbs where the proportion of blacks exceeded the national mean, four actually had black populations in excess of 60 percent. Robbins was more than 99 percent black, composed largely of workers in nearby freight yards.[7] Enveloped by predominantly white suburbs, then, the spatial distribution of these black suburban enclaves resembles patches of coal on a snowfield.

Black Status in City and Suburb

Clearly, there has been a marked shift in patterns of black migration. One shift is geographical as we have seen, but another is in the black's status or well-being. The black migrant's education was once minimal, and he (often, she) took whatever low-paying job could be found in or near the urban core. Lately, however, more blacks moving to northern and border-state cities are better educated. In fact, the average educational attainment and occupational standing of black migrants by 1960 exceeded those of the resident white population. In part, of course, this shift can be explained by the better education of outward-bound whites and the fact that much of the black migration has become intermetropolitan in character.[8]

Those black migrants who sought the suburbs were not like white suburban-ites, however, nor like fellow blacks remaining in the core city. In 1959, 50.9 percent of black suburbanites were below the poverty level as compared with 40.8 percent of the black city dwellers; by 1969, the figures in both places had almost halved, to 24.7 percent in the core and 23.2 percent in suburbia.[9] A more refined analysis shows that inner city blacks resembled urban whites more than suburban blacks resembled their white neighbors. This can be seen in Table 4-4 where these black-to-white ratios are shown for income and education meas-ures. An important racial distinction exists here, not merely between blacks and whites, but among blacks. Until the sixties, suburban blacks occupied a lower status than their core city brothers, but in the last decade the distinction was reversed. This change stemmed not so much from *more* blacks entering suburbia, but from more young, married couples with higher incomes, but not with better education.[10]

It is not hard to explain both intercensal improvements of black income and schooling as well as relatively larger improvements in the core as against the suburb. First, it is clear that large resources were applied during the sixties to assist blacks in lifting barriers which have been imposed on them throughout our history. This would account for the proportion of inner city blacks completing a high school education increasing from 43 to 62.5 percent during this decade.[11] Second, larger black-white ratios in the core city may be a function of the "white flight." As Farley notes, those whites fleeing are those most able finan-cially to do so, thereby subtracting from the higher income and schooling pool

Table 4-4

Ratios of Black to White for Income and Education, 1960 and 1970

| | Worker Earnings | | | Education | |
	Total Income	Service	Operatives	High School	4 Yrs. or More College
1970					
SMSA:	64.2	83.9	79.5	75.9	34.5
Core	69.3	88.7	83.8	80.6	36.3
Suburban	62.6	69.9	78.8	67.4	26.6
Non-SMSA	47.8	74.6	63.3	57.1	76.7
1960					
SMSA:	58.2	62.2	71.0	62.7	33.3
Core	61.4	65.8	75.6	64.7	34.1
Suburban	51.6	54.4	58.7	56.0	30.0
Non-SMSA	36.0	56.2	49.1	43.3	55.0

Source: Calculated and abstracted from U.S. Bureau of the Census, *Social and Economic Characteristics of the Population in Metropolitan and Nonmetropolitan Areas: 1970 and 1960* (Washington, D.C.: Government Printing Office, 1971), Current Population Reports No. 37, Table B at 3, and Table C at 4-5.

of the city and adding it to suburbs.[12] While blacks are also migrating to suburbs, as a group they start behind their fellow white migrants in status, are much fewer in number, and hence cannot remove the status gap between them and white suburbanites. In this move, blacks may change their post office and standard of living, but at the same time see a widening of status differences.

Not even the most intensive comparison of aggregate means can indicate the degree to which the black population has less resources and less success in our society. Table 4-5 shows clearly that in 1960 as the proportion of blacks rose in both city and suburb, various indexes of well-being also went down. Although these measures are weighted down by the extremely depressed status of southern suburban blacks, the striking feature of these coefficients is their roughly similar profiles for both central city and suburb. In both locales, blacks tended to live where more housing stock was unsound, crowded and aged, and where renting

Table 4-5

Zero-Order Correlation of Percentage Nonwhite with Selected Census Variables for Urban Places, 1960

	Locale	
Variables	Suburb	Central City
Income:		
Median Annual Family Income	−.34	−.46
Percentage Families with Annual Incomes Less than $3000	.57	.59
Percentage Families with Annual Incomes More Than $10,000	−.22	−.16
Standard of Life:		
Percentage Living in Sound Housing Units	−.56	−.39
Percentage Living in Crowded Units	.40	.46
Percentage Living in Owner-Occupied Units	−.37	−.35
Percentage Living in Units Built After 1954	−.29	.05
Median Value of Owner-Occupied Units	−.23	−.12
Percentage Units with Two or More Autos	−.27	−.07
Education:		
Percentage Completing Less than Five School Years	.54	.49
Median School Years Completed	−.35	−.21
Occupation:		
Percentage of Labor Force Unemployed	.41	.00
Percentage of Labor Force Male	−.30	−.33
Percentage in White-Collar Occupations	−.30	−.17

Source: Jeffrey K. Hadden and Edgar F. Borgatta, *American Cities: Their Social Characteristics* (Chicago: Rand McNally, 1965), 118-19.

was more likely than homeownership. City and suburb differed little in the way that increasing black population was associated with lower family incomes, fewer years of formal schooling, and fewer white-collar jobs. All standard 1960 measures of low status and depressed income appear with surprising consistency in both central city and suburb, suggesting the lack of any significant difference between the well-being of suburban and core city black. Where there were large differences in the coefficients, they showed suburban blacks worse off.

During the sixties, as Table 4-4 indicates, the situation of suburban blacks improved. In the Los Angeles area, for example,[13] blacks living in rapidly growing suburbs were more likely to own their homes than those living either in the central city in 1960 or in suburbs with many minorities in 1960. Thus, Inglewood's nonwhite population rose from 507 to almost 15,000 in the sixties; of the nonwhite newcomers, over 10,000 were black, of whom three of four families owned their own homes. Or, consider Pomona, whose nonwhite population rose from 1,208 to 12,444. Well over ten thousand of these were black, and 63 percent of the black families owned their homes. Meanwhile, blacks increased by 54 percent in the core city, but only 31 percent lived in their own homes. While suburbs with the most minorities were less well off than those with least minorities, only six minority suburbs had a higher percentage of families with incomes under $3,000 than did the county as a whole. Indeed, five of them were higher than the county average on median income, high income, and home values.

These findings should help dispel the argument that blacks have been bottled up in congested wards of the inner city solely because they are poor. Were this the case, blacks who have moved to the suburbs should be conspicuously better off than those left behind to molder in the central city. Yet the configuration of data in Table 4-5 strongly suggests—it does not "prove"—that the suburban black in 1960 was little better off than his big city counterpart. By 1970 he was in only somewhat better shape. (To be sure, there are prosperous blacks living in suburbs. But many well-to-do blacks live in residential enclaves of the inner city as well.) One other strand of evidence winds toward this provisional conclusion. Kain and Persky have demonstrated convincingly that, compared with blacks, a much higher proportion of poor white families live in suburubs.[14] If income alone were the only obstacle standing in the way of the suburban move, there should be no discernible difference between percentages of black and white suburban poor.

Constraints on Black Suburbanization

As is so often the case in accounting for social matters, no single cause explains the relatively small number of suburban blacks and their compression into a relatively few suburban neighborhoods. We will examine the constellation of causes more fully in the last chapter, but lack of black economic resources explains only part of it. During the sixties, black income actually increased much faster than prices, suggesting a surplus translatable into home purchasing power for some blacks. Other factors are also influential, for example, the rate of new housing construction, housing patterns reinforced by federal policy, and the speed with which economically available housing for blacks becomes actually available when discrimination is broken.[15] Even when they are not personally hostile to blacks, suburban realtors are under constant social pressure (whether "real" or merely felt) not to rent or sell to "social undesirables" who would allegedly defile the neighborhood. Even organizations established to integrate suburban neighborhoods work within constraints generated by these expectations. They try to control the infiltration of blacks on the assumption that whites will flee once the proportion of Negroes climbs above a carefully calculated peril point—the "tipping" level. Past this point, the operational code asserts, the integrated neighborhood will not be able to hold its mixed "pepper-and-salt" character.

Pressure to break this hold of realtor discrimination has been far from successful. Moral suasion changes few minds, and state or local legislation has had an effect which is

... mainly symbolic and ritualistic: Its existence holds aloft the explicit standard of equal opportunity in housing, confirming the American creed for all of us; but tacitly those who pass the law know that its provisions will not be enforced in a way which basically threatens white neighborhoods.[16]

A national law passed in 1968 against housing discrimination has not been vigorously enforced, its effectiveness deterred by antagonistic political and economic forces.[17]

It is the case here, as in every dispute over civil rights, that widely accepted basic values conflict. The policy goals of "integration" and "open occupancy" fill the public agenda of political issues on housing. There is obviously a private agenda at work, also, filled with fears and prejudices too familiar to explain here. Yet there also exists on this and other such issues a philosophical agenda containing a basic conflict over values of equality and liberty which is too rarely explicated.[18] Integrationists are appealing to the value in our national credo that men should—if not *be* equal—be equally treated, even if it takes law to compel that action. Advocates of "open occupancy" are appealing to the value of liberty, that men should be free to do as they will without the hindrance of law. Just as every other place in our history—rural township or county, small town, big city—has furnished a new context for this normative constitutional dispute in the past, so has the suburb in our time.

But discrimination alone does not explain suburban segregation, for also involved are changing economic conditions within the metropolis. Economists studying the relationship between housing location and job availability are undoubtedly correct in asserting that blacks who stay in the festering city or the black segments of inner suburbs pay heavily for their isolation. At one time, blacks who occupied run-down tenements in core city neighborhoods benefited economically from their accessibility to employers seeking unskilled service and manual labor in workshops of the city and the heavy-industry belt around it. Because of transient demands for casual service labor, women could find employment, if only at a rock-bottom wage scale. Even when they were unemployed, men and women alike could keep in touch with job opportunities by asking friends and neighbors or by going to public employment agencies.

But while the agencies are still there, many of the jobs have gone. As industry and retailing decentralize, the outward shift of job opportunities severely handicaps people bound to the inner city and its immediate environs. After examining the structure of employment demand in the twenty-five largest SMSAs, Mooney estimated that their central cities have lost about 340,000 jobs in manufacturing and another 250,000 in retail trade. More is involved than mere relocation, with one job springing up in suburbs for each one abolished in the core city. Thus in 1948, core cities accounted for 67.8 percent of all metropolitan jobs, but by 1963 their share had dwindled to 59.2 percent. Women, Mooney noted, were less likely than men to be seriously harmed by the outward migration. The jobs that have traditionally been filled by women (waitresses; secretaries, receptionists, and other office help; seamstresses and sewing machine operators) have been more successful in resisting the outward flow of jobs.[19]

The steadily accelerating attrition of job opportunities, particularly for men, poses a great problem for the future well-being of central city and inner suburb blacks. For whites, current prosperity and prospects for steady employment at high wages have *preceded* the decision to move to suburbs. But the diffusion of job opportunities suggests that the northern blacks will have to move out to suburbs in order to rise out of poverty, rather than the other way around. Some hint of this actually occurring is suggested in the earlier finding of the relatively lower status of blacks in the suburb. Compared with city blacks, suburban blacks had better incomes but lower education in 1970, a sign that lower status blacks have been moving outwards in order to find better paying jobs. Yet it is also true that suburban migration has drawn some better-off blacks, particularly young married couples. But most of these move just over the city's rim, as we have noted—from north Oakland to south Berkeley, from New York to Nassau County, and from Los Angeles to Inglewood.[20]

But we must not lose sight of a central demographic and human fact; there is not all that much of a better life for blacks in either city or suburb. As noted earlier, the proportion of blacks able to move to suburbia remains remarkably low and stable. As Frieden has pointed out, although it is true that jobs are growing faster in suburbs, the total number of jobs is still greater in central cities of America. Also, in most sectors the decline of the city is relative, not absolute; from 1957 to 1962, job losses in other sectors were offset by increases in government employment for eight of our largest SMSAs.[21] The 1970 census did not show any great occupational advantage for suburban blacks; whether in city or suburb, about the same percentage were unemployed or had to live beneath the poverty line.

These constraints on black suburbanization, whether stemming from discrimination or structural changes in housing and the economy, clearly call for something more than drifting with purportedly irresistible social forces. Public policy does make a difference in expanding life opportunities of any group, as farmers, businessmen, union members, and professionals can attest to from the history of economic policy. Such policy has made a surprising difference in the opportunities southern blacks now enjoy for voting and better education.[22] To do so, however, requires understanding of conditions under which law can affect social change. These are conditions of the kind of policy legislated, the vigor of administrative enforcement, and the degree of support and opposition from those benefiting and those losing by such policy.[23] This is a major undertaking, better held for our concluding section on suburban policy.

Conclusion: "Suburbia" or Suburbs?

In these two chapters, we have showed how a tendentious stereotype has blurred the diversity in suburban social forms. A suburb settled by workers manning shifts in a nearby factory differs sharply from a prestige suburb inhabited by bank presidents and account executives. Both, in turn, have little in common with the lower-middle class reservation with its beige curtains and monotonous tract housing. "Suburbia" is an abstraction which nullifies the striking heterogeneity among all the communities that shelve away from the border of a city. There is no archetypical suburb; as Dobriner has noted:

There is such a diversity of suburban forms it is misleading to label all suburbs 'homogeneous.' Suburbs differ greatly in the circumstances of their creation, in the price of their real estate, their degree of transiency, their size and institutional complexity, and the income, life style, occupation and educational level of their residents. . . . Unfortunately, many of the quasi-empirical studies which gave rise to the homogeneity myth focused on upper-middle class areas around large central cities.[24]

If so, what accounts for the popularity of the notion? With his customary astringency, Berger has argued that the myth of suburbia happily suited the ideological needs of tastemakers so diverse and hostile that they could agree on little else.[25] The Luce magazines used "suburbia" with its robust optimism, carefree children, material comforts, and apparent classlessness to bring the melting pot legend back for an encore. The city might be torn apart by ancient tribal feuds and jealousies, but in suburbs all the bases for social cleavage would vanish and a new American emerge. On the Left, critics used the myth to mount an assault on smooth provincial conformity and the erosion of cultural pluralism. In their view, Philistia had been transplanted from the Main Street of the twenties to the Suburbia of the fifties. Since the mere mention of working-class suburbs, black suburbs, and quiet retreats of the very wealthy would work to discredit *both* celebration and denunciation, both sides found it convenient to ignore them. Following Keynes, we may say that "there is no resisting a partial truth whose time has come."

Indeed, the wide disparities in status among suburbs prompts us to question the conventional procedure of comparing *whole cities with their suburban arcs.* Suburban heterogeneity is so great that any average calculated for the entire suburban band is bound to mask differences among the separate municipalities that make up the suburban surrounds. Urban neighborhoods are no less heterogeneous. Cities today, as well as in the past, contain enclaves where the wealthy and well-born reside in luxury high-rises or lovingly redone old brownstones; working-class districts of aging row houses and rundown tenements; and nests of white-collar workers with their wives and young children. In the ethnic checkerboard of inner city, anybody can pick out the urban habitat of Jew and Italian, black and Puerto Rican, Irish and Slovak, storefront and church proclaim the distinctive character of each urban locale. And, as Lieberson has shown, in the suburbs one can expect to find somewhat more diluted enclaves formed by children and grandchildren of the original white immigrant generation.[26] We have earlier noted that new generations of black, brown, and yellow citizens similarly found suburban retreats on the Los Angeles rim. Few distinguishable urban sections lack suburban counterparts. So long as differences are washed away in the process of aggregating different urban neighborhoods into the "city," or of compressing different suburban municipalities into the "suburban ring," similarities between the suburban community and the equally homogeneous urban neighborhood will not appear.

While no moat divides the city from its suburban bands, some differences between them still persist and can be expected to linger for some time. The city is still a port of entry for poor whites and blacks from the rural South and Puerto Rico. Though their position has been declining, cities still occupy nodes in the latticework of transportation and communication activities that spans the continent. As long as attorneys, stockbrokers, and securities men have to stay close to the stock exchange and courthouse, we can expect these activities to stay close to the heart of the city. For some time, the city will continue to play host to spectator sports and amusements of all kinds, because that is where the spokes and grids of the transportation network can assemble the most customers. For the same reason, lively arts are city arts. Spacious and specialized theatres, concert halls, and galleries all benefit from the central city's monopoly of access. When the Metropolitan Opera Company moved, it took up quarters in Lincoln Center a few blocks north, not in Manhasset or Massapequa Park.

If the suburban development of the last half-century meant merely the thinning-out of residential densities, proliferation of detached single-family housing, and gradual diffusion of industrial activity, it would have been interesting only to demographers, social ecologists, and city planners. It is only because suburbanization is supposed to exert effects on those who live there that the topic has intrigued sociologists and political scientists. Because suburban life is held to work such miraculous changes upon the political style of its inhabitants, it is time to look at suburbs in the broad context of national politics.

**Part 2
Electoral Behavior**

Political Competition in The Suburbs, 1948-1964

While the Illinois ballots were being tallied in 1952, Colonel Jake Arvey despondently noted impressive pluralities that General Eisenhower was rolling up in Cook County's suburban precincts. As the suburbs were counted in, Stevenson was being counted out; Arvey lamented that "The suburbs were murder."[1] Shortly afterwards, Senator Robert A. Taft joyously forecast that Democrats would never again occupy the White House unless they could find some magic to charm suburbanites away from the GOP. Four years later, his prediction was echoed in a paper Edward C. Banfield delivered to the American Political Science Association. In it, he prophesied a dismal future for the Democratic party. Assuming that Republicans would continue to harvest six of ten votes in suburban counties and giving Democrats the same proportion in the big city, he concluded that customary Democratic pluralities for metropolitan areas as a whole would vanish sometime between 1956 and 1960. By 1975, the GOP would have an enormous metropolitan margin of more than two million votes, certainly a formidable lead.[2] Given the inclination of downstate voters to continue voting Republican, it would probably become insurmountable; suburban migration would make Republicans the majority party.

Conversion and Transplantation: Two-and-a-half Theories in Search of Evidence

The Theories

Scholars and journalists confected a number of explanations for the Republican conquest of the suburbs during the fifties. Instantly popularized, they sought to explain away the rout of liberal presidential candidates in two consecutive American elections. Three divergent, but not necessarily inconsistent, explanatory accounts were advanced.

The first, and probably most popular explanation, held that urban Democrats change into suburban Republicans as soon as they forsake the city for their new environment. Supported mainly by impression and anecdote, the *conversion* hypothesis saw the suburb as a chrysalis, where men and women enter as Democrats and emerge as Republicans. Once tied to the party by occupational, ethnic, religious, and occupational bonds, the Democratic affiliation of the *émigré* begins to waver once he signs the mortgage note on his suburban ranch house. Sur-

51

rounded by new neighbors he wishes to emulate, he is overcome by a consuming desire to model his life on the social template furnished by people down the street, most of whom are Republicans. Thrown among new companions, both husband and wife begin to adopt their points of view. Politically, they become contemptuous of big-city Democratic machines that purportedly trade on patronage and irrelevant tribal loyalties. The new suburbanite also finds that Republicans are rather more solicitous of property rights. Now that he is a homeowner saddled with a whopping mortgage, this notion no longer seems windy rhetoric. So, he winds up voting for Republicans in state and national elections, as the older residents have always done. It is his way of signifying he has left the city behind; more than that, it consolidates his status as a man who is coming up in the world.[3]

As the conversion hypothesis puts it, settling the suburbs means more than reshuffling the metropolitan population. In this view, the demographer's "flight to the suburbs" encapsulates an entire process of social transformation and assimilation, a comprehensive change in social and political identifications. Loyalties that once were nurtured on the steaming asphalt pavements of the big city foam away, yielding to new preferences in consumer goods, leisure time activities, and political parties. These new attitudes ripen and intensify as the newcomer internalizes the distinctive suburban ethos, making it part of his own political perspective. As culmination of the general process, the urban Democrat metamorphoses into a suburban Republican.

Whether right or wrong, the conversion explanation had the appealing advantage of simplicity and clarity. Another thesis, which Wood dubbed the *transplantation* explanation, was not so clearly stated. In fact, though Wood labored hard to resolve the disparity, it came in two fundamentally distinct variants.[4] One was closely akin to the conversion theory; the other was radically different from it. The version that resembled the conversion thesis asserted that it was mainly people ripe for a political change who left the city for the suburbs. Upwardly mobile and having already acquired a middle-class self-image, they longed to blend in with what they conceived to be the political complexion of the suburb. Thus, the increasing suburban Republican vote was only part of a larger and more subtle process of social mobility.

The major difference between this version of the transplantation theory and the conversion theory lay in the timing of the decision to become a Republican. In the conversion theory, it came *after* the move to the suburbs; in the transplantation theory, it was made *in preparation for* the move. The man getting ready for the move to the suburb resembles the high school senior who starts to learn the words to "Fair Harvard" the day he gets his letter of admission. It is, so to speak, a process of anticipatory socialization.[5] It is fair to add that the two explanations overlap one another; they are not rivals at all. One could plausibly maintain that the homogeneous, social-psychological tenor of the suburb merely reinforces the decision made by the *émigré* before moving.

The other version of the transplantation theory was quite different. It affirmed that partisan attachments, once formed, show remarkable durability. A standing bargain to vote for a party is not likely to wither in transit from tenement to split-level. A big city Republican is likely to choose a Republican suburb, not necessarily because it is Republican but because it is composed of upper-middle class people like himself. Similarly, Democrats moving out of the city are likely to select a suburb whose inhabitants vote Democratic. In this variant, therefore, the social class of the migrant counts most. The political complexion of the suburb he prefers has no independent effect upon his party affiliation. The apparent growth of the Republican vote in the suburbs can be attributed to the greater propensity of the upper-class to move out of the city.[6]

The Contemporary Evidence

If any of the theories were correct, we would logically expect the Democratic share of the big city vote to fall as the GOP portion of the suburban vote increased. To be sure, the Republican share of the suburban vote did rise in the two presidential elections during the fifties. From 1948 to 1952 alone, suburban counties in the fifteen largest metropolitan areas more than doubled the pluralities they gave the GOP, going from 773,000 to almost 1.7 million. Moreover, they increased yet again in 1956.[7] Unfortunately for the symmetry of the explanations, as can be seen by inspecting Table 5-1, Eisenhower got a larger proportion of the big city vote as well, actually gaining *more* votes in the city than in the suburbs. This simple finding, readily available to both Whyte and Burdick, tends to cast doubt on all three theses. It is particularly devastating to advocates of the conversion thesis. From these data one might have concluded, with equal, or better, justification, that a massive conversion to the Republican party was taking place in core cities. Proponents of the conversion thesis did not so conclude, indeed they could not, for this would lead one to abandon the thesis which held that witless conformity is a distinctively suburban phenomenon.

Other evidence points up the fragility of the conversion thesis. In their study of a heavily Republican suburb of Kalamazoo, Manis and Stine found that only 23 of 203 interviewees had changed party affiliations. Of these, it is true, twenty had drifted away from the Democratic party. However,

Eight revealed that they had changed in 1951 or 1952, while only one person had changed since then. Since nearly half the interviewees had moved into the suburb since 1952, it may be assumed that the national situation rather than local influences was responsible for the changes.

Equally hard on the conversion thesis's notion that new suburbanites long to blend into the neighborhood was the fact that fewer than half the recent arrivals knew the political affiliations of the people next door, and not more than a fifth

Table 5-1

The Rising Fortunes of the Republican Party in Fourteen Big Cities, Presidential Elections, 1948-1956

CITY	GOP % of Major Party Vote in			Percentage Increase of GOP Vote from		
	1948	1952	1956	1948-1952	1952-1956	1948-1956
Baltimore	45.2	48.3	55.9	3.1	7.6	10.7
Boston	28.6	40.4	46.4	11.8	6.0	17.8
Buffalo	41.8	50.4	57.7	8.6	7.3	15.9
Chicago	41.4	45.6	51.3	4.2	5.7	9.9
Cincinnati	51.3	56.8	62.5	5.5	5.7	11.2
Cleveland	35.6	40.1	45.4	4.5	5.3	9.8
Detroit	38.1	39.5	38.2	1.4	−1.3	0.1
Los Angeles	46.8	52.1	50.9	5.3	−1.2	4.1
Minneapolis- St. Paul	39.1	48.2	49.7	9.1	1.5	10.6
New York	41.0	44.6	49.0	3.6	4.4	8.0
Philadelphia	51.1	41.6	43.0	−9.5	1.4	−8.1
Pittsburgh	38.9	43.9	47.7	5.0	3.8	8.8
St. Louis	35.4	38.0	39.1	2.6	1.1	3.7
San Francisco	48.8	53.0	51.8	4.2	−1.2	3.0
Mean Change				4.2	3.3	7.5

could remember ever having discussed the 1956 presidential race with their neighbors.[8]

In a similar vein, Berger's study of Milpitas, a working-class suburb of San Jose, provides more evidence against the conversion thesis. The tract Berger sampled was about 80 percent Democratic in registration, and, despite the alleged Republicanizing effect of suburban life, Eisenhower's vote actually *dropped off* between 1952 and 1956. Just as important, Berger's suburbanites did not know how their neighbors voted, or what party they favored. Only half the sample correctly labeled their surroundings as predominantly Democratic. Nor was politics a matter of great discussion and interest. Thirteen percent were entirely unaware of the party affiliation of their two closest friends, and another 11 percent did not know the political allegiance of even one close friend. They excused their ignorance on the grounds that talking about politics or religion was considered taboo.[9] It is difficult to see how party-switching by social pressure could have been so pervasive if suburbanites were ignorant of the partisan affiliation of their neighbors and were, in any case, reluctant to talk about politics.

As we have noted above, both the conversion thesis and the first version of the transplantation hypothesis assume a constant relationship among social mobility, suburban relocation and change in party identification from Democrat to Republican. But data in *The American Voter* show that the imputed sequences do not withstand detailed scrutiny. First of all, they show convincingly that the upward bound urban resident was just as likely to hold on to an address somewhere in the city as he was to exchange it for one somewhere in a suburban belt. Furthermore, those who clung to the core city were just slightly less likely to switch to the GOP than those who moved outside it, accounting in part for the increase in the Republican percentage of big city votes set forth in Table 5-1.

Most important of all, a change from Democratic to Republican partisanship was *not* uniformly associated with upward social mobility. True, of the upwardly mobile switching parties, just about 58 percent *did* move from the Democrats to the Republicans. But, among those suffering a decline in occupational status, 53 percent also went in the same direction. For whatever reason, people going up or down the occupational mobility scale were more likely to change their party identifications from Democrat to Republican than from Republican to Democrat, even though the difference in magnitudes was not large.[10] That is, status and changes in party affiliation were virtually unrelated. But since upward-bound people outnumbered those going down the ladder by a ratio of 2.5 to 1, the Republican party emerged as the major beneficiary of social mobility.

Suburban Voting in the Fifties:
Eisenhowerism or Republicanism

The discovery of the American suburb coincided with an electoral floodtide that twice swept Eisenhower into office, from which commentators hastily concluded that suburban environments transform Democrats into Republicans. Left uncertain was whether Eisenhower's pluralities signified only a fleeting attachment to an immensely popular candidate or durable loyalty to his party. A comparison of party identification and distribution of the presidential vote in three consecutive elections beginning in 1948 will help decide the issue.[11]

In the narrow Truman victory of 1948, only a relatively few Democrats broke party ranks to vote for Dewey. Among self-identified Republicans, very much the same pattern prevailed, even though proportionately more weak Republicans than tepid Democrats crossed party lines. The votes in that year thus reflected basic party loyalties with a high degree of accuracy.

The elections of 1952 and 1956 were different. What is important about them was the dissociation between party identification and actual distribution of ballots. Although the percentage of voters favoring the two *parties* changed very little if at all, Eisenhower scored two impressive victories. For a variety of transient reasons, no less important for being momentary, Eisenhower's two candidacies drew many Democrats across party lines. He received almost two-thirds of all votes cast by citizens who classified themselves as Independents or nonpartisans, 38 percent of the weak Democratic partisans, and 16 percent of the voters who still acknowledged strong affiliation with the Democratic party. By and large, the vast bulk of Republican party adherents stood fast.

But by 1960 it was clear that the surge of Democratic voters had flowed only temporarily to Eisenhower and not permanently to his party. The dominant division of basic party loyalties had not been disturbed by defections during the fifties, for by 1960, the 1948 pattern had more or less reasserted itself. The large suburban pluralities for Eisenhower, as we shall show, were surprisingly volatile thereafter.

Despite the supposed ubiquity of suburban nonpartisanship in local affairs, defenders of the conversion thesis assumed that all votes cast in *national* elections are motivated by enduring partisan loyalties, rather than a momentary attachment to a particularly attractive candidate. In a typical presidential election year, the inference would not have been a bad one to draw. Normally, the pattern of party preferences follows the distribution of voting choices (except for self-declared Independents). But 1952 and 1956 were not normal years, and so the inference proved treacherous.

Data from *The American Voter* corroborate this finding for suburban voters, at least for native-born whites in the North. In 1956, 67 percent of the suburban migrants from the city voted for Eisenhower. Among this group we find a somewhat higher percentage of Republican than Democratic partisans, 38 to 32 percent. But for those who had grown up in a suburb, the excess of Republican identifiers was even greater, 43 to 27 percent. The same disparity between vote and party affiliation was visible in big cities as well. Among lifelong inhabitants, 54 percent voted for Eisenhower in 1956, but only 23 percent counted themselves as Republicans. Of those living in core cities but brought up elsewhere, the difference was greater still, 67 to 38 percent.[1][2]

Read one way, voting data assembled during the fifties point to a booming Republican vote in both city and suburb. But seen in the context of data which gauge the tenacity of partisan affiliations, they are better interpreted as a transient groundswell of support for the man who just happened to be the Republican candidate for president in every election held during the fifties.

As The Suburbs Go . . .

The Thesis of Party Realignment

In recent years, just how Republican has the suburban vote for president been? Has the Republican vote been rising in suburbs while suffering a decline in cities they surround? Given the vast increase in the size of the suburban electorate, these questions are important to tackle. If an increasingly Democratic core city is splitting off from an increasingly Republican suburbia, it might well mean that the American polity is veering towards a massive critical realignment.

Speculating on the significance of a continued rise in the suburban Republican vote, one can easily imagine the GOP inheriting suburbs with their growing electorate while a disintegrating Democratic party desperately hangs on to its legions in the shrinking cities. Aligned with habitual rural Republicans all over the country, suburban Republicans could conceivably become major partners in a dominant new party coalition exploiting conflicts already breaking to the surface of contemporary American life.

With poor black and white bottled up in the cities and urban welfare rolls already soaring, it is not entirely implausible to imagine some of the domestic policies which managers of this emergent coalition would market to its steady clientele.[13] Rhetorically lashing out at "welfare chiselers" and "improvident men and women too lazy to work," these managers would very likely proclaim their hostility to any kind of federal "handout"—public housing, income maintenance proposals, socialized medicine, and all the rest. In a word, they would oppose all redistributive measures designed to make cash and services flow to impoverished big city residents.

To be sure, the polarization between city and environs would not be altogether complete. Democrats would still be able to mobilize some cosmopolitans who happen to reside in suburbs, e.g., social activists who work in universities and on federally-subsidized projects at research centers. Suburban Jews would also fight to resist the Republican tide. Neither would Republicans be completely shut off from dependable sources of urban voting strength. They would be able to pick up votes of (mainly white) construction and production workers pinched by spreading black wards. They could also count on the faithfulness of elderly city-dwellers who had always voted Republican.

All past coalitions have been heterogeneous to a degree; what counts are the major linkages between party loyalty and dominant elements of an emerging stratification system. It may be, as Apter has argued, that the stratification system produced by industrialism is giving way under impact of the post-industrial economy. In the most advanced sectors of the economy, Apter proposes, the classic blue-collar, white-collar differentiation has been superseded by a class structure of "technologically competent," "technologically obsolescent," and "technologically superfluous." Burnham has further conjectured that a new mode of party alignment may spring from this stratification system once it takes hold. Signs are already visible. The technologically competent and superfluous (chiefly the hardcore poor), he suggests, are natural allies against the "threatened middle." As antipathies become politicized (as they already are, to a degree), coalitions may become institutionalized in new party alignments.[14]

Presidential Voting as an Indicator
of Realignment

In this section, we seek to examine whether recent presidential elections point toward this possibility. We will concentrate on five presidential elections beginning with Truman's narrow victory in 1948 and closing with Johnson's lopsided triumph in 1964, We will look at patterns displayed within eleven key states: Illinois, Maryland, Massachusetts, Michigan, Minnesota, Missouri, New Jersey, New York, Ohio, Pennsylvania, and Wisconsin. All are outside the South and have historically oscillated between the parties in presidential elections. None can fairly be regarded as a "safe" state; between 1948 and 1964, no state in the collection presented either party with an unbroken string of electoral successes. Only in Missouri did a party win as many as four of the five elections; of the set of 55 contests, Republicans won 27 and Democrats 28—as even a division as it is possible to get. The states are populous, accounting for approximately half the nationwide electorate in each of the five elections (Table 5-2).

For this analysis, each state was divided into three grand divisions:

1. *Core Cities*: The central cities designated by the Bureau of the Census as the focus of a SMA (for the elections of 1948, 1952, and 1956), or a SMSA (1960 and 1964).
2. *Suburbs*: The non-core city portion of either the SMA or SMSA.
3. *Downstate*: The non-metropolitan residual; roughly, the rural and semi-rural portions of the state.[a]

Table 5-2 shows the relative size of the electorate in each of the three grand divisions, election by election. By 1960, the sheer size of the suburban electorate overtook that of their core cities. However, the downstate share remained relatively constant over five elections. Thus, reshuffling of the electorate reflects gross population shifts we pointed to in the last section: the fading away of the big city, the growth of suburbs, and relative stability in the downstate population.

Table 5-2
Growth of Suburban Presidential Vote in Eleven Large States, 1948-1964

Percentage of Votes Cast in:	Year				
	1948	1952	1956	1960	1964
City	44.2	41.5	38.4	35.9	34.8
Suburb	29.0	32.5	35.9	38.6	40.2
Downstate	26.8	26.1	25.7	25.5	25.0
Total State Electorate	26,718,239	32,996,533	33,216,821	35,827,623	35,048,188
Percentage of Nationwide Vote	54.8	53.6	53.5	52.0	49.6

[a]As already noted, outer boundaries of the SMSA extend far beyond the more densely settled urban fringe to take in territory that is virtually indistinguishable from the rural downstate area. A bias thus results from combining votes cast by citizens of this region with ballots cast by residents of suburban municipalities nearer the core city. However, since the effects of the bias inflate the proportion of Republican voters in suburbs, it is not serious. If it were possible to eliminate the distortion, our case would be strengthened, not weakened.

Figure 5-1 traces the fluctuations in the Republican vote over the five elections. As can easily be seen, the pitch and incline for all three lines parallel one another with remarkable fidelity, almost as though they were chained together. With the exception of 1948, when suburbs had a slightly greater percentage of Republican voters than downstate (55.3 to 53.1 percent), the three grand divisions appeared in the same order throughout the series. In each election but the first, downstate voted most heavily Republican, cities most heavily Democratic, and suburbs occupied a middle position.

More important still, as can be seen by inspecting the *width* of the band dividing core city from suburb, percentage differences between the two remained

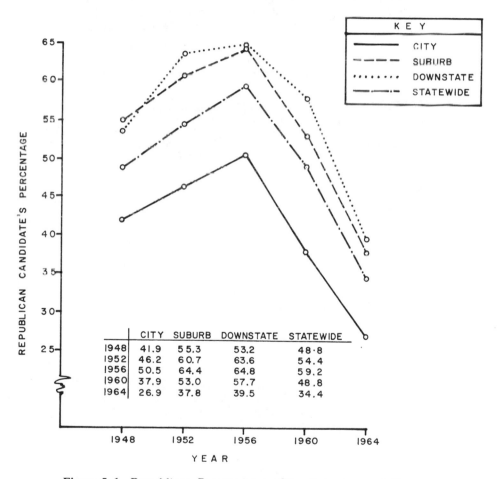

	CITY	SUBURB	DOWNSTATE	STATEWIDE
1948	41.9	55.3	53.2	48.8
1952	46.2	60.7	63.6	54.4
1956	50.5	64.4	64.8	59.2
1960	37.9	53.0	57.7	48.8
1964	26.9	37.8	39.5	34.4

Figure 5-1. Republican Percentage in City, Suburban and Downstate Areas of 11 States, Presidential Elections, 1948 to 1964.

relatively constant. In fact, the disparity between percentages was less in the Goldwater-Johnson contest than it was in any of the four preceding elections, a devastating test of the supposition that suburbs throughout this era were becoming more conservative.[b] It can, after all, be plausibly argued that Eisenhower's conspicuous lack of any clearly defined ideological posture inhibited the turnout of suburban conservatives who were confronted by a meaningless choice between Eisenhower's Tweedledeedee and Stevenson's Tweedlededum. Yet, when choice supplanted echo, the Republican vote in suburbs dropped off even more precipitously than the Republican vote in core cities.

So, far from revealing an ever-widening moat between city and suburb, our probing uncovers a great similarity between the two. The strikingly uniform rhythm detected in the rise and fall of all three trend lines suggests a *secular* shift, not a segmental one. Each grand division responded uniformly to the mixture of short-term forces characteristic of each election; throughout, there was a notable absence of polarization along metropole-suburban lines. Whatever the new pattern of party realignment waiting in the wings, it will most likely *cut across* grand divisions rather than polarize them.[15]

[b]For elections conducted between 1948 and 1960, the mean difference between suburban and big city Republican vote amounted to 13.2 percent. The smallest difference in these four elections was 13.4 percent in 1958. Both mean and low differences are greater than the 11.9 percent difference recorded in 1964. Hence, suburban and big city candidate preferences reached their point of maximum convergence in the 1964 election.

Suburban Characteristics and the Vote for President, 1948-1964

So far we have shown how Republican votes in the urban, suburban, and down-state areas of eleven states tended to rise and fall together. The procedures we followed forced us to slice through time and space with a certain degree of reck-lessness. In particular, because we computed only mean Republican votes for the suburban ring taken as a whole, our analysis neatly suppressed any variation in voting patterns *among* individual suburban communities. As we saw in earlier chapters, suburbs are not perfect replicas of one another but rather display wide variations in socioeconomic character. Almost needless to say, status attributes are not randomly distributed among all communities of the suburban ring, so that all have about the same proportions of blue-collar workers or of the very rich. For a number of reasons, people of similar occupational standing, income, and education tend to congregate in the same community, producing an observ-able strain towards homogeneity within the suburb.

One reason is income level. Even though a very wealthy suburb may contain a blighted corner where gardeners and domestic workers live, high prices for hous-ing tend to exclude machinists and clerks. The outcome is that the community as a whole is recognizably "upper-crust." Manual laborers are similarly isolated in distinctive communities, perhaps joined by lower echelons of service workers and a sprinkling of aged people who cannot afford more expensive housing. There is more to it than the cost of real estate, of course. Workers with only a high school education would find it uncomfortable to live among account execu-tives, most of whom have completed college. As a result, suburban communities, particularly smaller ones, tend to take on characteristics which remain relatively stable over the short run. For this reason, we shall show linkages between voting behavior and socioeconomic attributes of entire *municipalities*, rather than be-tween the vote and individuals having these same characteristics.

A Methodological Note

It is important to note that the associations are based on individual suburbs rath-er than on suburban individuals. Statistical measures based on many millions of individual citizens living in American suburbs would almost certainly diverge from those we shall report in the rest of this chapter, as Robinson has shown in a justly famous essay.[1] It is hazardous to make inferences about the behavior of discrete individuals on the basis of measures that refer to whole communities.

Individual and collective measures do not refer to the same units of aggregation, and it is important to remember this point.

Risky as aggregative associations are, however, they must be used to interpret past elections. Without them, any effort to reconstruct political history is bound to be incomplete. In discussing electoral data, we shall pause to show how our aggregate measures tend to parallel results of investigations using individual voters as basic units of analysis. As the two different streams of data converge on the same conclusion, our confidence in each is amplified.

Since our aim was to test for linkages between suburban social characteristics and electoral performance, we chose only those suburbs with over 10,000 in population for which reliable and complete election data could be assembled. Abundant voting data are available for virtually all U.S. counties, but securing election information for smaller units is only slightly less difficult than getting a verbatim transcript of politburo meetings. Through several years, however, we did collect data from correspondence with local and state election officials, from official manuals, and from a colleague, Joseph Zikmund. Even then we could not get data from all the big states. Texas and Missouri are two spectacular cases; they report election data by wards and by whole counties, with nothing in between.

We finally had data for the presidential elections of 1948 and 1952 in 400 suburbs, and for the elections of 1956-1964 in 407. Overall, we had complete data for all five presidential elections in 389 suburbs. A state-by-state summary is presented as Table 6-1. Regrettably, this adventitious sample is far from optimal; it is plagued both by patchiness and regional biases. Suburbs in states publishing good election records had a much better than average chance of winding up in our sample, accounting for the heavy representation of suburbs in New England, Middle Atlantic, and North Central states.

Even so, suburbs in eight of the ten most populous states are included; only Texas and Florida are missing from the inventory. Quite apart from having many inhabitants, states looming largest in our sample have a history of alternating between parties in presidential elections, assuring us of reasonable heterogeneity in their voting behavior. As of 1960, the *Municipal Year Book* listed 736 suburbs with at least 10,000 inhabitants.[2] Our 407 represent better than 53 percent of that total.

Suburban Movement in Presidential Voting

In Table 5-2, we showed how the Republican presidential vote in suburban rings of eleven large states tended to inscribe the same pattern as core cities and downstate areas. The same profile emerges from an examination of individual suburban municipalities, as seen in Table 6-2, which presents a bird's-eye view of this distribution in each election between 1948 and 1964.

Table 6-1

Distribution of Suburbs Included in the Analysis, by State

| | Presidential Elections[a] | | |
	1948-1952	1956-1964	1948-1964
Maine	2	2	2
Massachusetts	46	46	46
Rhode Island	9	9	9
Connecticut	14	14	14
New York	25	27	24
New Jersey	102	104	102
Pennsylvania	70	69	69
Ohio	54	56	54
Indiana	2	0	0
Illinois	3	1	1
Michigan	20	23	20
Wisconsin	13	15	13
Minnesota	16	18	16
Iowa	1	0	0
Missouri	2	2	2
Virginia	1	1	1
Colorado	1	0	0
Washington	2	0	0
California	17	20	16
N =	400	407	389

Sources: State legislative manuals, reports of the Secretary of State, and communications from local election registrars.

[a]Totals vary because some suburbs were not incorporated until after the 1952 presidential elections, because data were missing, and because some suburbs dropped below the 10,000 population level between 1950 and 1960.

Change in the relative position of the median suburb from one election to another is a simple but informative measure. If suburbs were actually socializing ex-city dwellers to become loyal to the Republican party, the median suburb should fall in a higher Republican bracket each year. At least, it should not fall in a lower one. Yet, as we see, the path etched by the median suburb from election to election looks very much like the single-peaked profile earlier seen in Figure 5-1. From 1948 to 1952 and again from 1952 to 1956, the median suburb climbed up one notch. But after the GOP attained its 1956 peak, Nixon and Goldwater toppled down the other side, dropping two notches in each subsequent election. If the rise can be legitimately described as a gradual ascent, the fall deserves to be called bonecracking. In about half the communities, fewer had 30 percent of their registered voters sided with Goldwater.

The five cumulative arrays in Table 6-2 tell us more about the distribution of suburbs among the intervals. What stands out with startling clarity is the absence

Table 6-2

Cumulative Distribution of Selected Suburbs by Percentage Republican Vote, Presidential Elections, 1948-1964

Percentage Republican	1948 (N=400)[a]	1952 (N=400)[a]	1956 (N=407)[a]	1960 (N=407)	1964 (N=407)
70.1+	100.2%	100.1%	99.9%	100.0%	100.0%
65.1-70.0	81.7	76.1	67.8	94.8	99.3
60.1-65.0	72.2	65.1	*52.6*	88.7	98.8
55.1-60.0	61.4	*51.1*	39.8	79.9	96.6
50.1-55.0	*51.1*	38.6	26.0	63.9	94.4
45.1-50.0	42.8	28.8	17.2	*52.1*	91.2
40.1-45.0	30.5	18.8	9.6	40.1	82.8
35.1-40.0	22.5	10.3	4.9	27.3	70.0
30.1-35.0	12.5	6.8	2.7	16.7	*55.7*
0-30.0	6.5	2.5	1.5	11.0	40.0

Note: The group containing the median suburb is in italics.

[a]Totals may be more or less than 100.0 percent due to rounding.

of any long-term continuity in the patterns. Whatever else may be said of inter-election transformations in the shape of the distributions, the changes are too abrupt to be described as gradual or crescive.

From one perspective, the pattern of surge and shift traced over five contests was extremely volatile. From another vantage point, however, the rhythm and pace of the movement between one party and another was remarkably regular. Most important of all, the mixture of long-standing partisan attachments and transient short-run forces at no point polarized suburban municipalities into two sharply dissimilar groups, one as strongly Democratic as the other was Republican. Rather, as is evident from changes in the shape of cumulative distributions from one election to the next, suburban voters circulated between parties in a strikingly uniform way.

Thus, Democratic suburbs of 1948 moved towards the Republican candidate in 1952, while suburbs Dewey had carried were voting even more heavily Republican than they had in 1948. A mirror image of this broad and comprehensive secular movement can be detected in the last three elections in the series. In 1956, three-quarters of the suburbs bunched up in the Republican half of the cumulative array, a distribution produced by an accentuation of the movement that occurred between 1948 and 1952. Four years later, top-heavy Republican portions of the array had begun to sag downward toward the Democrats. Almost half the suburbs still retained Republican majorities, but they were more evenly dispersed throughout the upper half of the distribution. Meanwhile, marginally Republican and barely Democratic suburbs of 1956 were enrolling substantial majorities for Kennedy in 1960. By 1964, the Republican rout was complete, with most suburbs falling into the dense lower tail of the array.

Suburban Social and Electoral Linkages

1948-1952

To determine these suburbs' structural and electoral configurations, we split the five elections into two segments, 1948-1952 and 1956-1964, which gave us the closest possible fit between elections and the most current census. Optimally, interpolation between censuses would have provided better measures of suburban social dimensions for the two intercensal elections, but this proved impossible. About a quarter of our suburbs appeared for the first time in the 1960 Census of Population and Housing. In addition, that census deepened its coverage of American municipalities by adding a much wider array of descriptive measures about each one. Even so, because no election is more than four years away from any one census, distortions should be minimal.

Electoral profiles are set forth in Table 6-3. Each suburb has been first classified according to the combination of majorities it registered in the presidential elections of 1948 and 1952. By far the larger share of suburbs stayed with the same party in the two elections. Even so, the top row of Table 6-3 highlights the magnitude of Eisenhower's personal appeal. Slightly more than a third of the suburbs that were Democratic in 1948 defected to him, as compared with only five suburbs which supported Dewey in 1948 and Stevenson in 1952. As is evident from the table, all but the smallest group of suburbs moved toward Eisenhower. In fact, his percentage edge over Dewey was greater in the 110 suburbs that voted Democratic in both elections than it was in the 224 suburbs chalking up Republican majorities in both years. Further, the variability around the mean of the distribution was less in 1952 than it had been in 1948, as can be seen in the shrinking of the coefficient of variability (expressed as the ratio of the standard deviation to the mean).

Considered as individual units, suburbs moved towards Eisenhower as though they were chained together. In so doing, they duplicated a pattern found by others in a national opinion survey:

. . . groups strongly Democratic in 1948 were but weakly Democratic in 1952, groups evenly divided in 1948 were likely to be clearly Republican in 1952, and groups predominantly Republican in 1948 remained strongly Republican in 1952.[3]

It is noteworthy how these two analyses tend to reinforce one another, despite differences in units of analysis. The survey discerned a trend towards Eisenhower in each conventional demographic layer formed by stratifying voters according to their education, occupation, and income. Rich and poor, blue collar and white, schooled and unschooled—all these components of the electorate flowed massively towards Eisenhower and gave him towering majorities in two consecutive presidential races. Our analysis, on the other hand, is based on the gross

Table 6-3
Suburban Characteristics and the Vote for President, 1948-1952

Majority in 1948 Majority in 1952	D D	D R	R D	R R	All Suburbs	Mean r with Percentage GOP 1948-1952
	(N=110)	(N=61)	(N=5)	(N=224)	(N=400)	
Electoral Data:						
% GOP, 1948	36.2	46.4	52.9	65.5	54.5	
Standard Deviation	10.5	7.6	a	11.0	16.6	
% GOP, 1952	42.5	55.1	46.8	68.0	58.8	
Standard Deviation	12.1	4.7	a	9.9	14.9	
	(N=100)b	(N=48)b	(N=4)b	(N=157)b	(N=309)b	
Socioeconomic Characteristic:						
Median Age	30.2	31.1	31.4	33.4	31.9	
Standard Deviation	2.2	2.9	a	3.1	3.2	
% Aged	6.7	7.4	7.7	8.3	7.6	.53
Standard Deviation	2.2	2.8	a	2.3	2.4	.31
Median School Years Completed	9.6	10.4	9.5	11.3	10.6	
Standard Deviation	1.0	1.3	a	1.3	1.4	.59
% Unemployed	5.7	4.1	4.9	3.3	4.2	
Standard Deviation	2.3	1.8	a	1.5	2.1	
% Employed in Manufacturing	47.4	40.0	39.9	32.4	38.5	-.48

Standard Deviation	12.9	13.4	a	11.3	14.1	-.47
% Housing, Owner-Occupied	56.9	62.6	64.9	66.4	62.7	.28
Standard Deviation	16.5	17.1	a	15.4	16.6	
% Housing, one-unit	50.1	56.7	52.2	62.5	57.1	.25
Standard Deviation	23.6	23.4	a	21.4	23.4	
% New Housing (Built 1940-1950)	20.7	28.6	14.3	24.9	23.9	.06
Standard Deviation	21.1	24.1	a	19.0	20.7	

Source: *U.S. Census of Population, 1950*, and *U.S. Census of Housing, 1950*.

[a]The number of cases is too small to calculate a meaningful standard deviation.

[b]The number of cases differs from those presented for the voting data because of omissions in the census reports

division of the vote within entire communities rather than on responses volunteered by individual citizens. That the two sets of findings parallel one another indicates that evidence of a secular surge towards Eisenhower is unrelated to the type of unit used in the analysis.

The bottom of Table 6-3 summarizes the pattern of association between socioeconomic characteristics of 309 suburbs in the 1950 census and their electoral performance. (Ninety-one suburbs did not appear in that census, which accounts for the difference in the case base.) As both the profile of correlation coefficients and the means tabulated for each group clearly show, American suburbs in this period were not a homogenized pulp, either socially or in their political preferences. What does emerge clearly from the table is the way disparities in suburban demography were reflected in the presidential vote. Thus the familiar connections between status level and partisan affiliation are found again in suburbia.

Even a brief inspection of the figures recorded in each row reveals the linearity of the relationship, seen also in the sign and magnitude of coefficients calculated for all 309 suburbs. As one goes from left to right across columns from least to most Republican groups of suburbs, the median age and mean proportion of elderly inhabitants (over 65 years of age) both rise.[a] The coefficient of .59 for education and Republican voting was the most robust of all. These findings affirm the conclusion advanced by survey analysis that age and education were two important correlates of the Republican vote in 1948 and 1952.[4] Since their conclusions were based upon a nationwide sample of individual voters, the similarity in our findings is all the more noteworthy.

The next two rows of Table 6-3 deal with candidate preference as a function of occupational composition and gross level of unemployment. In both rows, the size of the mean dwindles as the eye sweeps from left to right across columns, a monotonic progression neatly summed up by the inverse correlation between each index and the division of the vote in these two presidential elections. Suburbs casting majorities for Truman and Stevenson had the most unemployment and topped all groups in the proportion of the labor force employed in manufacturing industries. Peaking in the uniformly Democratic group, the means for each measure decline until they hit the bottom in the group of 157 suburban municipalities.[b] Our findings again coincide with those reported by survey analysis that laborers were least likely of all urban occupations to vote Republican in 1948 and 1952. By contrast, professional and managerial workers in white-collar cadres turned in the greatest majorities for Dewey and Eisenhower.[5]

[a]These two measures are technically dependent; the simple correlation was .70. With the effects of the correlation between these two removed by partialling, the relationship between median age and Republican vote still stood at .46.

[b]The level of unemployment bore little relation to occupational composition; the simple correlation was only .19. Controlling for unemployment dampened the original relationship between occupational composition and the vote from a −.47 simple to a −.44 partial correlation.

Despite Harris's contention that the mere fact of owning a new suburban home disposed citizens to vote Republican, the relationship between housing measures making up the final three rows of the table is clearly flimsy. After all, in even the most Democratic suburbs almost 57 percent of the houses were owner-occupied, a figure not even ten percent smaller than the value recorded for the most Republican suburbs. Within each group, variances were substantial, producing a simple correlation coefficient of only .28. Essentially the same lack of pattern may be seen between the Republican vote and the share of the housing stock in single-unit dwellings. The smallest correlation of all links construction of new housing stock with electoral patterns, for the profile of means actually inscribes a curvilinear pattern, contributing to the .06 correlation. The 48 suburbs casting majorities for Truman in 1948 and for Eisenhower in 1952 had the greatest proportionate amount of new housing construction.

It should be noted that new housing construction is a better proxy measure of net migration than sheer population increase. The latter measure fails to distinguish between population growth due to formation of new households and "natural" growth due to childbirth. Thus, the astoundingly low correlation between home construction and Republican share of the presidential vote may be read as indicating the disassociation between migration patterns and suburban Republican vote. As we saw in the last chapter, both conversion and transplantation theories postulate a high correlation between suburban migration and a large Republican vote.

The inference seems unavoidable that the vast increase in the suburban population had virtually nothing to do with the partisan division of vote in the two presidential elections. The general configuration of the correlation profile indicates that education, age, and occupational composition provides a much firmer explanation. This account is of course strengthened by parallels we have drawn with the analysis presented in *The Voter Decides*.

1956-1964

The second analysis treats presidential elections from 1956 to 1964. Methodologically, this combination is optimal in its variation. The first and last elections in the series are mirror-images of one another, a Republican and a Democratic sweep, with the candidate not only winning but making inroads into many states that had traditionally voted for the opposition. The election of 1960 is the midpoint, both chronologically and politically, for Kennedy barely nosed past Nixon. So, three elections give us, in turn, a Republican avalanche, a hairline Democratic victory and a resounding Democratic triumph. With a sample of only three elections, no better mix of outcomes is possible. The social and electoral data are provided in Table 6-4.

The first point to notice is that only one-half the combinations mathematical-

Table 6-4
Suburban Characteristics and the Vote for President, 1956-1964

Majority in 1956	D	R	R	R	
Majority in 1960	D	D	R	R	
Majority in 1964	D	D	D	R	All Suburbs
	(N=70)	(N=141)	(N=160)	(N=36)	(N=407)
Electoral Data:					
% GOP, 1956	41.5	58.8	71.3	78.6	62.5
Standard Deviation	7.1	12.3	6.9	9.0	14.6
% GOP, 1960	34.0	43.1	58.6	72.2	50.2
Standard Deviation	8.5	10.9	5.1	6.2	14.3
% GOP, 1964	23.7	31.6	40.7	58.5	36.2
Standard Deviation	7.3	12.8	6.1	6.1	15.9
Socioeconomic Characteristics:					
Median Age	29.0	31.5	32.3	33.5	31.6
Standard Deviation	4.9	3.9	4.4	4.5	4.5
% Aged	7.4	8.8	9.2	9.2	8.7
Standard Deviation	3.4	2.9	3.1	3.6	3.2
% Young	37.4	35.0	34.4	35.2	35.2
Standard Deviation	5.9	5.0	5.3	4.7	5.4
Median School Years, Adults	10.5	11.0	11.8	12.6	11.4
Standard Deviation	1.2	1.1	1.0	1.0	1.2
% High School Graduates, Adults	39.6	44.2	53.4	67.2	49.2
Standard Deviation	11.0	11.4	12.1	12.6	14.0
% Employed in Manufacturing	42.8	40.0	32.9	28.6	36.5
Standard Deviation	10.2	10.0	9.6	7.5	11.0
% White-collar	38.9	44.4	54.1	67.4	49.4
Standard Deviation	8.3	9.1	10.9	13.0	12.9
% Unemployed	4.1	3.9	3.3	3.3	3.6
Standard Deviation	1.0	1.1	1.0	1.7	1.2
Median Annual Family Income	$6372	$6769	$7745	$9762	$7368
Standard Deviation	$ 992	$ 885	$1892	$2553	$1811
% Annual Family Income Less than $3000	12.1	9.6	8.5	7.2	9.3
Standard Deviation	6.5	5.0	4.2	4.5	5.1

% Annual Family Income					
More than $10,000	15.2	19.1	27.9	44.7	24.3
Standard Deviation	7.1	7.3	13.2	15.4	13.5
% Housing, Owner-Occupied	76.2	71.8	76.0	87.6	71.4
Standard Deviation	20.0	23.3	17.9	11.1	16.7
Median Value, Owner-					
Occupied Housing	$12,336	$14,361	$17,250	$22,242	$15,912
Standard Deviation	$ 3,583	$ 3,479	$ 5,064	$ 5,859	$ 5,164

Source: *U.S. Census of Population, 1960* and *U.S. Census of Housing, 1960.*

ly possible actually occurred. In no suburb did a Democratic victory in 1956 or 1960 precede a subsequent Republican win, further evidence of the broad movement towards Democratic candidates throughout the sequence. In the banner Republican year of 1956, Eisenhower captured all but 70 of the 407 suburbs. Four years later, 141 suburbs abandoned the GOP to cast majorities for Kennedy, leaving Nixon with 196 communities, somewhat fewer than half the total. The surge to the Democratic candidate in 1964 was even more pronounced; only 36 suburbs stuck with Goldwater. Overall, the precipitate Republican decline may be gauged by the fact although Eisenhower was able to capture 83 percent of the suburbs, Goldwater could manage only 8 percent. The most compelling evidence of Republican decline can be seen by inspecting the top three rows of Table 6-4. In each of the four types of suburb, Nixon fell behind Eisenhower, while Goldwater, in turn, lagged behind Nixon.

We can again detect a basic secular rhythm in the circulation of suburban voters from one party to another. From 1948 to 1952, the largest net Eisenhower shift came in suburbs that had cast majorities for Truman in 1948. This pattern was repeated in reverse from 1956 to 1960 and again from 1960 to 1964. In each pair of elections, suburbs switching from one party to another recorded the greatest net movement of voters from Republicans to Democrats. As a whole, the rotation resembles the swing of a pendulum, where the bob traverses more space than a point located on the stem. This is a metaphorical way of reasserting a point we have made before, that at no point in our two electoral sequences have American suburbs veered in the direction of increasing polarization, with one group becoming more Democratic at the same time as the other became more Republican. On the contrary, interelection movements have been remarkably diffuse and uniform.

What social characteristics differentiate the four varieties of suburb? As Table 6-4 shows, the more affluent and better educated its inhabitants, the greater the likelihood the suburb held fast to Republicans over the course of three elections. On the other hand, the most Democratic suburbs had the lowest family incomes as well as the greatest proportions of impoverished households and the smallest of prosperous families. Staunch Republican suburbs had the heaviest representation of white-collar workers in the labor force, the smallest in manufacturing, the highest scores on two educational measures, and the largest proportions of owner-occupied housing.[c] Looking at these means as they move from left to right across the rows, we find that candidate preferences in these elections were regularly associated with these gross social measures; with few exceptions, the means tilt monotonically in the same direction noted in Table 6-3. These findings make it difficult to escape the conclusion that presidential preferences of suburbanites are better expressed as a function of clear-cut socioeconomic distinctions among types of suburbs than they are of suburban residence *per se*.

We can carry this analysis one step further by correlating primary census variables with the Republican percentage in each of the five contests, as set forth in Table 6-5. Particularly striking is the diminishing importance of age composition in accounting for variations in this vote. Our analysis employed three dimensions of age structure which in 1948 and 1952 showed a correlation with Republican voting.[d] But over the course of the last three elections, these coefficients steadily tapered off to around zero.

On the other hand, indexes reflecting class stratification hold up much better as salient variables. As Table 6-5 shows, there were substantial simple correlations between Republican voting preferences and two measures of educational attainment, three measures of occupation, and three intercorrelated measures of suburban income distribution.[6] Although all correlations were conspicuously weaker in the last three elections in the series than in the first pair, they were (with one exception) somewhat stronger in 1960 than in 1956 or 1964.

Though these findings are problematic, they do not have to be shunted aside as embarrassing anomalies. As so often happens in social science, the problem can be tackled by looking elsewhere for a solution; in this instance, the changing relationship between status polarization and candidate preference which has

---

[c]The vast boom in suburban residential housing construction during the fifties may be seen in a swift comparison of the appropriate data rows in Tables 6-3 and 6-4. Note that the suburbs with Republican pluralities in 1948 and 1952 actually had a *smaller* proportion of owner-occupancies than suburbs uniformly Democratic between 1956 and 1964. Overall, the percentage of owner-occupancies climbed from 57.1 to 71.4. Despite the appeal of the journalistic correlation linking homeownership to fondness for Republicans, our data show a long-term secular decline in the percentage of suburbanites voting for Republican presidential candidates.

[d]Another methodological caution. All measures in Table 6-5 refer to whole communities rather than discrete individuals. Indeed, John Smith's "median age" or "median family income" is a perfect absurdity, as is "the percentage of John Smith's labor force employed in manufacturing." It is illegitimate to force inferences concerning individuals from propositions dealing with divisible collectivities, a statistical variant of the logical fallacy of division. In general, group correlations are larger than correlations founded on individuals, because aggregating procedures tend to average out large deviations around the mean.

In the present instance, however, our findings run parallel with data presented in *The Voter Decides*, which show that Truman's appeal was concentrated among younger voters and fell off sharply with increasing age. All age groups moved Republican in 1952, with the largest net shifts of all occurring among voters who had not passed their thirty-fifth birthday. Campbell, et al. (see note 3, p. 65). These findings are compatible with the correlations recorded for median age in Table 6-5.

Table 6-5

Selected Correlation Coefficients and the Vote for President, 1948-1964

	Zero-order Correlation Coefficient with Percentage GOP in:				
	1948	1952	1956	1960	1964
Median Age	.56	.49	.27	.13	.08
% Aged	.31	.31	.15	.07	−.04
% Young	−	−	.14	−.02	−.03
Median School Years Completed	.60	.57	.41	.50	.38
% High School Graduates	−	−	.42	.53	.42
% Employed in Manufacturing	−.48	−.46	−.34	−.39	−.26
% White-collar	−	−	.50	.56	.44
% Unemployed	.49	−.46	−.23	−.26	−.17
Median Annual Family Income	−	−	.43	48	.42
Family Income, Less than $3000	−	−	−.32	−.29	−.27
Family Income, More than $10,000	−	−	.49	.52	.44
N⁻	309	309	407	407	407

been graphed in *The American Voter*. Using a measure of status polarization based on differences in occupational esteem, those authors set out to test the proposition that electoral conflicts divide American voters along class or status lines. In Marxist theory and post-Marxist exegesis, interests springing from class relationships to instrumentalities of production erase all competing planes of social identification. Though originally dispersed, these interests will coalesce under the impact of capitalism until they divide society into two mutually antagonistic classes.

In testing this proposition, the authors of *The American Voter* proceeded in the following way. If status polarization alone determines political preference, then high-status voters will unanimously prefer one candidate and low-status voters will rally behind his opponent. When this occurs, the correlation between status polarization and dominant lines of political cleavage will attain its maximum (Tau-beta) value of 1.00, another way of stating that status location perfectly predicts candidate preference. If, however, candidates get exactly the same proportion of votes cast by both high- and low-status groups, the complete dissociation between status polarization and electoral conflict will drive the correlation down to zero. Under such circumstances, it is futile to predict candidate preference from status position. There are also intermediate cases, which we may call oblique divisions. If one candidate draws a disproportionately large share of the votes cast by one status group and only a small share of the ballots cast by the other, the value of the coefficient will fall somewhere between zero and 1.0.

Using occupational variables as an index of social status, Campbell *et al.* showed that the status-GOP correlation climbed from .22 in 1944 to a modest peak of .44 in 1948. Over the next two elections it declined precipitously, falling to .20 in 1952 and to an astoundingly low mark of .12 in 1956, indicating the virtual absence of an electorate split by class or status divisions. Translated into more familiar terms, the progressively weaker associations reflect Eisenhower's renowed ability to capture votes of many low-status citizens who had preferred Truman in 1948.[7] As we have noted before, the shift from Truman to Eisenhower swept along voters from every conceivable occupational, educational, and income grouping. Fanning across status (or class) lines, Eisenhower's broad appeal devastated the hasty equation linking status polarization and candidate preference. In American politics, major voting divisions are oblique, occurring *within* and not *between* demographic strata. That educated people sometimes think otherwise testifies to the extraordinary vitality of "class" doctrines which plow such a wide swath in ideological musings and such an irregular furrow through real life.

Seen in this context, the continuous deflation in the size of the three coefficients between 1948 and 1956 becomes readily explicable. It bears upon a point we have made before, that the behavior of suburban voters parallels the behavior of voters living elsewhere. Not only did Eisenhower's two candidacies increase the Republican presidential vote in suburbs and nation, but demographic correlates show the decreasing dependence of voting divisions on variables defining social status.

Although these coefficients were somewhat milder in the last three elections than in the first two, note that they bulged up slightly in 1960 before deteriorating once more in 1964. With but one exception, the same slight peaking is also evident in the larger set of coefficients covering elections between 1956 and 1964. As Campbell has remarked, the election of 1960 resembled the contest of 1948 more than its two immediate predecessors, both of which were deviant because relatively large numbers of Democrats abandoned their party to vote for Eisenhower.[8]

Just as self-acknowledged Democrats broke with their party to vote for Eisenhower, so did many Republicans make the same momentary decision to vote for Johnson. We may speculate that this involved a diffuse movement of upper-class voters which lessened the polarization of vote along class lines. In his study of Delaware County in Philadelphia's suburban ring, Burnham discovered a similar profile of correlation coefficients for the presidential elections of 1960 and 1964. While every area within the county drifted towards Johnson, the shift was particularly accentuated in upper- and upper-middle class segments of the region, thereby depressing the overall association between class and vote. (It will be recalled that the earlier movement towards Eisenhower was proportionately stronger in *lower* status segments of the electorate.) Using the percentage voting Democratic as his criterion, Burnham found that simple correlations between vote and class moved in a regular direction between the two elections; with median family income the correlation shrank from −.68 to −.58, and with the percentage in professional-managerial occupations from −.74 to −.60.[9]

Thus, these data conform to our major contention that the relationship between status and voting in presidential elections is subject to broad fluctuations. It tends to dissolve under the impact of transient, short-term forces which mark a particular campaign. There is little doubt that high-status suburbs are likely to register high Republican votes and lower-status suburbs heavily Democratic ones. But they also show that the vote division in any particular election is likely to reflect national patterns with remarkable fidelity. In 1952 and 1956, many low-status Democrats temporarily cut themselves loose from traditional party moorings and cast ballots for Eisenhower, while in 1964 many high-status Republican voters defected to Johnson.

The strong match of status and vote is not perfect, then, for short-run factors can shove the whole continuum of status in one direction or the other. This status-vote match is like bedrock which occasional earthquakes move only slightly—but some, nevertheless—while extreme strata move farther and more often. Party identification with its status roots holds most partisans, particularly those of strongest feeling, to their party's candidates, while those with minimal identification swing more erratically.

This bedrock quality is visualized in Figures 6-1 and 6-2. In each, we employ a score for each suburb derived from an analytically extracted factor we have labeled Affluence.[10] It combines familiar status variables of income, education, occupation, etc., which we have treated separately up to this point. Figure 6-1 displays a very high degree of association between the Affluence Factor score and the median GOP presidential vote in 1956, 1960, and 1964.[e] If the association were perfect between high status and Republicanism, all dots in Figure 6-1 would lie along the 45° diagonal. As it is, the clustering is tight and the configuration sharp enough to portray dramatically a syndrome of suburban life styles. With gratifying regularity we can see low status suburbs giving Republican presidential candidates little support, just as affluent suburbs backed them strongly—the more affluence the greater the support. The use of the median vote in Figure 6-1, however, conceals variations, as we note in Figure 6-2. Here suburbs are aggregated by partisan divisions in each of these 3 elections (DDD, RRR, etc.) and by the spread of each division's factor score (measured by the standard deviation). The result is a picture of the overlap of suburban sociopolitical life styles. Republican suburbs (RRR and RRD) covered a wide range of Affluence, from highest to middling (+2.3 to −0.3). Democratic suburbs, however, reflected a narrower range of Affluence (+0.3 to −1.5), not descending so far down the Affluence scale as GOP suburbs extended up it.

These figures show not only the broad sweep of gradations of suburban life styles but the smallness of step from one to another as well. Figure 6-1 suggests, from the length of its diagonal, the extensive range of both presidential

[e]Partial coefficients of the Affluence Factor with these 407 suburbs' Republican percentages in the three elections were, respectively, .53, .54, and .42. Similar coefficients were obtained for congressional Republican vote in the elections of 1958, 1960, and 1962, where N = 166.

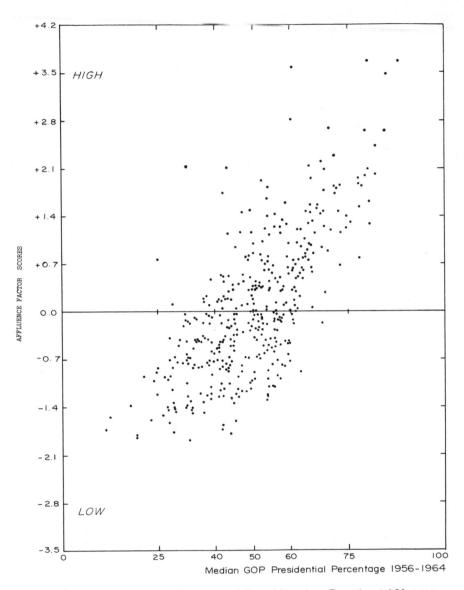

Figure 6-1. Suburban Affluence and Republicanism, Presidential Vote, 1956–1964.

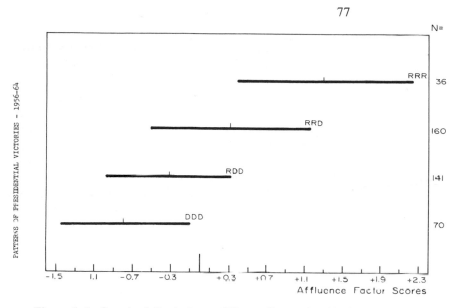

Figure 6-2. Standard Deviations of Factor Scores for 407 Suburbs by Pattern of Presidential Victories.

voting and Affluence in American suburbs, and, from the clustering around the 50 percent GOP line, the overlap of status and political styles. There are anomalies in all this, of course. Deviant cases, marked in Figure 6-1 by dots straggling well away from the diagonal, are accounted for in part by high-status suburbs with large Jewish populations and a Democratic affinity. Or, in Figure 6-2, suburbs with scores of about 0.0 could be one of several kinds of partisanship— DDD, RDD, or RRD. Yet after recognizing such contraindications of the thesis, it is the sweep and cluster of the scattergram which tells us most about the variety—not the homogeneity—of suburban politics.

**Sampling Errors and Faulty
Inferences**

Widespread misconceptions about the rise of Republican partisanship in suburbs sprang from three closely related methodological errors. The first was the assumption that two resounding Eisenhower victories added up to a sample drawn from a homogeneous population of elections. The second was to ignore shifts simultaneously taking place in voting behavior of those in core cities. As though these were not enough, writers routinely assumed that all suburbs were perfect replicas of one another. Let us discuss each in turn.

With results of the 1952 and 1956 elections still fresh in their minds, commentators confidently foretold continued Republican successes in the suburbs. Yet, it would be a challenging task to dream up a more bizarre pair of contests to use as a baseline for extrapolation. The Eisenhower triumphs were eccentric, even abnormal. In suburbs as elsewhere, Eisenhower was an enormously popular candidate, but the affection voters expressed for him could not be transferred to either of his two successors, as we have shown. Commentators had hastily misinterpreted a robust suburban vote for Eisenhower as a sign of suburban Republicanism. There was also an error of omission. Observers correctly took note of Republican successes in suburbs but lost sight of heavy gains Eisenhower chalked up in core cities. Ignoring the latter tempted the conclusion that Eisenhower's appeal was confined to suburbia. However appealing, the inference was false. Over the course of the five elections we have traced, city and suburban electorates moved along in tandem, rising from 1948 to 1956 and plummeting between 1956 and 1964.

The shared dynamics of these inter-election movements expose the flimsiness of both conversion and transplantation hypotheses. Both sought to explain why the gap between city and suburban electorates would continue to widen at an accelerated pace. This, however, has not happened; in social science it always pays to get the facts straight before stretching to explain them. Although Republican presidential candidates continue to poll higher votes in suburbs than in core cities, the net *difference* in the percentage of Republican ballots cast by the two electorates has remained remarkably stable over five elections. Even though our aggregate data do not permit us to see how newcomers responded to the cues presented in an unfamiliar suburban environment (a later chapter will employ survey data to this end), they are powerful enough to refute major implications of both conversion and transplantation hypotheses.[11]

Furthermore, the stereotype of a predominantly Republican suburb was produced by research strategies which managed to conceal variations in status and voting characteristics. One strategy simply assumed out of hand that all suburbs were perfect replicas of Whyte's archetypical Park Forest, with all inhabitants earnestly striving for upper-middle class status and all voting Republican in every election—thereby begging all the important empirical questions. Another tactic was to compute the partisan division of the vote for the entire suburban ring of a metropolitan area. Treating the suburban band as an undifferentiated aggregate pulverized all possible differences, social and electoral alike, among individual towns and villages along the rim of the core city. As Figure 6-1 clearly notes, there is no suburb, only suburbs. Comparing averages, but blissfully ignoring deviations, commentators correctly noted that residents of the outer band averaged higher scores on all status measures than inner city inhabitants. They also observed, again correctly, that the average Republican presidential vote was higher in suburbia than in core city. They then concluded, this time incorrectly, that every suburb was both prosperous and Republican.

In the last chapter, we pointed to the wide diversity in suburban status. Building upon these distinctions, this chapter has traced the linkages between social status and electoral behavior. Although the strength of correlation between measures of social status and electoral partisanship responds to short-term forces in suburbs as it does elsewhere in the nation, it is generally true that Republican presidential preferences and increased social status are positively related. Nevertheless, many of these suburbs were strongly Democratic, even in the face of a powerful Republican candidate. Thus the variety of suburban status is accompanied by a closely matching political variety. While this is true for the most visible office in American politics, does it hold for lesser ones? The query is the concern of our next chapter.

7

Lesser Elections and Party Competition in the Suburbs

It is a sign of the ballyhoo surrounding presidential elections that, even during Eisenhower's ascendancy, little was written about the performance of Republican candidates for lesser offices. If either the conversion or transplantation theories were true, there should have been a marked increase in suburban voting for Republican candidates for Congress and the state house. Only a handful of these over 500 lesser elections are pursued by television commentators or even *The New York Times*, whether in off years or in presidential campaigns. Though they go virtually unnoticed, these elections are no less important for what they reveal about patterns of party allegiance.

Suburbs and Lesser Elections

Scholarly writing also reflects the lack of interest in lesser elections. For every piece written about Congressional and gubernatorial races, one can find many more dealing with presidential elections. Evidence of the division of the suburban vote for lesser offices has been spotty, but generally it fails to support the hypothesis that suburban growth is associated with Republican growth. Some case studies are illustrative. Edson unearthed a marked increase in votes for Democratic Congressional candidates in suburbs of St. Louis County between 1946 and 1954. Some localities added three new Democratic voters for every single new Republican. Indeed, the rate of increase in Democratic voting strength was greatest in suburbs experiencing the *most* rapid population growth. When he surveyed individual voters, Edson found that the suburban move had not transformed customary partisan allegiances. Most people carried their partisan affiliations intact; social class and parental party preference best accounted for patterning of the vote. Only young executives on the make showed any tendency to break away from the Democratic party.[1]

Janosik found very much the same pattern in Bucks County, Pennsylvania. No poor rural settlement, Bucks County in 1950 had the third highest median income in the state. Drawn to the county by a new steel plant and by a Levitt planned suburban village, most of the new suburbanites registered as Democrats. From 1951 to 1954, Democratic registrations grew by 1,500 percent, while Republican registrations barely doubled. Voting behavior apparently conformed with party registration. In local elections of 1951, Republican candidates swept into office by a lopsided vote of 14,000 to 2,500. However, when gubernatorial elections were held in 1954, the suburban growth, which had quadrupled the number of ballots cast, enabled the Democratic candidate to draw to within a thousand votes of the Republican.[2] On the standard conversion theory, the predominantly Republican political environment should have stimulated widespread ticket-switching. "Why," as Harris put it rhetorically, "risk social ostracism when everyone knows that the town had an eight-to-one Republican registration?"[3] A hypothetical answer might be, "Why not, when nearly 80 percent of the new families are Democratic?"

Wallace's investigation of Westport, Connecticut, one of New York City's most prestigious suburbs, also torpedoes the notion of growing suburban Republicanism. Like Edson, Wallace found that most of the new arrivals voted the way their parents always had. Thereby, Westport became conspicuously less Republican, largely because many newcomers were Jews, whose loyalty to the Democratic party has always been tenacious.[4] Closer to New York City, four bedroom counties (Nassau and Suffolk on Long Island, and Westchester and Rockland on the mainland) gained both population and increased Democratic voting strength throughout the fifties.[5]

Working with towns around Boston, Wood discovered that suburbs with relatively large Democratic pluralities in 1954 had been giving Democratic candidates pluralities as early as 1940.[6] At the same time, towns with the largest current Republican pluralities had been firmly Republican from the start. Not a single suburb with a Democratic majority in 1940 had defected to the Republicans, but thirteen localities that had been Republican in 1940 were casting majorities for Democratic candidates by 1954. Compared with the Democratic suburbs, the Republican towns had more homeowners, enjoyed higher incomes, occupational prestige, and rentals, and were further away from downtown Boston. Wood speculated that a comprehensive pattern of population movement accounted for patterning of the vote. As lower-income families moved across the Boston city line into the inner ring of suburban towns, older residents, predominantly well-to-do Republicans, dribbled further out to smaller suburbs on the metropolitan rim. City line suburbs gained Democrats, while those further out absorbed displaced Republicans. Hence there was no party switching, no mass abandonment of old party affinities; there was merely a reshuffling of partisans within the entire metropolis. Wood inferred that the exodus of lower-income Democratic families to the inner ring largely accounted for observable increases in suburban Democratic voting. At the same time, Republican losses in older towns closer in were offset by Republican gains in villages further away.

**Suburban Vote for President and
Lesser Offices, 1948-1964**

Though few, these scattered studies question whether suburban residence resulted in a uniformly Republican schedule of voting preferences. Rather, they indicate that Democratic votes for lesser offices *swelled* as a result of the sub-urban flight, even during the decade of Eisenhower's enormous suburban plural-ities. However, there is no way of knowing whether suburbs of Boston and St. Louis, as well as four suburban counties of New York City and one of Philadel-phia, add up to a representative sample of all American suburbs. Moreover, the data were all collected during the fifties, and it is possible that the newcomers did shed their loyalty to their parents' party as they became more attuned to the political and social attitudes of the old settlers.

To check the implications of these studies against a broader sample of sub-urbs, we compiled data on congressional and gubernatorial races between 1948 and 1964. A state-by-state summary is presented as Table 7-1. There are dispar-ities between the number of units reported in presidential elections (Table 6-3) and those listed in Table 7-1. One reason is that some states, e.g., New York and Pennsylvania, hold their gubernatorial elections in off-years; hence, there are more suburbs reporting data for nonpresidential years than for presidential years. Also, Ohio at one time conducted gubernatorial elections biennially. Be-ginning with the election of 1960, Ohio eliminated gubernatorial elections in presidential years. These constitutional changes explain the sharp drop in lesser elections. Another explanation is that election registrars are generally more lax in keeping files on lesser elections.

Figure 7-1 presents a synoptic view of the longitudinal movement of the sub-urban vote for lesser office. As in the last chapter, we have treated each suburb as a discrete unit. Since the arithmetic mean masks variation, we have also indi-cated the standard deviation for each election. One valid objection to averaging Republican voting percentages from large and small suburbs is that one loses sight of variations in voting patterns that can be attributed to sheer size. In line with Wood's argument, it is plausible to contend that larger suburbs, particularly those just over the city line, are likely to have proportionately greater numbers of Democratic voters. Therefore, in treating suburbs as though they were all one standard size, we have in effect understated the true proportion of Democratic voters in the entire suburban electorate. As will be seen, however, this bias logi-cally works against our hypothesis; in short, we are not arbitrarily stacking the decks to produce a meretricious proof of our contentions.[a]

Figure 7-1 traces the fluctuation in the mean Republican vote for lesser of-fices between 1948 and 1964. The dashed sawtooth line tilted slightly upwards from 1948 to 1952 before slumping in off-year elections of 1954. From there it soared to its apex, reaching almost 59 percent in Eisenhower's second electoral

[a]The zero-order correlation coefficients between population size and the Republican share of the two-party vote are all negative, but their magnitude is small. From 1956 through 1964, the correlation averaged $-.11$; in no election did it exceed $-.20$. Thus, at no point did sheer population size account for more than 4 percent of the variance in the vote. For all elections between 1948 and 1964, intercensal population growth showed a small but posi-tive correlation with the Republican vote. On the average, it accounted for about 5 percent of the variance in division of the vote.

Table 7-1
Distribution of Suburbs Included in the Analysis, By State and Type of Election

	1948		1950		1952		1954		1956		1958		1960		1962		1964	
	Cong.	Gov.	C	G	C	G	C	G	C	G	C	G	C	G	C	G	C	G
Me.	2		2		2		2		2				1		2		2	
Mass.		46		46		46		46		46		46		46		46		46
R.I.		9		9		9		9		9		9		9		9		9
Conn.	14		14		14		14		14		14		14		14		14	
N.Y.	3		3	23	3		3	23	3		3	23	3		3	23	3	
N.J.	102		102		102		103		104		104		104		104		104	
Pa.				62				63				63				63		
Ohio[a]		53		55		55		56		56		56				56		
Ind.	2		2		2		2		2									
Ill.	3		3		3		2		3		1		1		1		1	
Mich.		20		20		20		22		22		22		22		22		22
Wis.		13		13		14		14		15		15		15		15		15
Minn.	18		18		18		18		19		20		20		19		20	
Iowa	1		1		1		1		1		1		1		1		1	
Mo.	2		2		2		2		1		1		2		2		2	
Colo.	1		1		1		1		1		1				1		1	
Wash.	2		2		2		2		2		1				1		1	
Calif.	16		16		16		19		18		16		17		18		19	
Total:	165	141	165	228	167	144	169	233	170	148	161	234	161	92	165	234	168	92
	306		393		310		318		395		235		399		260			

Sources: State legislative manuals, reports of the Secretaries of State, and communications from local election registrars.

[a] Ohio eliminated biennial gubernatorial elections after 1958.

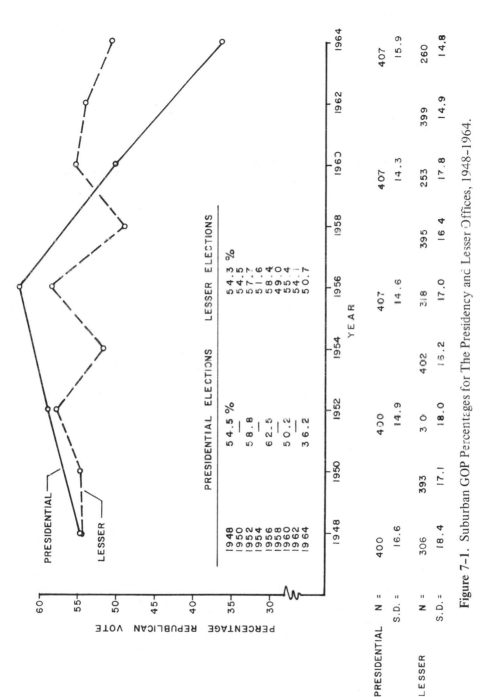

Figure 7–1. Suburban GOP Percentages for The Presidency and Lesser Offices, 1948–1964.

triumph. The trend line then plummeted to its lowest point in mid-year elections of 1958, shot up in 1960, and sagged again between 1960 and 1964.

Clearly the pattern of surge and decline in Figure 7-1 cuts against both conversion and transplantation hypotheses because according to either the final result is the same—a steadily swelling Republican vote in the suburbs. That is simply not the case for these data. For not only had suburban migration built up to full flow during the fifties, but the earlier wave of migrants also had many opportunities to conform to the partisanship of the more established residents. But Figure 7-1 shows a steady decline in the Republican share of the vote.

There is always a problem of deciding which level of election best measures party allegiance. Because they are unusually susceptible to short-term forces, presidential elections are notoriously misleading as surrogate measures for party identification. Eisenhower's unexpected popularity and Goldwater's predictable lack of appeal both resulted in violent oscillations of the presidential trend line around 52.4 percent, the mean for the presidential series. Eisenhower's two candidacies induced many normally Democratic voters to abandon their party, but only momentarily, as is shown by the diminished Republican vote for lesser offices in the mid-year elections immediately following. Even so, the candidate exerted a much greater tidal pull than the party; in both 1952 and 1956, candidates for lesser office trailed behind Eisenhower. The gap was particularly large in 1956, when Eisenhower led the rest of the ticket by more than four percentage points. Goldwater produced large but transient defections in the other direction. That the dramatic shift in Johnson's favor did not mean a correspondingly gross shift in partisan dispositions can be demonstrated by the much higher vote cast for Republican candidates contesting lesser offices in the same year.

Thus, if one were to infer partisan loyalties *solely* from presidential votes during the fifties, he would detect a long-term movement of Republicans swamping the suburbs. On the other hand, the sharp drop in the presidential trend line from 1956 to 1964 would lead to the opposite conclusion. Based on a misleading measure of party identification, both inferences are equally faulty. As Converse has argued, congressional votes oscillate much less hectically than presidential votes and thus come closer to matching the actual division of partisans in the electorate.[7] A comparison of the two trend lines of Figure 7-1 shows this difference clearly, for the presidential vote was much more volatile than that for lesser office. Overall, the difference between highest and lowest presidential votes was almost 23 percentage points, more than twice as large as the 9.4 percentage points separating the most extreme votes in lesser elections.

More important than the rise or fall of the line between any consecutive pair of elections is the height of the line over the horizontal axis at the beginning and the end of the series. Sixteen years intervened here between the first and last presidential elections, plenty of time for conversion to work its alleged magic. It is also enough time for Republican migrants from core cities to make their presence known in election returns. Yet the percentage of Republican votes cast for lesser office in presidential years was almost four points lower at the end of the series than at the start. If we take off-year elections as our critical sampling points, it is immediately apparent that Republican percentages were almost exactly the same—54.5 percent in 1950 and 54.1 percent in 1962. So, far from increasing according to transplantation and conversion theories, the Republican share of the suburban two-party vote has been remarkably stable.

A comparison of demographic correlates of the presidential vote (see Table 6-5) and those recorded for lesser elections shows little difference between the two sets. Age variables were positively correlated with Republican percentages for lesser offices throughout the period, but the magnitude of the coefficients steadily drifted towards zero, just as they did in the presidential series. In lesser elections from 1948 to 1964, the correlation between median age and Republican vote dropped from .34 to .16, while corresponding figures for the percentage of aged people in the population were .29 and .08. As with presidential voting, the division of the vote in lesser contests has become progressively dissociated from the age distribution of suburban communities.

Although higher in off-year elections when turnout is smaller, status variables show a consistently strong relationship with Republican voting in lesser elections. Between 1956 and 1962, the correlations with Republican vote were .37 and .56 for median annual family income, .44 and .62 for annual family income in excess of $10,000, and .45 and .67 for white-collar worker proportion. To round out the picture, educational variables (percent completing high school and median years of formal schooling) trace the same pattern, climbing from a 1956 low to a 1962 high.

Nowhere was the discrepancy between presidential and lesser office votes so wide as in 1964. Fortunately for the Republican party, Goldwater did not drag his running mates down to defeat with him, as may be seen in Figure 7-1. As a result, the correlation between status variables and Republican share of the vote dwindled for the presidential election while they remained consistently high in lesser elections. In the presidential race, for example, the coefficient between the percentage of high school graduates and the vote was .42, compared with .63 for lesser races. For median annual family income, the corresponding coefficients were .42 and .54, and for percent white collar, .44 and .52, respectively. In short, Johnson's ability to draw votes from every class stratum weakened the correlations between electoral and status measures. Because the vote for lesser offices was more nearly a party vote, the magnitude of these same coefficients remained high.

Party Competition in Suburbs

The Concept of Competition

Normative and empirical democratic theorists alike have stressed the crucial role which competitive parties play in organizing and domesticating political conflict.[8] In democracies, constitutionally protected opposition parties challenge the incumbents by offering the electorate a rival set of candidates in public elections. No dictatorial regime has long permitted opposition to contest public offices; indeed, the lack of party competition is an indispensable criterion of non-democratic polities.

Despite the importance conceded competition, there is surprisingly little agreement on how best to measure it. As always, the extreme cases present no problem at all. The Soviet Union, the so-called "Peoples' Democracies," and Hitler's Germany have never permitted opposition parties, much less competitive elections. Where there is only one party, it is fatuous to talk about party competition. In such countries as Great Britain, the United States, Israel, Western Germany, and Sweden, a number of organized and relatively permanent parties regularly contest presidential and legislative office. This is not to say that party competition is uniform throughout all the constituencies making up the nation. There are many congressional districts in the South where Republicans run only for the exercise, and many others elsewhere present equally bleak prospects to the Democrats. (Between 1914 and 1954, no Democrat won a public election in Vermont.) Even in democracies, the vitality of party competition varies from one constituency to another. Sometimes, the variations are only incremental; on other occasions, they are very sharp indeed. The problem is to devise a scale that will accurately reflect these variations.

Sifting through much writing on the subject, one finds a broad area of agreement on the meaning of "party competition." Schlesinger asserts that in a competitive party system, "there are at least two parties . . . which are viable means to political office." Where party competition is fierce, a newcomer to politics will have just as good "a chance to get into office either as a member of party A or of party B."[9] In much the same vein, Dawson and Robinson declare:

The degree of inter-party competition refers primarily to the extent to which both parties possess the opportunity of gaining control of . . . various offices. In a competitive situation there must be a possibility of the 'out-party' to become the 'in-party.'[10]

Proceeding further, they assert that a constituency in which the minority party regularly polls between 30 and 49 percent of the votes cast is significantly more competitive than one where the minority party gets no more than about a fifth of the votes.[11] Along the same lines, Sorauf proposes that, "in a general sense the political party is competitive if it has a genuine chance of winning elective office."[12]

All the definitions hinge on "expectations," "chances," and "likelihoods." However, in devising empirical measures of party competition, referents of "expectations" and "chances" quickly recede from view. Measures of party competition deal with past performance and past performance alone; all shy away from calculating probabilities of success in winning future elections. And, although the definitional consistency seems almost perfect, operational rules used to join historical data with summary measures of party competition differ from one effort to another. The variation is understandable. "Party competition" is a derived concept. There are no indivisible units of "competition" that can be identified and summed like apples and potatoes. Necessarily, measures of "party competition" must be *calculated* by arithmetically manipulating discrete units and events in order to rank constituencies or whole polities from most to least competitive. Most measures, naturally enough, are fashioned from the proportion of votes cast or offices won in a continuous sequence of elections; some attempt to combine the two. Further, the basic data come to us already quantified. A vote cast or an office won is a unit that is as hard and indivisible as a grain of sand or a ton of steel. It is in the mathematical combination of the basic data into summary indices that the definitional consistency gives way to a diversity of measures.

The first dimension of party competition is the pattern of alternation in party control of offices. Consider two states, North and South Gladiola. From 1946 to 1964, each state has elected five Republican and five Democratic governors. It would be tempting to conclude that both are equally competitive, since control of the highest elective office in the state has been equally divided between two major parties. Closer scrutiny reveals, however, that North Gladiola elected Democratic governors from 1946 to 1954 while the Republicans won five consecutive races after that. In South Gladiola, on the other hand, control of the governor's office intermittently shifted back and forth between two parties, with Democrats winning in presidential years and Republicans in off-years. Nobody could reasonably dispute calling South Gladiola a competitive state. However, party control of the governor's office in North Gladiola changed only once over the course of the period, so North and South Gladiola are not equally competitive. Therefore, as Schlesinger first noted, an informative measure of party competition should take account of the frequency with which the contending parties alternate control of elective office.

The first dimension has to do with the distribution of offices; the second deals with the distribution of votes. There are two partly separable components of the vote: direction and magnitude. "Direction" refers to the party which gets more votes than its competitors; "magnitude" refers to the size of its plurality. Suppose we have two adjacent congressional districts. In the first, the Democratic vote varies between 47 and 49 percent. In the neighboring district, Democrats never get more than 35 percent of the vote. Although Democrats are the minority party in both districts, their performance is distinctly better in the first. A scale of party competition must reflect these differences in magnitude.

Ranney and Kendall proposed one of the first measures of inter-party competition.[13] For each American state they computed the percentage of minority party victories in races for president, governor and United States senator (but not congressman) on a single continuum. The clustering of percentages indicated that states fell into two main groups, the first from 0 to 22.8 percent and the second from 27.2 to 48.8 percent. For this reason, Ranney and Kendall called "one-party states" those in which the minority party won fewer than a quarter of the contests. All the rest were "two-party states." Since this method of classification considered only the division of offices, they proceeded to a finer classification based on a division of the vote within one-party states. In a "modified one-party state," the majority party received at least 30 percent of the votes in more than 70 percent of the contests, and at least 40 percent of the votes in over 30 percent of the races. Pure "one-party states" consisted of the remainder. Thus, the minority party in "modified one-party states" did no better than simple "one-party states" in splitting offices, but considerably better in winning votes.

As important as this effort was in beginning to develop a standard for classifying inter-party competition in various constituencies, it was faulty nonetheless. For one thing, it depended too heavily on the existence of "natural" cutting points between clusters, the justification for which is atheoretical if not fortuitous. But the most important flaw is that it is completely insensitive to patterns of alternation; despite palpable differences between them, both North and South Gladiola would have been assigned to the two-party category.

A year and a half later, Schlesinger, noting this defect, proposed to remedy it by explicitly taking account of "the rapidity with which the parties alternate in their control of an office."[14] The scheme he devised is presented as Figure 7-2. This plots the relative frequency with which parties alternate in holding a given office against an "overall" dimension. The "overall" dimension is split down the middle by a solid vertical line intercepting the horizontal axis at the 50 percent victory mark.

If a given constituency gives Republicans more electoral victories than Democrats, the plot is placed to the left of this line; if Democrats have been triumphant in more than half the contests, the plot falls to the right. The horizontal distance from the midpoint of the symmetrical range is determined by the actual percentage of races won by the dominant party. The vertical axis is calibrated to reflect the percentage of contests in which control of the office(s) under consideration passed from one party to another. In the limiting case where the dominant party wins all the elections, the plot will coincide with the horizontal axis. If no party holds on to any office for two consecutive terms, the plot will fall right at the top of the vertical axis. In general, the location of a political unit on the vertical axis is determined by the expression:

$$\frac{\text{Total number of elections in which control alternates}^{b}}{\text{Total number of elections} - 1}$$

Schlesinger's scheme deals only with the distribution of electoral victories and the pattern of party succession in office. Unlike the scheme of Ranney and Kendall, it ignores how the vote was divided between parties, either in a single

---

[b]In any series of n elections, there are only n-1 possibilities for any given office to change hands. It is not clear whether Schlesinger uses n or n-1 elections as the denominator.

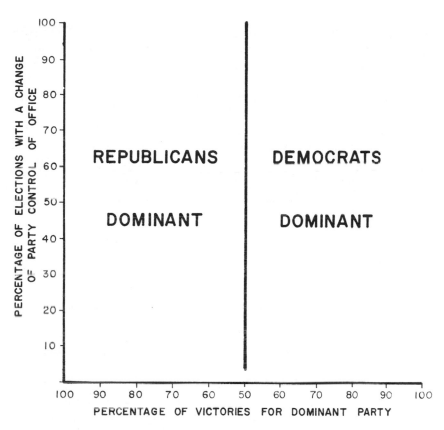

Figure 7-2. The Schlesinger Two-Dimensional Scheme for Measuring Party Compeition.

election or over a series of elections. Whether a party steals into office with a slim margin or rolls in on an avalanche is unimportant; all that matters is the identity of the winning party and its predecessor in office.

Apart from the loss of information as to the partisan vote division, there is a flaw in the Schlesinger model. For axes to be drawn at right angles to one another, the pair of variables they are intended to represent must be logically or technically independent. That is, the range of variation possible on one axis should be logically unrelated to the range of variation possible along the other.[c]

[c]For example, income and racial attitudes are examples of two variables that are technically independent, for income logically entails nothing about racial attitudes. No empirical possibility has been foreclosed by the way the terms have been defined. The rich, in fact, may be more bigoted than the poor, less bigoted than the poor, or there may be no discernible empirical relationship between income and racial attitudes towards minority groups. On the other hand, a strong positive relationship between proportion of high school graduates and median number of years of schooling completed by adults is factitious because the variables are technically dependent. A high proportion of high school graduates automatically pushes up median years of schooling; the way the variables are defined guarantees a robust correlation between them. What is billed as an empirical correlation is actually a tautology.

But once the number of minority party victories in any series has been ascertained, the number of possible alternations is not free to vary between the extremes of zero and one fewer than the number of elections contained in the series.[d]

A little arithmetical probing will show why this is so. In the special case where one party has managed to win all the elections in a series, the number of alternations must *necessarily* equal zero. No additional information is disclosed by the location of the vertical plot. Now consider the general collection of possibilities where a minority party has won at least one election. Suppose that in a series of n elections, the minority party has been victorious in x contests ($x<n/2$ where n is even and $x<\frac{n+1}{2}$ where n is odd). The number of alternations mathematically possible must lie somewhere in the range between one and $2x$. For any series of elections in which the minority party wins any elections at all, the minimum number of possible alternations will always be one. This will occur when the minority party's victories are consecutive and either inaugurate or conclude a series. If the consecutive victories occur at some point within a series, the number of alternations will necessarily equal two. The number of alternations logically possible will reach its maximum value when the minority party never wins a pair of consecutive victories. This number, however, can never exceed $2x$ when the majority party wins the first election and $2x$-1 when the minority party leads off the series with a victory.

In general, then, the closer two parties approach an even division of elections, the more are constituencies free to vary along the vertical axis.[e] The power of the vertical axis to discriminate among electoral units recedes rapidly as one moves away from midpoint of the horizontal axis; it becomes largely redundant. Although Schlesinger's two dimensions are conceptualized as independent of one another, analysis clearly shows that the range of variation along one of the axes is logically constrained by the degree of variation along the other.

A Spatial Model of Party Competition

With the strengths and limitations of previous efforts in mind, we propose a spatial model for charting differences in party competition among a number of comparable electoral jurisdictions.[15] The perpendicular reference axes drawn on

[d]To simplify exposition, we deal with the absolute number of alternations and elections rather than with relative percentages. Since percentages are easily calculated once the number of elections in the series is known, all we lose is an unnecessary complication.

[e]We do not wish to deny Schlesinger's contribution. It is important to know the diversity in alternation patterns as parties approach an even division of electoral successes. However, we think it unlikely that the minority party would poll fewer than 40 to 45 percent of the vote in any election held in such constituencies, so the superiority of Schlesinger's scheme over the Ranney-Kendall measure is a moot point.

Figure 7-3 can be used to locate any constituency for which continuous electoral records are available. Running from left to right across the graph is a horizontal axis which separates the constituencies according to identity of the dominant party. If Republican candidates have won more elections than Democrats, the electoral unit falls above the line; if Democrats have won more often than Republicans, the constituency is located beneath it. (Ties present a special problem considered below.)

Once the dominant party has been ascertained, the vertical dimension, which is perfectly symmetrical above and below the horizontal axis, is used to plot

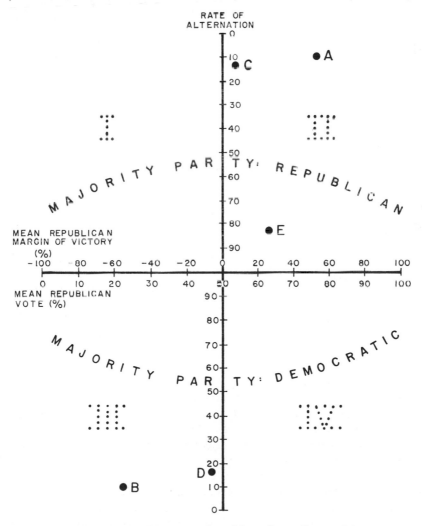

Figure 7–3. The Measurement of Inter-Party Competition.

alternations in party control of a set of offices. In any continuous string of n elections, there are $n-1$ occasions for the office to pass from one party to its competitor. This number is divided into the actual number of alternations and the resulting quotient is multiplied by 100 percent to give the rate of alternation, or the percentage of all elections in which there has been a shift in party control. In the extreme case where a party has won every election in the series, the rate of alternation will necessarily be zero. In the sequence of party victories DRDRDRD, there are as many alternations as there are opportunities. The quotient which expresses the turnover rate would therefore be 100 percent, and the electoral unit would fall somewhere on the plane formed by the horizontal axis.

For contrast, consider another sequence in which Democratic candidates have been successful in four contests of seven: DDDDRRR (or RRRDDDD). Here there has been only one shift of party control in the six possibilities that form the series, and the rate of alternation will be 16.7 percent. Thus, the dispersion of points along the vertical axis measures differences in the rate of alternation. The further away from the horizontal axis a plot falls, the longer have been spells of uninterrupted control by the majority party in the electoral jurisdiction.

The vertical dimension maps distribution of offices between the parties; the horizontal dimension charts actual division of votes between parties over time. The actual share of votes going to the minority party says much about the ferocity of competition. Victories can be wide or narrow, and tight races are qualitatively different from narrow ones. As Sorauf has remarked:

the party consistently polling 40 to 45 percent of the vote in a two-party system is not, in the narrow sense, more competitive than the party that struggles along at 20 to 25 percent of the two-party vote. It does, however, exert a greater impact and check on the campaigns, candidates, and policies of the winning party, even though it never wins an election. And if it has consistently flirted with the 45 percent mark in the past, its future possibilities cannot be lightly dismissed."[16]

In short, a party system where a permanent minority party loses by a slender margin is more competitive than one where it is trounced election after election, even though that fact cannot be measured by party control of elective office.

This dimension may be measured in two ways using the mean Republican vote. The first is simply to take this mean for a given constituency and plot it on the horizontal axis; percentages calibrating this measure are located immediately beneath the horizontal axis and range between zero and 100 percent. A mathematically equivalent system of calibration also appears above the horizontal axis in Figure 7-3. These numbers measure the arithmetic difference between Republican and Democratic shares of the vote averaged across elections in the series. When the margin favors Republicans, the difference will be positive and the plot will fall on the right-hand side of the vertical axis. If the mean Republican vote is less than 50 percent, the difference will be less than zero and the plot will be located to the left. As the difference between mean Republican and Democratic vote approaches zero, the constituency is increasingly competitive.

The primary virtue of this scheme is that the degree of variation along one axis is only slightly limited by the range of dispersion along the other. Only the extreme corners of Quadrants I and IV are logically empty, for it is impossible for a party to win all, or nearly all, elections with an average vote close to zero percent. Apart from these exceptions, any electoral unit may occupy any portion of space enclosed by the graph.

Consider some of the possibilities. The most competitive constituencies, with a high rate of alternation and a small margin of victory, would lie close to the intersection of the two axes. Point A marks the location of a strong Republican constituency, where the mean Republican vote is 80 percent and the rate of alternation only 10 percent. Point B signifies a predominantly Democratic electoral unit with the same characteristics.

As a further illustration, suppose that a constituency is closely divided in every section but so stable in its voting patterns that alternations in party control rarely occur. Such a constituency would be represented either by points C or D, depending on which is the majority party. In constituency E, a less likely case, party control of office shifts back and forth with great rapidity but Republicans win elections with much larger margins of victory than Democrats win theirs.

Our method has two defects. First, it cannot handle electoral units where each party has won exactly half the elections. It will not do to let the plot coincide with the horizontal axis at the point where the turnover rate attains its maximum value of 100 percent. This solution is faulty because it is logically possible for two parties to win an equal number of elections and have a turnover rate that is considerably less than 100 percent, as may be illustrated by the sequences DDDRRR or RRRDDD. One obvious way around this difficulty would be to choose an odd-numbered sequence of elections, but this is not always possible. A better way, particularly if there are many ties, would be to plot separately the rate of alternation against the mean Republican (or Democratic) share of the vote for such constituencies.

A second, and much more serious, problem arises from discontinuities in the vertical scale. The horizontal axis is perfectly continuous. Because a party's share of the vote in any reasonably populous constituency may range anywhere between zero and 100 percent, it follows that its mean vote over a series of elections may fall anywhere within the same interval. This is not true of the vertical dimension. The denominator of the fraction expressing the rate of party alternation will always be one fewer than the number of elections contained in the series. Because of this, the minimum spread between any two points on the vertical scale will be the reciprocal of this number, and the number of possible points on the vertical scale will always be $2n$ 1. (It would not be $2n$ because the midpoint of the vertical scale will be the same no matter which party has won just one more than half the elections in the series.)

In a series of 11 consecutive elections, for example, there would be 21 possible positions on the scale, with an interval of ten percentage points between any adjacent two. In general, points representing constituencies will always appear on one of the possible $2n-1$ planes cutting through the vertical axis at right angles. As the number of elections contained in the series increases, the smaller becomes the spread between two successive values measuring the rate of party turnover. Only in a very long series, for example, congressional voting over an entire century, would the scale become virtually continuous.

This problem becomes particularly distressing when one wants to compare constituencies with an unequal number of elections during the same time period. Some states hold gubernatorial elections every two years, and others every four. Suppose we have two states. In the first, we have ten elections and in the other only five. In each, two Democratic governors are followed by a Republican who can hold on to his office for only one term before losing it to the majority party. For the state holding elections every two years, the rate of party turnover would measure 67 percent. For the state having quadrennial elections, the rate would be only 50 percent despite the identity in the patterns of alternation. The same pattern of party turnover in office will usually produce different rates of alternation if the number of elections contained in the series is unequal.[f]

It is this model which we employ to demonstrate the degree of suburban party competition and hence test both transplantation and conversion theories. In the last chapters, we showed how the Republican share of presidential votes rose and fell in response to candidates in each campaign, soaring during Eisenhower years and falling just as drastically in 1960 and 1964. Earlier in this chapter, we showed how Republican voting strength in lesser elections has moved along a relatively flat plateau since 1948, a period of enormous growth in the suburban electorate. Using a modified version of the graphic scheme in Figure 7-3, we will now draw together the separate strands of our discussion so far. Table 7-2 presents this information.[g]

---

[f]To standardize the vertical scale for unequal numbers of observations, we have followed a procedure suggested by Professor Ben W. Bolch of the Department of Economics at Vanderbilt University. Assume we have gubernatorial data from two sets of states. In both, the Democratic party has won a majority of the elections. The first set contains twelve elections, with a standard deviation in the turnover rate equal to $S.D._1$. The second set has six elections; its standard deviation is symbolized as $S.D._2$. The first step is to calculate a correction factor $\frac{S.D._1}{S.D._2}$, which is simply the ratio between the two standard deviations. The second is to multiply the actual turnover rate of each state in the second set by this correction factor. The product is the adjusted alternation rate.

[g]For simplicity in exposition, we have superimposed intervals on both vertical and horizontal axes. Although this procedure sacrifices some information that would be presented in a scattergram, the clustering of observations makes for some ease in interpretation. Seventeen of the original 407 suburbs have been omitted from this table because of data missing within the series. Where we lacked data at the beginning of the series, rates of alternation were adjusted according to the procedure specified in the last footnote.

Table 7-2

Party Competition in American Suburbs: Presidential and Lesser Elections, 1948-1964

Majority Party Republican

Mean Republican Percentage in Elections 1948-1964

Percentage of all elections in which parties alternated	0-29.9	30.0-34.9	35.0-39.9	40.0-44.9	45.0-49.9	50.1-54.9	55.0-59.9	60.0-64.9	65.0-69.9	70.0-100.0	Percentage of Total	Cumulative % of Total
0-10					2	5	32	24	27	39	58.6	58.6
11-20					1	4	17	11	1	1	16.8	74.4
21-30				1	1	9	11	4			12.1	86.5
31-40				1		7	7	1			7.4	93.9
41-50					2	5	3				5.1	100.0
											(N=214)	
100												
100												
70-61					1	1					1.1	100.1[a]
60-51					4						2.3	99.0
50-41				4	15	8					15.3	96.7
40-31			1	11	7	1					11.4	81.4
30-21			5	14	6	1					14.8	70.0
20-11		5	12	14	7	1					22.2	55.2
10-0	14	22	16	4	2						33.0	33.0
											(N=176)	
Percentage of Total	3.6	6.9	8.7	12.6	12.3	10.3	17.6	10.3	7.2	10.3		
Cum. % of total	3.6	10.5	19.2	31.8	44.1	54.4	72.3	82.6	89.8	100.1[a]		

50.0

Majority Party Democratic

[a] Cumulative percentages slightly in excess of 100 percent due to rounding.

The first conclusion which may be drawn from this table is that, between 1948 and 1964, Republicans won more races than Democrats in only 55 percent of 390 suburbs included here. "Only," of course, is a relative term, but the size of the margin fails to sustain the impression that the flight to the suburbs pitched the Democratic party into a deepening crisis. As for alternation between parties, what is most striking is the generally low turnover rate in all constituencies. Look at the dispersion of suburban municipalities along the vertical midline and the summary distributions presented on the right-hand edge of Table 7-2. Almost 60 percent of the suburbs dominated by Republicans alternated party victories in fewer than 10 percent of the opportunities presented by consecutive elections, as compared with nearly a third of the constituencies in the Democratic group. In light of the speculation during the fifties, the second datum is more surprising than the first. It is tantamount to saying that 58 of the 390 suburbs gave majorities to Democratic candidates election after election, a finding that clashes sharply with the received image. These data show that there were permanent suburban Democratic strongholds as well as constituencies (twice as many) which constantly produced Republican majorities.

As might be expected from the utter lack of observations in the most competitive segments of the vertical axis, the mean rate of alternation is very low, 16.5 percent for all the suburbs tabulated during this period. Largely because of Eisenhower's appeal to regular Democrats, the mean rate of alternation for Democratic suburbs was nearly twice as large as that for Republican suburbs, 21.1 versus 12.6 percent. Based solely on their ability to win elections in the suburbs, parties were highly unequal in strength.[h]

The horizontal array is equally informative. Although there is the expected inverse relationship between the gross turnover rate and the size of the winning party's average margin, what is most arresting is the presence of a relatively large group of suburbs with an exceedingly low mean Republican vote. Seventy-five, or almost one-fifth, of all the suburbs had an average Republican vote smaller than 40 percent, clearly Democratic suburbs. At the other end of the scale, the number of suburbs where the mean Republican vote surpassed 60 percent was barely more than a quarter of the total. Indeed, the mean Republican vote in 88 of the 390 suburbs fell within the narrow range marked off by the two intervals flanking the vertical midline of the table, from 45-54.9 percent. And, in eight of the Republican suburbs, the mean Democratic vote actually exceeded the mean Republican vote.

As might be expected from the correlations in these chapters, the suburbs fanning out to the northeast corner of Table 7-2 differed sharply from Democratic suburbs in the opposite region. The increasing polarization of vote be-

[h]In her study of gubernatorial party competition, Kennedy discovered much the same pattern. Based on division of the vote, party competition was negligible, with only five states having turnover rates in excess of 60 percent. As measured by division of the vote, competition was much more intense. The virtue of our method of graphing party competition is that it allows us to present both dimensions simultaneously and see at a glance the relationship between the two.

tween the parties accentuates the differences between the socioeconomic characteristics of the communities. Republican suburbs had higher median incomes, a larger share of white-collar workers in the labor force and more years of formal schooling.

The Failures of Prophecy

During the fifties, when the Democrats were reeling after two losses to Eisenhower, observers conjectured that the march of population across city lines would eventually bring an end to the Democratic ascendancy. Anticipating a book that Phillips would later write, Banfield and Whyte asserted that a firm national Republican majority would sooner or later emerge from huge suburban pluralities. The presumption was that accelerating change in the spatial distribution of the nation's population would give rise to a comprehensive and persistent change in party identification. This prophecy failed to hit the mark for two major families of reasons, one methodological and one theoretical.

The observers' poor aim was partly due to improper sampling. Commentators stumbled upon a small collection of suburbs, generally middle-class colonies so new that the curbstones were laid in place just shortly before the newcomers took possession of their split-level ranch houses—and sometimes not even then. There they found a grey crushing conformity and an appalling other-directedness that relentlessly ironed out individual differences.[17] Noticing large Eisenhower pluralities registered in these compounds, they hastened to generalize their findings to all suburbs. The error was both crude and devastating, like trying to estimate the mean height of all undergraduates from a sample consisting only of basketball players.

Commentators also erred in projecting a linear trend based on only three consecutive presidential elections. Seeing a sharp Republican rise in suburban vote they were prone to push the trend line forward to voting patterns in future elections. Extrapolating a linear trend line based on a handful of observations is faulty even when a mathematical equation is used to extend it. Under the best of circumstances, the procedure is bound to misfire because the paucity of observation points leaves too few degrees of freedom in calculating the angle of inflection of a smoothed trend line.

To make bad matters even worse, the projections took off from the worst possible data. Fluctuations in presidential voting were simply too gross to isolate any sort of overriding central tendency in the configuration of widely spaced points; there were too many uncertainties. Not the least of them was the meaning of a large vote for Eisenhower. Quite possibly it portended a gigantic shift in partisan affiliations, but equally possible only a momentary defection of committed Democrats. The commentators sided with the first interpretation. But they failed to test their leading hypothesis against division of the vote in lesser elections. Less disturbed by dramatic though momentary oscillations than the presidential trend line, lesser elections are more reliable barometers of impending shifts in partisan balance. Projecting this trend line forward in time would have made scholars and commentators late in the fifties more chary of forecasting an emerging suburban Republican majority.

The forecasts also discarded accumulated empirical political knowledge. Ingrained partisan affiliations are rather firmly fixed. Though partisans may occasionally drift away to vote for a candidate of the opposing party, partisan attachments remain firm. Once rooted, they are likely to loosen only under the impact of drastic social change. Thus, the necessary initial conditions for a gross shift in party commitments were completely absent in Eisenhower's two candidacies. The forecast of an imminent shift in party loyalties perched on a combination of faulty methodology and dubious empirical theory.

**Part 3
The Suburban State of Mind**

City-Suburb Attitudinal Differences in the National Population

Some Cautions on Methodology

Our inquiry into the character of suburban political behavior has to this point dealt only with voting in national and local elections. We need to examine data on attitudinal characteristics of individual metropolitan residents to help explain their political behavior. Such data have usually been provided by survey research. In fact, much of our discussion of suburban voting has been informed by our knowledge of relationships between attitudes and voting derived from survey research in the general population. Surprisingly little of this research, however, has focused on suburban attitudinal patterns. Despite recent interest in "contextual analysis," systematic investigation of city-suburb locale effects on political attitudes has been virtually ignored.

One exception is a secondary analysis of national survey data from 1952 to 1964 reported by Zikmund.[1] His comparison of party identification and general political orientation patterns for city and suburb respondents yielded statistically significant locale differences only for partisan attitudes. Zikmund did not present data on the effect of individual attributes on party identification; thus we cannot estimate the impact of suburban residence as an independent variable from his data. As a result of additional analyses of variance on these variables, Zikmund suggests that *intra*-metropolitan studies of the impact of suburban residence may demonstrate a stronger effect of locale on non-party-related variables such as political trust and political interest.

A six-metropolis survey of attitudes reported by Hawley and Zimmer did find such intra-areal differences.[2] Suburbanites were generally less satisfied than central city residents with their governments' services, and viewed their local government officials as less competent than central city officials. Yet the suburbanites expressed greater trust in their officials. Still, the crucial question again left unanswered by this study is whether suburban residence has any independent effect on attitudes not attributable to individual social attributes.

For example, Orbell found that an apparent suburban locale difference in feelings of anomie in a sample of Columbus, Ohio, metropolitan residents was partially attributable to individual social class of the respondents.[3] City-suburb differences in racial attitudes of this sample were similarly explainable in terms of both individual and community social class.[4]

Clearly further investigation of intra-metropolitan locale effects is necessary. Logically, differences in general orientations towards local government should be

studied within tho metropolitan context, where the researcher can relate objective data describing individual local governments and communities to subjective
survey results. In the following chapter, two such metropolitan case studies, utilizing survey data, are presented. In this chapter, however, we focus on national
city-suburb differences. For while inter-metropolitan dissimilarities may obscure
the overall national impact of suburban residence on individual attitudes, much
of the current national political rhetoric is based on assumptions about the suburban state of mind which require empirical investigation.

National survey data collected by the University of Michigan Survey Research
Center in 1968 permit examination of three crucial aspects of the suburbanite's
political frame of mind: political party identification, presidential candidate
preference, and racial attitudes.[a] In analyzing these data we must continue to
limit ourselves to the census-derived definition of city and suburb. The respondent's place of residence was coded by 1960 size, metropolitan location (central
city, suburb, outside of metropolitan area), and census designation as "urban" or
"rural" place. About one-quarter of the sample lived in central cities, one-third
in suburbs or exurbs of varying size, 17 percent in urban places outside of
SMSAs and about 24 percent in rural areas. Characteristics of respondents in
these locales are shown in Table 8-1. The analysis below excludes rural and
urban respondents residing outside major metropolitan areas. Demographic data
on respondents' locale are not included in this dataset. Thus, we cannot directly

Table 8-1
Residential Location and Respondent Characteristics

	Metropolitan (SMSA)				Non-metropolitan			Total
	Central City	Suburb 50,000+	Suburb 10,000-50,000	Suburb 2,500-10,000	Exurbia	Urban	Rural	
% White	76.1	97.9	98.8	91.6	94.5	92.6	95.0	89.7
% Both Parents Native Born	54.3	61.7	68.5	71.9	68.3	78.6	82.7	70.2
% Family Income $10,000 and above	27.1	44.7	47.9	47.4	41.3	26.1	19.9	31.6
% Some College Education and above	29.6	34.1	31.1	35.7	26.4	34.8	17.1	28.4
% White-collar, Managerial and Professional	39.6	44.7	47.5	52.3	45.7	39.3	22.7	38.6
% Married, children under 18	32.5	59.6	48.2	52.6	59.3	35.7	41.7	42.3
% Homeowner	45.7	59.6	70.4	77.1	85.9	56.4	74.2	64.2
Total N	351	47	129	184	100	237	328	1375

[a]1968 survey data were made available through the Inter-University Consortium for Political
Research. The total number of respondents was 1,482; since blacks were over-sampled, a
weighted sample of 1,375 is used in this analysis.

measure compositional contextual effects (such as community social class or ethnic composition) on individual attitudes. Nor can we separate independent effects of these compositional contextual variables from more global effects of residing within a suburban milieu.[5] The analytic technique used is multiple regression analysis. This method permits a more precise estimate of independent effects of multiple variables on a dependent variable than is possible using more familiar cross-tabulation techniques.[6] Tabular presentations are used to illustrate attitudinal differences between samples.

Party Identification and Candidate Preference

Since the 1968 survey focused on the presidential campaign of that year, many of its questions were devoted to party identification and candidate preference. These data permit us to examine the extent of contemporary suburban Republicanism. Candidate preference is always of central concern in understanding partisan political behavior. Table 8-2 shows the relationship between candidate preference (reported in a post-election interview) and locale, controlling for education as an indicator of social class.

Table 8-2
Percentage Reporting Vote for Nixon, 1968 By Locale and Education

| | Total Metropolitan | | White Metropolitan | |
Education	City	Suburb	City	Suburb
Less than H.S. grad	32.7	50.6	45.3	55.0
H.S. grad	41.7	54.1	50.8	55.0
Some College +	53.5	65.0	59.4	66.7
% of Total	42.6	57.3	52.4	59.5
N[a]	(238)	(326)	(185)	(309)

[a]N's in parentheses indicate total numbers of respondents reporting vote for either Nixon or Humphrey.

If we confine our investigation to respondents who preferred either Nixon or Humphrey, we find what appears to be a substantial locale difference, with Nixon receiving far more "votes" in suburbs than in central city. In fact, an average of 14 percent more suburban respondents at all three educational levels report voting for Nixon than their class counterparts in the central city. However, when we turn our attention to the white-only column we can see that most of the difference between central city and suburban residents is apparently accounted for by race. With nonwhites excluded, Nixon remains the favorite of suburbanites, but at every educational level differences between the two locales drop to an average of 7 percent.

Multiple regression analysis permits us to more precisely estimate the independent additive effects of individual social attributes and suburban residence on candidate preference. Regression results indicate that race and religious background were the most important social background variables in determining candidate preference of the metropolitan population in 1968. Compared to non-whites, whites were 43 percent more likely to prefer Nixon; compared to Protestants, Jews were 59 percent less likely, and Catholics 24 percent less likely, to prefer Nixon. Controlling for individual education, religious background, race and ethnicity, we find that the estimated difference in preference for Nixon between city and suburban residents was 6 percent.[b]

In 1968 the third-party campaign of George Wallace, particularly his appeal to voters outside the South, attracted considerable interest. Some observers have suggested that the Wallace phenomenon may have obscured the character of a current Republican trend in national politics which is based in part on Republican resurgence in suburbia. However, Table 8-3 shows that there was virtually no city-suburb difference in reported Wallace support outside the South, indicating that his candidacy was not related to city-suburb differences in preference for Nixon.

The metropolitan distribution of party identification is in general similar to that for candidate preference. Republican identification is apparently associated with suburban residence at all education levels for the total metropolitan population, as indicated in Table 8-4. However, as in the case of candidate preference, these differences are considerably smaller within the white metropolitan population. (Respondents were classified as Republicans or Democrats if they described themselves as "strong" or "weak" identifiers or as "Independents leaning" towards one party. When Independent "leaners" are excluded, the proportion of "Independents" is about the same—approximately 10 percent—at each educational level among central city and suburban residents. Thus, differences in proportions of Republican identifiers reflect two-party splits.)

Table 8-3

Percentage Reporting Vote for Wallace, 1968 By Locale and Education, Among Non-Southern Whites

Education	City	Suburb
Less than H.S. grad	5.9	7.1
H.S. grad	10.9	8.6
Some College +	4.1	4.9
% of Total	7.1	6.8
N[a]	(155)	(279)

[a]N's in parentheses indicate total numbers of respondents reporting vote for Humphrey, Nixon, or Wallace.

[b]95 percent confidence interval = ± 8 percent.

Table 8-4

Percentage Republican Party Identifiers, 1968 By Locale and Education

Education	Total Metropolitan		White Metropolitan	
	City	Suburb	City	Suburb
Less than H.S. grad	18.0	28.3	25.0	30.7
H.S. grad	28.2	38.5	34.4	39.5
Some College +	40.1	56.3	45.6	57.6
% of Total	28.0	41.0	35.4	42.9
N[a]	(346)	(452)	(263)	(429)

[a]N's in parentheses indicate total numbers of respondents responding "Republican," "Democrat," or "Independent" to party identification questions.

Multiple regression results indicate that race, religious background, and social class have significant independent additive effects on party identification, with race and religion playing a predominant role in determining preference. Controlling for level of education, occupational status, religious background, race and ethnicity we find an estimated 6 percent difference in Republican party identification between city and suburban respondents.[c]

Some discussions of the suburbanite in politics see him as an Independent, rather than as a Republican or Democrat. This image may derive from the non-partisan character of local suburban politics, discussed in chapters 10-12. However, cross-tabular and multiple regression analysis of these national survey data show virtually no locale difference in the proportion of self-defined "Independents" in 1968. But, if we classify as Independents those who fail to perceive differences between the issue positions of the parties, there are some significant locale differences.[d] Table 8-5 presents by locale and education the proportion of those who found no difference between the major parties' positions on five or

---

[c]95 percent confidence interval = ± 8 percent. For obvious reasons, there is little survey material on attitudes of black suburbanites; collection of these data will require surveying several metropolitan areas utilizing carefully stratified samples.

[d]Respondents were asked which party would be more likely to favor government action in ten domestic and foreign policy areas. Some did not know the parties' positions on the issue or felt there was no difference between them; others saw Wallace's AIP as the only party having a clear stance. Respondents who answered in any of these three fashions were categorized as perceiving no difference between major parties on that issue, and a "no difference" score was assigned to each respondent by summing the number of times he indicated this perception.

Considering the general lack of constraint among public policy issue orientations for the American public, the average .25 correlation among ten binary variables derived this way is not surprising. See Philip Converse, "The Nature of Belief Systems in Mass Publics," in David Apter, *Ideology and Discontent* (Glencoe, Ill.: Free Press, 1964). The summing method used here obviously provides only a crude measure of one perceptual dimension of party independence. On another dimension—split-ticket voting—we find no important locale differences. However, the variety of local elections referred to by respondents increases the difficulty of interpreting such findings.

Table 8-5

Percentage Perceiving No Difference Between Major Parties on 5 or More Issues, By Locale and Education, Among Whites

Education	Central City	Suburb
Less than H.S. grad	15.1	28.8
H.S. grad	19.0	30.6
Some College +	27.5	23.1
% of Total	21.1	27.5
N[a]	(185)	(309)

[a]N's in parentheses indicate total numbers of white metropolitan respondents, excluding Wallace supporters.

more issue questions. Suburban residents were more likely than central city residents to perceive party positions as essentially the same; this is true at every educational level except those with college experience. (Wallace partisans who see their own party as taking a clear stand on issues were excluded from this analysis.) Regression results indicate that, controlling for class, religion, race and ethnicity effects, there is an estimated difference of 9 percent between city and suburban respondents in proportion "Independent" measured in this fashion.[e]

Whether Democratic suburban emigrants changed party identification after 1952 has been discussed earlier through analysis of voting data. The 1968 study enabled us to search for such evidence in survey data as it included the question, "Was there ever a time when you thought of yourself as (the opposite party)?" The level of reported stability in identification is very high (never under two-thirds answering "No"), and the range of difference by locale or education is only a few percentage points. Table 8-6 shows that there is somewhat more shift-

Table 8-6

Percentage Changing to Republican Party Identification, 1968 By Locale and Education, Among Whites

Education	Central City	Suburb
Less than H.S. grad	50.0	61.9
H.S. grad	72.4	62.9
Some College +	62.1	76.1
% of Total	61.9	66.9
N[a]	(84)	(124)

[a]N's in parentheses indicate total numbers of respondents reporting change in party identification.

[e]95 percent confidence interval = ± 8 percent.

ing from the Democrats to the Republicans (two-thirds of the shifters), but that the direction of shifting is not significantly related to either education or central city-suburban residence. We can conclude that the rate of shifting from one party to the other is low, and that neither rate nor direction is affected by suburban residence.

In general, then, the 1968 survey data demolish the notion that strong Republican support or pro-Nixon sentiment in the suburbs is directly attributable to locale. Clearly, suburban exclusion of nonwhites and city-suburb differences in social class, ethnicity, and religious distributions produce many of the apparent differences in partisan political attitudes between the two locales. Suburbs did in fact vote more strongly for Nixon in 1968, but the absence of greater Democratic support in white suburbia is not primarily a result of the impact of suburban residence on attitudes.

On the Expansion of the Rights
of Blacks

Voting research has clearly shown that the bases for party affiliation are firmly laid at an early stage of political life and intimately tied to social background variables. Moreover, this affiliation is the most powerful long-term predictor of presidential candidate choice.[7] Thus the overall absence of locale effects upon party identification and candidate preference should not surprise us once we have rejected the popular mythology of suburban politics.

Yet, it is true that suburbanites live in an environment which is visibly different from that of the central city dweller. Just how different is becoming increasingly debatable,[8] and, as we have attempted to demonstrate, differences among suburbs may be more important than differences between city and suburb. We must then ask whether suburban experience leads to any different perspective on issues than that held by city residents. Specifically, are there locale differences in political policy attitudes which are not explainable in terms of individual social background? The 1968 interview included questions about the federal role in guaranteeing nondiscrimination in jobs and schooling, neighborhood exclusion, and desegregation in general. Concern about blacks' encroachment in the cities is often presumed to have produced a contemporary "white flight" to the suburbs. Thus, if locale has any differentiating effect upon political outlook, it should extend to these issue orientations.

Our analysis of the white metropolitan population outside the South as shown in Table 8-7, indicates that locale attitudinal differences on questions of the rights of blacks are relatively small. However, the proportions opposing expansion of the rights of blacks are not small. This is brought home by large numbers who favor "strict segregation" or something in between the latter and desegregation. Suburbanites at every education level are somewhat more likely

Table 8-7

Percentage Opposing Expansion of the Rights of Blacks, White Metropolitan Population Outside the South, 1968 By Locale and Education

Issue	Less than H.S. grad		H.S. grad		Some College +		Total	
	City	Suburb	City	Suburb	City	Suburb	City	Suburb
Federal gov't should *not* guarantee fair treatment in jobs to blacks	46.0	57.6	50.9	54.1	42.1	43.5	46.3	51.1
Federal gov't should *not* guarantee school integration.	40.4	50.6	50.0	50.9	35.2	45.9	42.1	48.9
Whites have right to exclude blacks from neighborhood.	18.5	23.0	10.8	18.1	10.5	17.4	13.1	19.2
Favor some degree of segregation.	68.3	72.2	60.6	65.0	42.1	42.1	57.5	59.1
Total N	63	90	66	120	57	115	186	325

than city respondents to oppose Federal action to guarantee blacks' rights. Among the least educated there are notable locale differences in attitudes on employment and education. Among high school graduates, locale differences are largest for housing integration; among those with higher education, for school and housing integration.

Again multiple regression analysis permits us to more precisely estimate the independent additive effects of individual attributes and locale on racial attitudes. Social class (measured by income, education, and occupational status) has little effect on these dependent variables. The largest regression coefficient for class appears in the regression equation for neighborhood segregation attitudes and shows only an estimated difference of 5 percent[f] in segregationist support between white- and blue-collar workers. Religious background has a much stronger effect on racial attitudes; for each of the dependent variables the estimated difference in segregationist support between Jews and Protestants is about 20 percent.

Controlling for these social attributes, we find that individuals with a general politically conservative outlook are 12 percent less likely to support federal school intervention compared to more "liberal" individuals.[9] This variable has little effect on neighborhood and general segregation attitudes, suggesting that federal intervention *per se* is a significant source of controversy over integration. More opposition to neighborhood integration might have been voiced by these

[f]95 percent confidence interval = ± 6 percent.

respondents had the national survey asked for opinions on federal housing intervention.[g]

Finally, controlling for individual attributes mentioned above, we find that suburbanites are 4 percent more likely to oppose Federal intervention in the areas of education and employment.[h] The estimated city-suburb difference for general segregation attitudes is an even smaller 2 percent.[i] However, on the neighborhood integration issue, suburbanites are 9 percent more likely to take a negative view.[j] Thus, our findings are consistent with those of another recent national study of racial attitudes in fifteen American cities by Campbell and Schuman:

The one point at which suburban people show a special sensitivity is in the area of segregated housing. They are more likely [than city residents] to support the proposition that white people may properly keep Negroes out of their neighborhood if they wish and they show more resistance to the prospect of having a Negro family living next door. These differences are small, less than ten percentage points, but they are not chance.[10]

The Special Issue of Residential Segregation

Much has been said about the efforts of suburban whites to exclude blacks from their communities. Their success was noted earlier in chapter 4, which showed

[g]Questions on employment, education and neighborhood integration were worded as follows:

"Some people feel that if Negroes are not getting fair treatment in jobs, the government in Washington should see to it that they do. Others feel that this is not the Federal Government's business. Have you had enough interest in this question to favor one side over the other? (If yes) How do you feel? Should the government in Washington—

  1. See to it that Negroes get fair treatment in jobs.
  3. Other, depends.
  5. Leave these matters to the states and local communities."

"Some people say that the government in Washington should see to it that white and Negro children are allowed to go to the same schools. Others claim this is not the government's business. Have you been concerned enough about this question to favor one side over the other? (If yes) Do you think the government in Washington should—

  1. See to it that white and Negro children go to the same schools.
  3. Other, depends.
  5. Leave these matters to the states and social communities."

"Which of these statements would you agree with:

  1. White people have a right to keep Negroes out of their neighborhoods if they want to.
  5. Negroes have a right to live wherever they can afford to, just like anybody else.
  8. Don't know, depends."

[h]95 percent confidence interval = ± 10 percent.

[i]95 percent confidence interval = ± 10 percent.

[j]95 percent confidence interval = ± 8 percent.

that suburban blacks are as residentially segregated as central city blacks. Data suggesting that residential integration may arouse feelings among suburbanites not engendered by job and school integration led us to investigate opinions on this issue further.

At first thought, it seems reasonable that homeowners would be more resistant to neighborhood integration than renters. Fears over blacks "lowering property values" would affect the former more than the latter. Yet, multiple regression analysis shows that, after controlling for individual class and residential locale, metropolitan homeowners are 7 percent *less* likely to favor neighborhood segregation as compared to renters.[k] Hahn's study of white voters in California and Detroit also found renters more negative on neighborhood integration, although his study did not treat locale effects.[11] Our regression analysis shows that, after controlling for income, education, and occupation, core city homeowners are indeed 5 percent *more* likely to favor neighborhood segregation as compared to renters. However, among suburbanites, controlling for class, *renters* are as much as 15 percent more likely to favor segregation as compared to homeowners.[l] Table 8-8 shows this distinction sharply. Among homeowners at every educational level, locale differences are small. Among renters, however, suburbanites are much more likely to support neighborhood segregation than are city residents. Controlling for class, the estimated city-suburb attitudinal difference for renters is 21 percent.[m] Because renters comprise a minority of the suburban subsample (about 25 percent), the overall level of resistance to neighborhood integration in the suburbs does not appear so high; however, we seem to have isolated in suburban renters a core of resisters.

In sum, regression results afford insufficient evidence for generalizations on

Table 8-8
Percentage Supporting Neighborhood Segregation By Locale and Education, Among White Homeowners and Renters

| | Homeowners | | Renters | |
Education	Central City	Suburb	Central City	Suburb
Less than H.S. grad	17.9	20.0	19.2	29.6
H.S. grad	15.2	11.6	6.3	36.7
Some College +	12.5	14.1	9.8	29.2
% of Total	15.6	14.7	11.1	32.1
N[a]	(77)	(232)	(99)	(81)

[a]N's in parentheses indicate total numbers of respondents.

---

[k]95 percent confidence interval = ± 9 percent.
[l]In both locales, 95 percent confidence interval = ± 10 percent.
[m]95 percent confidence interval = ± 12 percent.

suburban segregation attitudes which have appeared in the popular press. Supposedly crucial variables—class, ethnicity, homeownership, family structure—
together shows little association with neighborhood segregation attitudes
(R=.30). Although we find that suburban residence is related to opinions on this
issue, we are unable to explain more than 10 percent of the total attitudinal
variance among city and suburban respondents. Substantial additional research is
needed before we will be able to understand the nature of resistance to suburban
integration.[12]

The Case of the Inner Suburb

A necessary ingredient of such analysis will be the ability to differentiate among
suburbs. Here we are bound to our national survey's categorization of respondents by size—not location or status—of suburb. As noted previously, we find few
demographic differences among these categories; respondents from the largest
suburbs are somewhat more likely to be white "ethnics" (less likely to have
native-born parents) and much more likely to be renters. However, Table 8-9
shows that size of suburb is associated with racial attitudes, with the most negative attitudes appearing among respondents from the largest suburbs. The pattern is less clear for attitudes on equal employment, but it is marked on other
issues. Controlling for individual attributes (class, religion, family status, conserv
ative outlook, and homeownership), residents of large suburbs are 25 percent

Table 8-9
**Percentage Opposing Expansion of Rights of Blacks By Size of Suburb, Among
Non-Southern Whites**

Issue	Suburb 50,000+	Suburb 10,000- 50,000	Suburb 2500- 10,000	Exurb under 2500 rural
Federal gov't should *not* guarantee fair treatment in jobs to blacks	51.4	46.5	47.3	55.9
Federal gov't should *not* guarantee school integration	68.8	53.5	46.5	34.5
Whites have right to exclude blacks from neighborhood	35.5	22.0	16.0	12.7
Favor some degree of segregation	81.8	60.0	52.5	58.5
Total N	33	105	122	65

more likely to take a segregationist stance on education, housing, and general policy as compared to city respondents.[n] Residents of medium-sized suburbs are 10 percent more likely to take a segregationist stance, as compared to city respondents.[o] Residents of smaller suburbs and exurbia are, on the average, less likely than city respondents to support segregation. The possibility that this locale difference is an artifact of racial composition was explored by including respondent's perception of neighborhood racial makeup in the regression equations. This changed regression coefficients for locale variables slightly, but the overall picture remained the same.

We have insufficient data to interpret this locale pattern, but a conjecture may be offered. Large suburbs are most likely to fall in the inner suburban belt of the nation's larger cities where there are higher proportions and numbers of black residents. While white residents of large suburbs have fled the city, they are probably closer to its problems and obviously closer to its racial minorities than other suburbanites. For example, we find that 34 percent of these large suburb respondents cited law and order as the most important problem facing the country in 1968. This was somewhat higher than the proportion of city whites citing this problem (30 percent) but differed more with the views of other suburbanites (24 percent). Suburban segregationists, whom we find more frequently in large suburbs, were also more likely than their opposites to view "urban unrest" as a very important factor in their 1968 presidential vote. Our data on the effects of locale and homeownership support Hahn's speculation that:

For an individual who has not yet achieved the station of homeownership and who may live in closer proximity to Negroes, the fear of Negro dominance in the neighborhood may be more severe than for homeowners who are ensconced in the relative security of their domains. The maintenance of existing patterns of housing discrimination, therefore, may be more critical for a renter who has not yet satisfied the dream of owning his home.[13]

A crucial question for policy makers is whether those who are most resistant to integration can be treated as a minority of the national suburban population or must be recognized as representatives of a particular type of suburb on the rim of the city in the path of black movement.

Conclusions

Our analysis of national survey data shows that apparent city-suburb differences in partisan political attitudes are primarily attributable to demographic differ-

---

[n]95 percent confidence interval = ± 20 percent. Note small sample sizes.
[o]95 percent confidence interval = ± 12 percent.

ences between the two locales. On the other hand, we find that suburban residence does have an effect on racial attitudes which is not merely a consequence of demography. One underlying theme of these data is that racial exclusion is intimately tied to suburban attitudes. Another is that, despite the increasing number of attributes which these locales share, suburban residence may remain important for those who feel they have "made it" to suburbia and wish to defend their concept of suburban life-style. Finally, with regard to both partisan and racial data, it should be noted that sociological explanation does not vitiate political implications of attitudinal distribution. Clearly these attitudes will contribute a key issue for partisan politics of the seventies and a basis for conflict between city and suburb, and among suburbanites.

9

Orientations Toward
Community and Politics

Design and Focus

Previously cited research has suggested that the magnitude of locale differences in attitude may be greater within individual metropolitan areas than in the national population and may apply for a broader spectrum of attitudes. Considering the degree of heterogeneity within the suburban population which has been demonstrated, this might be the case. However, shifting attention from the national to the metropolitan scene does not simplify the analytic problem. In order to evaluate the impact of suburban residence on attitudes we must be able to distinguish effects of individual attributes and interaction between individual and contextual variables, from global effects of suburban residence. For example, Orbell and Sherrill have demonstrated the existence of interactive effects of individual and community class on racial attitudes within the Columbus, Ohio metropolitan area.[1] In addition, analysis of intra-metropolitan locale effects must consider differences *among* suburbs, as well as differences between the central city and the suburban ring. Thus, in a pilot survey of orientations towards local government in selected Philadelphia suburbs, Williams and his colleagues found attitudes varying with individual and community class.[2]

Large-scale collection of both aggregate and survey data for a sample of metropolitan areas stratified by region, stage of development and demographic characteristics, would be needed to rigorously investigate the impact of suburban residence on attitudes. Such an undertaking is not likely in the immediate future. Instead, contextual analysts may have to adopt the "case study" strategy of traditional political scientists and attempt to derive findings through examination of attitudinal patterns in a fortuitous sample of areas.

In this chapter we suggest the direction for such analysis by examining data from two areas, Boston and Los Angeles. The Boston SMSA is northeastern, with many of the attributes of that regional culture. It is comprised of a centuries-old central city surrounded by suburbs which were likewise established in pre-Revolutionary days. Boston suburbs are highly differentiated by income, occupation, ethnicity and even religion; in degree of differentiation this area appears to match the Philadelphia region studied by Williams *et al*. Almost polar in character is the Los Angeles SMSA, which is much larger, southwestern in culture, and which has developed at a later point in time. Los Angeles epitomizes urban sprawl, with a central city that incorporates downtown areas, inner city ghettoes, beach communities and residential sub-divisions at all income levels.

117

The region has only recently emerged from a period of rapid growth. Thus, while data analyzed here cannot be said to represent the entire range of metropolitan diversity, they have been drawn from two quite different areas, which makes the similarity of findings reported below all the more interesting.

Suburban Boston data are drawn from a 76-communities study conducted in 1967. We found two types of suburbs as measured by the ratio of professional and managerial to blue-collar occupations (the white-collar level was relatively constant across communities). These two also differed in income and education, and their voting and expenditure patterns during the sixties appear to demonstrate genuine differences in modal community values. Thus, class differences between the two seem to signify differences in life styles. Four upper-middle class professional (PROFSUB) and four affluent blue-collar (WORKSUB) suburbs were selected for more intensive study. A highly stratified probability sample of 165 married males between 30 and 60 was interviewed in a design which permitted measurement of independent and interactive effects of individual and community class. Analysis of these data focuses on *inter-suburb* differences.[a]

Los Angeles data were drawn from a large-scale survey of the metropolitan area conducted in 1970.[b] The highly clustered sample of 963 was not designed to reflect inter-community differences within the metropolis. Respondents were divided *post hoc* into five groups which roughly correspond to sociopolitical regions. About half the sample are Los Angeles city residents. Sixty percent of these are from tracts that are heavily black or predominantly Mexican-American, generally renter-occupied, and low income, located in the southeast sections (INNERCITY). The remainder, while inside the city, fit the "suburban" stereotype; these are virtually all-white, high-income tracts in the western and San Fernando valley areas where homeownership predominates (OUTERCITY).[3]

Respondents outside the city are almost equally distributed across three regions: Southeast INNERSUB (low to medium income, owner-occupied tracts from one predominantly black and several white blue-collar suburbs), West/Southwest MIDDLESUB (white, medium income, renter/owner ratio about 2:1), East/Northeast OUTERSUB (white, medium-income, 90 percent homeowner). Suburbs in the western and eastern SMSA range in size from 30,000 to 100,000 and include areas from the more urban moderately industrialized (MIDDLESUB) to the more exurban and totally residential (OUTERSUB). Southeastern IN-

---

[a]This survey was conducted by the Boston Area Survey Project (Harvard-M.I.T. Joint Center for Urban Studies) for Deborah and Carl Hensler as part of their dissertation research. Because of financial constraints only a small sample of residents in each town could be interviewed. Respondents were screened for occupation, sex, ethnicity and age, using the local police lists plus interview questions to limit the number of control variables in the data analysis stage. Thus results are not generalizable to the total resident population of these suburban types; instead analysis focuses on locale effects for an important subpopulation.

[b]This survey (LAMAS) is an omnibus, shared-time survey of approximately 1,000 SMSA residents, fielded semiannually by the UCLA Survey Research Center. Questions analyzed in this chapter were contributed by Deborah Hensler. LAMAS data become part of the Center's public archive two years after survey completion.

NERSUB's, adjacent to central city ghettoes, are in the line of minority group movement; to local politicoes this is "Wallace country." These Los Angeles data permit analysis of city-suburb locale effects on attitudes. The absence of objective data on specific individual social contexts precludes intensive investigation of interactive effects, but *intra*-city and *inter*-suburban comparisons permit us to approximate these.

Three attitudinal complexes were selected for this analysis. The first of these—*orientation toward community*—examines one aspect of our national mythology, that an individual can find a stronger "sense of community" and a more satisfactory life in suburbia. Suburban social homogeneity is frequently cited as the basis for the development of such community attachment.[4] Our findings in the last chapter on suburbanites' views on excluding minority groups have led us to investigate the relationship between suburban residence, preference for homogeneity, and community satisfaction and attachment.

A second complex of attitudes we analyze is *orientation toward local government*. The suburban polity has been described as a "miniature republic."[5] The suburbanite is thought to believe that he can affect local government more easily than his city brethren, that he has traded corrupt urban officialdom for leaders he can trust, and that his local government has the power to protect and maintain the social character of the community. While some empirical studies report survey findings consistent with this picture, the Boston and Los Angeles data permit us to more precisely estimate the independent effect of locale on these orientations.[6] There is a special utility in this exploration. We need to know more about suburban political perceptions in order to predict community reaction to national policy changes in areas such as housing integration.

In a third attitudinal area we examine *perceptions of community problems*. We need to learn more about the role that anxiety about urban crime, social disorder and racial conflict plays in determining the suburban state of mind. In our analysis we will focus upon the impact of suburban residence *per se* upon the perceptions of social problems and the issue orientations of metropolitan residents.

Orientations Towards Community

The hypothesized special affection of the suburbanite for his community is not found in our study. Neither the Los Angeles nor Boston data provide evidence of differential rates of general *satisfaction* by type of community. Rather, a respondent's satisfaction with his community is equally high in widely varying areas of Los Angeles. Regression analysis of Los Angeles data indicates no important individual class, ethnicity or city-suburb locale effects on this variable. Similarly, Boston suburbanites demonstrate high levels of community satisfaction, with results unvarying by community class. However, Table 9-1 shows that

Table 9-1

Percentage Satisfied with Community, By Individual Class and Locale, Boston Area Survey, 1967

Individual Class	Profsub	Worksub
Professional	67	49
Blue-collar	67	76
N	(48)	(48)

those who resemble the modal community resident are more likely to be satisfied with their towns than those who are demographically different.[c]

We find no evidence of locale, class, or ethnic effects on respondent's community *attachment*. About two-thirds of the Los Angeles respondents regard their community as their "real home—the place where they really belong." Boston data show a similar pattern of strong community attachment across class levels in both locales.[d]

Perceptions of intra-community differences are a potential source of a type of social friction which is said to distinguish city life from suburban. Writing about sources of "urban unease" Wilson has speculated that:

the concern for community is less the "need" for "belonging" . . . than the concerns of any rationally self-interested person with a normal but not compulsive interest in the environment of himself and his family. . . . Because of these considerations [that persons different from oneself will not behave appropriately] the members of a community have a general preference for social homogeneity and a suspicion of heterogeneity.[7]

Such preferences and fears are assumed to be a motivating force in suburban opposition to racial and class integration. Boston and Los Angeles interviews focused on the question of tension over ethnic and class relations as a threat to the individual's "sense of community." Analyses of these data show that bases for community attachment do differ according to individual and community class but that there is no simple relationship between perceptions of social heterogeneity and sense of community.

Table 9-2 summarizes these results for professional and blue-collar respondents in the two Boston suburb types. The relationships of objective measures of integration (such as association membership and neighboring) to community attachment seem to depend on the individual's social position in town. In particular, none of these measures is strongly related to the statistically deviant blue-

[c]The "community satisfaction" measure was derived from a factor analysis of community evaluation items including responses to closed and open-ended questions.

[d]In Boston, "community attachment" was measured by asking the respondent to place his feelings about the town on a five-point scale ranging between "I feel very much a part of this town" to "I don't feel much connection with what goes on in this town."

Table 9-2

Correlates of Sense of Belonging, By Individual Class and Locale, Boston Area Survey, 1967

Locale:	Profsub		Worksub	
Individual Class:	Professional	Blue-collar	Professional	Blue-collar
Independent Variables				
Neighboring	.38	−.10	−.03	.24
Local Friendship	.63	.04	.62	.46
Local Association Membership	.24	.18	.49	.04
Perception of Social Similarity	.15	.34	−.43	.44

collar respondent's degree of attachment in PROFSUBs. A *subjective* measure of integration (feeling like or unlike other residents) is related to community attachment, but this relationship is not straightforward. Blue-collar respondents are, in both suburb types, more likely to exhibit attachment to the town if they feel similar to the modal town resident. However, professionals in WORKSUBs are *less* likely to identify with the town if they feel similar to the mode.

What explains these diverse effects of individual and suburb class on the relationship between perception of social similarity and community attachment? Open-ended responses indicate that the general picture of the community carried in each resident's head varies with his social position in town. The latter apparently affects modes—rather than degree—of adaptation to the community, how—rather than whether—he adapts. For the professional in a WORKSUB, it is functional to recognize social differences; his is a realistic picture of the town's social structure, in which he holds a superior position. Blue-collar respondents in a PROFSUB, however, tend to exaggerate the extent of the town's social heterogeneity which then permits them to feel more like other residents. Perhaps respondents are thinking about their own more similar neighborhoods instead of the larger community when they respond to these questions. However, the items emphasized the town referent; thus a respondent who substitutes a more immediate referent may be indicating that he does not wish to think about the social reality of the entire town. However explained, the deviant blue-collar worker's tendency to see townspeople as "all working men" and to ignore occupational differences between himself and modal residents is positively related to his degree of community attachment.

Among Los Angeles respondents we find no evidence that perceptions of social differences among community residents are directly related to an individual's attachment to his community. For white Los Angeles respondents, almost all of whom live in racially segregated communities, vague descriptions of life-style are the most frequently articulated basis for perception of similarity or dissimilarity to their neighbors. In the total white population, race and ethnicity are rarely mentioned in this context. However, where residential integration is a fact, respondent's perceptions in such areas reflect reality. Controlling for respondent's race and social class, INNERCITY respondents are 29 percent more likely to describe their communities in terms of race and ethnicity, as compared to OUTERCITY respondents.[e] Controlling for race and class, INNERSUBURB respondents are somewhat more likely than MIDDLESUBURB and OUTER-SUBURB respondents to mention race. But perception of racial dissimilarity between self and community is not related to community attachment in any of these locales.

Finally, in both the Boston and Los Angeles analyses, we identified as "uneasy" (in Wilson's sense) those respondents who showed both a preference for a socially homogeneous community and a perception of heterogeneity within their present community. However, we find no evidence that such respondents are less satisfied with, or less attached to their communities, regardless of locale.

Generally our analysis of both Boston and Los Angeles data suggests that class integration and attendant social heterogeneity in a community are not threatening *per se*; instead what is important is the message that the latter carries about the individual's own social position. Attitudes on housing integration in the national sample of suburbanites suggest that racial integration would be threatening to many. We cannot draw from these metropolitan data any conclusion about how future perceptions of suburban racial heterogeneity will affect satisfaction with suburban life. However, we find no evidence that suburbanites' perceptions of or attachment to their communities are significantly different from those of urban residents. The pattern of orientations to community among different social classes and in city and suburban locales suggests that acceptance of integration will depend on residents' evaluation of the effect of racial heterogeneity on their community and individual social position.

Orientations Toward Local Government

Suburbanites' ability to promote or oppose community social change will depend in part on their attitudes toward political participation. Suburban residents are often depicted as more participant and feeling more effective than their big city counterparts. Suburban governments are typically nonpartisan with broad scope for citizen participation. For example, our Boston area suburbanites have a town meeting form of government which permits them to take direct part in discussion of policies and decision-making. The realities of nonpartisan political styles in suburbia will be discussed in chapter 11. Here we focus on individual orientations toward local government, on how effective suburbanites feel work-

[e]95 percent confidence interval = ±16 percent.

ing within it, and what they think of it, i.e., what are termed personal political efficacy and system evaluation.

Hensler has found that political efficacy and evaluation form two distinct attitudinal factors.[8] Individual social class, in particular educational level, is strongly related to personal political efficacy but not to system evaluation. Political efficacy, but not system evaluation, is strongly related to involvement and participation at both local and national levels. Further, political efficacy is strongly related to general personal efficacy. This correlational pattern suggests that sense of political efficacy is a product of early socialization rather than a response to specific governmental attributes.

Table 9-3 shows that political efficacy in the Los Angeles white population is indeed related to educational level and not to city-suburb locale. Multiple regression analysis reveals that, controlling for race, income, and occupation, college-educated respondents are 19 percent more likely to feel efficacious compared to those with less education.[f] Controlling for these individual attributes, we find no important locale effect on efficacy. However, it is interesting to note in Table 9-3 that the members of one white suburban group—those with high school education—*are* much more likely to feel efficacious than their big city counterparts.

Boston survey data repeat the general pattern of strong individual class effects and limited independent locale effects on political efficacy. Respondents in both suburban locales indicated high levels of efficacy and participation. Sixty-three percent of those in PROFSUBs and 43 percent in WORKSUBs reported attending general town meetings and Board of Selectmen meetings, "almost always voting," and frequently discussing town politics. There is marginal evidence of individual and community class interactive effects on efficacy; blue-collar workers in PROFSUBs and professionals in WORKSUBs are somewhat less likely to feel efficacious than demographically conforming respondents.

Table 9-3
Percentage of White Los Angelenos Politically Efficacious, By Locale and Education, 1970

Education Level:	Inner City	Outer City	Inner Suburb	Middle Suburb	Outer Suburb	Total City	Total Suburb
Low	41.7	37.0	50.0	38.5	45.8	38.5	43.0
Medium	33.3	40.7	60.0	56.8	65.1	39.4	60.9
High	80.0	66.7	79.3	66.7	57.1	69.0	65.9
Total	53.8	52.3	65.3	54.5	57.8	52.6	58.3
N	(39)	(153)	(75)	(121)	(116)	(192)	(312)

Note: Totals represent number of white, non-Spanish surname respondents replying to question.

---

[f]95 percent confidence interval = ±12 percent.

Our findings are consistent with other more general research. Schuman and Gruenberg reported an absence of inter-city effects on *personal* efficacy, and Orbell found no intra-metropolitan differences for *political* efficacy in Columbus, Ohio.[9] While we conclude that locale has no apparent independent effect on this political orientation, further research with larger sample sizes is necessary to investigate the possible interactive effects of individual class and locale.

When we consider variables associated with political system evaluation we find a rather different pattern. In their study of attitudes in fifteen American cities, Schuman and Gruenberg report that the largest proportion of explained variance in government evaluation is attributable to intercity locale differences rather than to individual attributes.[10] While that study deals only with cities, and large ones at that, we find a similar pattern within the Los Angeles SMSA. Table 9-4 shows suburbanites here are very much more likely to say "local government is run the way it should be" than are city residents. Multiple regression analysis confirms this, showing an estimated 19 percent difference between suburbanites and city respondents, controlling for income, education, occupation, and race. The latter individual attributes have no measurable effect on system evaluation.[g]

Interestingly, we find no intra-city locale effects on evaluation in Los Angeles, and an absence of inter-suburb differences in government evaluation in both Los Angeles and Boston. Table 9-5 shows that satisfaction with town government is extremely high in both Boston suburban locales and is not strongly related to individual or community social class. We find the same pattern for items tapping trust in political officials and other such measures of diffuse system evaluation.

Table 9-4

Percentage of White Los Angelenos with Positive Evaluations of Local Government, By Locale and Education, 1970

Education Level:	Inner City	Outer City	Inner Suburb	Middle Suburb	Outer Suburb	Total City	Suburb
Low	43.5	14.3	69.2	64.9	52.0	27.5	61.3
Medium	35.0	38.3	52.0	54.3	48.6	37.3	51.6
High	35.0	37.3	50.0	54.8	60.9	36.8	56.3
Total	37.5	33.1	54.8	57.9	54.7	34.5	56.0
N	(64)	(142)	(62)	(114)	(106)	(206)	(282)

Note: N's, weighted to adjust for sampling rate differences, represent number replying to question.

[g]95 percent confidence interval = ±10 percent. The racial variable included in this regression contrasted white Anglos with blacks, Chicanos, and Orientals. Had we confined our analysis to black/white Anglo attitudinal differences, we might have found a stronger race effect.

Table 9-5

Percentage Boston Area Suburbanites Replying Local Government Is "Worth the Taxes," By Individual Class and Locale

Individual Class	Profsub	Worksub
Professional	92	72
Blue-collar	83	83
N	(48)	(48)

Recently political observers have pointed to a "tax-payers' revolt" in suburbia, and cited this as a basis for increased frequency of bond referenda failures. The latter phenomenon has been observed in Los Angeles as elsewhere, Given this concern, and considering that we had found higher levels of satisfaction with local government in suburban Los Angeles than in the central city, we investigated specific correlates of satisfaction further. Los Angelenos were asked how they felt about various local government services. In contrast to the findings for diffuse government evaluation, we find no locale differences in average ratings of these services.[h] We do find some limited independent race and education effects; nonwhites are 5 percent more likely than whites to give negative service evaluations,[i] and high school and college-educated respondents are 6 percent more likely than the lesser educated to respond negatively. Thus critics of urban services in Los Angeles are not generally distinguished by their residence but by their color and status. The most critical—regardless of place—are nonwhites and whites with better than average education.

Some locale differences do appear when we consider services separately, however.[j] Controlling for class, race, and homeownership, suburbanites are 21 percent more likely than city residents to say that sanitation services are "not worth the taxes,"[k] and OUTERSUB respondents are more likely than other suburbanites to feel this way about park and recreation facilities. There is no evidence of independent class or race effects on these specific evaluations except in the case of police services; within Los Angeles, high-income respondents are more likely than low-income counterparts to think police services are not worth the taxes paid. This is surprising, considering the higher incidence of crime in low-income areas. Varying findings on class and locale effects on specific service evaluations probably reflect locale differences in service levels. However, feelings about these differences apparently bear little relation to individuals' over-all satisfaction with local government. Suburbanites in some parts of the Los Angeles area are highly

[h]Respondents were asked to rate police, fire, and sanitation services, as well as schools, parks, and recreation; a service evaluation score was obtained by summing and averaging these ratings.

[i]95 percent confidence interval = ±4 percent.

[j]95 percent confidence interval = ±4 percent.

[k]95 percent confidence interval = ±16 percent.

dissatisfied with specific services—and conceivably might express such dissatisfaction by negative voting on bond referenda—but there is no evidence of a general "loss of faith" in suburban government in these data.

Government evaluation has an impact on general community satisfaction of those living inside the city or on its rim. We found no locale differences for the latter variable; how satisfied one is with the community is in no way traceable to residence in city vs. suburb. However, *within* Los Angeles city, when other individual attributes are controlled, those evaluating local government positively are 21 percent more likely to be generally satisfied with their community, compared to those with negative views.[l] But this relationship of government satisfaction with community satisfaction is not repeated in the suburban sample. There, however, we observe an interesting effect of political efficacy on community attachment. Controlling for other individual attributes, suburbanites who feel efficacious are 13 percent more likely to evidence community attachment, compared to inefficacious respondents.[m]

In general, then, the picture of the suburbanite as a more contented and efficacious political man is apparently accurate. He is more generally satisfied with his local government than the big city resident, despite some displeasure with specific services. However, differences between city and suburban residents on these dimensions are more a consequence of the kinds of people suburbanites are than where they happen to reside in the metropolitan area.

Issue Orientations

In seeking locale differences in political attitudes we have thus far focused on general orientations to the political world such as efficacy, evaluation and satisfaction. Now we turn our attention to some specific current issues. The 1970 Los Angeles survey provides data on respondents' identification of major community problems. It also permits us to examine candidate preference in a gubernatorial compaign which was widely viewed as articulating major political concerns of the 'seventies. Table 9-6 shows that city-suburb locale differences are remarkably slight in priorities regarding community problems. Unemployment, "crime and violence in the streets," air pollution, and property tax levels were selected as "most important" by majorities in both locales. Spontaneous references to problems "bothering" the respondent repeat this pattern, although concern about crime, vandalism, and disorder is voiced less frequently.

[l]95 percent confidence interval = ±14 percent.

[m]95 percent confidence interval = ±12 percent.

Although we focus on community satisfaction as a dependent variable, we clearly cannot determine the direction of causality in this relationship. Although political efficacy and system evaluation appear as independent dimensions in national survey data and in our Los Angeles city data, we find a correlation of .19 between these two variables in the suburban subsample.

Table 9-6

Percentage Los Angelenos Regarding Selected Problems as "Most Important," By Locale

Selected from Problem List	City	Suburb
Unemployment	67	59
Crime	58	50
Air Pollution	50	57
Property Taxes	34	49
Poverty	20	14
Race Relations	18	21
Quality of Schools	16	18
Spontaneous References		
Environmental	23	24
Social Disorder	9	4
Problems Attributed to Specific Social Groups	8	6
N	423	397

Multiple regression analysis shows that it is race, education, and homeowner-ship—rather than locale—which have the greatest effect on respondents' priorities. In particular, after controlling for other individual attributes, we find that nonwhites are 15 percent more likely than whites to select unemployment as a crucial problem and whites are 23 percent more likely than nonwhites to select air pollution.[n] Respondents concerned about crime and violence are more likely to be renters than homeowners and lack college education. On the other hand, the quality of schools and race relations in general are concerns of the better-educated; concern about the level of property taxes is, not surprisingly, most strongly affected by homeownership.

Although we find no independent city-suburb locale effects on priorities we do find intra-city differences which are independent of class, race and homeown-ership. OUTERCITY respondents, who live in areas less smoggy than those of INNERCITY residents, are nevertheless 23 percent *more* likely to spontaneously mention pollution problems as most "bothersome."[o] INNERCITY respondents, as compared to OUTERCITY residents, are 18 percent more likely to say they are bothered by social disorder and 14 percent more likely to attribute the cause of community problems to the young, other ethnic groups, hippies, etc.[p] Within

[n]95 percent confidence interval equal, respectively, ±10 and 12 percent.
[o]95 percent confidence interval = ±16 percent.
[p]95 percent confidence interval equal, respectively, ±12 and 10 percent.

the suburban region, after controlling for individual social attributes, we find that residents of the poorer INNERSUBs are somewhat more concerned about school quality than other suburbanites. Residents of the smoggier eastern basin are—realistically enough—more concerned about air pollution than other sub-urbanites.

Generally then, intra-city variations plus inter-suburban agreements on prior-ities indicate that city-suburb differences in the Los Angeles metropolis are dampened by the inclusion within the central city of a large area similar in social character to the suburban ring. Our data suggest that in metropolitan areas with more homogeneous inner cores we may find greater city-suburb divergence in problem identification and policy priorities. However, in cities with such a quasi-suburban sector, we would expect to find a dampening effect on attempts to build a solid city-wide coalition to promote action on urban welfare problems in the face of conflicting suburban demands.

An important framework for judging such issues could be the suburbanite's orientation to change as against retention in political affairs. In their analysis of metropolitan attitudes toward school district reorganization, Hawley and Zim-mer report that suburbanites are more likely to oppose change than are city resi-dents.[11] In pursuing the question of conservative orientation, Los Angeles resi-dents were asked whether they generally feel it is better to "stick to proven ways you already know about" or "look for new ways of doing things." Of those expressing a viewpoint, only 17 percent of city and suburban respondents alike took the generally conservative position.

Electoral returns indicate a rather different finding on conservatism within the Los Angeles public, but a similar lack of support for the thesis of a distinc-tive suburban conservatism. Considering the analysis and projections of Republi-can party strategists, these findings are of some interest.[12]

The Los Angeles survey was conducted immediately following a gubernatorial campaign in which incumbent Ronald Reagan was widely viewed as representing a conservative approach to government. Table 9-7 shows that an apparent city-

Table 9-7

Percentage Los Angelenos Reporting Vote for Reagan, By Locale and Education, 1970

Education	Total		White	
	City	Suburb	City	Suburb
Low	31.2	40.2	56.7	47.5
Medium	39.3	46.5	51.2	53.6
High	43.2	68.3	52.1	74.4
Total	38.6	54.6	53.1	62.0
N	(337)	(348)	(147)	(200)

Note: Totals equal number of white respondents reporting voting and preferring Reagan or Unruh.

suburb locale difference in candidate preference is mainly an effect of racial distribution in the metropolitan area. Regression analysis found—after controlling for income, education, occupation, race, and homeownership—that there is no measurable effect of locale on preference. Furthermore, this pattern is repeated for party identification. Additional analysis shows that Reagan's appeal to non-Republicans is likewise unaffected by locale. In sum, Los Angeles data repeat the finding for national survey data: suburbanites are more likely to support Republican candidates but this phenomenon is not directly attributable to locale.

Conclusions

Analysis of intra-metropolitan locale differences in two regions provides little evidence of the purported independent effects of suburban residence on attitudes. The common view that people in city and suburb do diverge in their orientations toward community, polity, and current issues does receive some support. But suburban attitudes upon closer analysis are revealed as correlates primarily of race and social class and not characteristic of the suburbanite *qua* suburbanite. Further, perception of social heterogeneity within city and suburban communities is not distinctively associated with dissatisfaction. Most intriguing is the evidence that there exists a greater satisfaction with local government in suburbia. Lacking more detailed survey data on such orientations we can only speculate about the effects of positive evaluation and political efficacy on suburban politics.

Is There A Suburban State of Mind?

In our exploration of the suburban state of mind, we set out to discover the nature of suburban political culture. Much has been written about this culture, both in the popular press and in academic journals. The national and metropolitan survey data analyzed in these two chapters provide some support for the image of suburban political culture as more Republican and more resistant to social change in the area of race relations, than its urban counterpart. Los Angeles suburbanites tend to be more participant, more efficacious and more positively-oriented toward local government than their urban neighbors. Data from a Boston area survey suggest these feelings are typical of suburbanites in both blue-collar and upper-income communities.

However, the magnitude of differences in the distribution of attitudes among urban and suburban populations is small enough to cause us to question the notion of *a* distinctive suburban political culture. More important, our failure to find measurable independent locale effects on attitudes, once we have "partialled-out" the effects of individual attributes, suggests that the dynamics of attitude formation in urban and suburban populations are the same. The suburban "climate of opinion," while different from that of the city, does not seem to play a significant role in determining individual political orientations. Suburbanites' attitudes are different from those of their urban counterparts because of the kinds of people they are, *not* because of where they live.

Our null findings, while perhaps disappointing to aficionados of contextual analysis and cultural historians, might be of little practical interest were it not for the projections of some political party strategists regarding the role of "the new suburbia" in the formation of new party coalitions. The potential is certainly there, but a conservative politician might take note of the relative strength of education, religious background and ethnicity effects versus suburban locale effects before directing his campaign appeal to the suburbanite *qua* suburbanite.

Part 4
Local Political Conflict

10 Revenues and Expenditures

Apart from guaranteeing each state "a Republican form of government," the Constitution has virtually nothing to say about the operation of state government, and cities are not so much as mentioned. In a legal sense, local governments may accurately be described as minor wards of the state, perennially subject to restraints and limitations specified by state legislatures and administrative agencies. It would be a mistake, however, to conclude that city hall is run entirely from the state capitol. Within limits established by the state, suburban municipalities are free to select forms of government. They are also free to build schools, invest more heavily in "academic" rather than "commercial" high schools, and adopt land-use controls to preserve the distinctive "character" of residential neighborhoods. They may also alter tax regulations to attract industry, or adopt zoning codes to keep industry out.

Because men will differ over such issues, there exists everywhere a local politics. The outcome of such politics is mediated by numerous variables. In this chapter, we shall demonstrate how the distribution of resources affects the fiscal policy outcomes of suburbs. The following chapter notes the special effect of the election process upon local suburban politics. The last chapter in this section notes the intervening impact of differing values in the special politics of land-use and schools. The mix of resources and values makes for a varied tone and fervor in suburbia, as it does in other American communities. Our major concern in these chapters is not to demonstrate some special quality about suburban local politics. Rather it is to note that that part of the stereotype which assumes blandness in suburban politics—or in other elements of life there—does not stand up well in the face of the variety we will show. Given the social variety discussed in earlier chapters, it is not surprising that suburbanites differ from place to place—and within each place—on who gets what, when, and how. The result is a politics that is less fondue than stew.

Raising the Money and Paying the Bills

Tax-Expenditure Loads and Land-Use Patterns

Municipal governments spend a great deal of money (during fiscal year 1966-1967 almost $19.2 billion)—with education, law enforcement, and high-

133

ways heading the list.[1] Despite all the feverish talk about an encroaching federal government peeling away functions from local governments, the number of civilians employed by Washington has leveled off over the last quarter century at the same time as the number of people working for local government has almost doubled. Military expenses aside, local governments spend more money each year than the national government or the fifty states. If local governments have become comatose, the figures fail to disclose the severity of the malady.

Providing local services requires money. Suburbs, particularly those anticipating or desiring rapid growth, have to pay heavily for the long-run capital facilities that constitute the community's social overhead. This tends to create a worrisome fiscal imbalance, for most of the bills have to be covered before new families arrive. And the capital facilities are invariably expensive, particularly if the community wishes to lure more affluent newcomers. It costs more to put up a new school building decked out with a music room, audiovisual aids and data processing machines than it does to maintain an obsolescent structure built a half-century ago in a blighted section of the central city. Affluent parents concerned with their children's welfare will settle for nothing less. Also, before new families move into a subdivision, roads have to be graded and surfaced, sewer mains and water pipe trenched and installed, and curbstones laid. Then, too, police and fire stations have to be built and outfitted, to say nothing of libraries and sewage treatment plants. Some of these facilities can be built in stages nicely timed to the arrival of newcomers, but most have to be completed before they can produce any services at all.

Blocked by state laws from raising much money from sales and income taxes, suburban municipalities have had to rely on the real property tax for revenue. Property taxes during 1968 and 1969 accounted for slightly over a third of all revenues spent by municipal governments, and for over 85 percent of all the money raised by local taxes.[2] But real property taxes carry a number of inherent liabilities. First, they are not as productive as might be supposed. Tax codes generally stipulate that assessments be pegged at a proportion of market value, but they seldom keep pace with the prices determined by the calculus of supply and demand. Second, many state laws place a ceiling on total revenue that can be raised by the property tax. Moreover, certain classes of property, most notably that owned by educational institutions, churches, and other nonprofit organizations, are given exemptions by state law. Third, efforts to raise the tax *rate* on real property are politically vulnerable. When mayor and council start talking about the "regrettable necessity" of boosting tax rates, homeowners and landlords are likely to stimulate a defensive alliance with business proprietors. From the standpoint of equity, property taxes are regressive, imposing a greater burden on low or moderate income households than on those relatively well off. Since the latter have a larger share of income left over after their shelter costs are met, the property tax inevitably takes a larger slice from incomes of poorer households. The sales tax has the same regressive incidence, and for the same reason.[3]

In a local political economy, the relationship between the yield of real estate taxes and the cost of providing municipal services helps explain why affluent suburbs resort to land-use and zoning controls to repel low and moderate income households. Local governments have a clear fiscal interest in maintaining high residential property values because so much of their income derives from taxes levied on real estate. However, a rise in these taxes that is not offset by improved public services tends to reduce the market value of homes. The common presumption is that the taxable land value is a negative function of residential densities. At the same time, the costs of producing and distributing public services are positively related to residential densities, since unit costs tend to be more nearly proportional to the number of consumers.[4] Therefore, once population densities surpass a variable and ill-defined peril point, high-income households will pay out more in taxes than the value of the services they receive.

When this critical threshold is attained, suburban governments must either hike the tax rate or curtail services. Higher taxes unaccompanied by improved services will not be popular with high-income households because the market value of their homes will decline. As a consequence, both high-income households and suburban governments (insofar as they are separable) both strive to keep residential densities thin; the former to maintain the market value of an important capital asset, the latter to maintain a favorable ratio between income and outlay.

There are other considerations as well. It is thought that property values decline as low-income families stream into a suburb, a consideration that heightens incentives to preserve restrictive land-use controls. As a consequence, housing opportunities of low-income families dwindle, compelling them to settle for less attractive communities. This pattern of population distribution by social class further aggravates disparities among suburbs, increasing homogeneity within suburbs at the same time as it widens the differences among them. It also leads to severe imbalances in fiscal capacity. Wealthy suburbs have a tax base that is sound enough to generate high-quality public services; those settled by low-income households have to run hard just to stay even.

Taxes on industrial and commercial property provide other streams of income for suburban governments' services. Assessors in communities with a large industrial or commercial base find they have a particularly productive source of revenue.[5] These taxes are partial substitutes for levies imposed on residential properties, creating additional incentives to lure business to suburbs. Increasingly, business establishments once moored to the city fail to renew their leases and shift to suburban locations thought free of congestion and crime. Top executives and the technologically skilled welcome the move because it cuts commuting time.

Then, too, suburban residents have managed to overcome their earlier resistance to the growth of business. A gleaming new office building, its facade of tinted glass framed in sculpted steel, is rather attractive to the eye. In its architectural design, it is just as appealing as a new nonprofit hospital, which pays no taxes. Light industry creates little noise and less grime. Tucked away in a vacant corner of the suburb close to the interstate connection, it makes no unsightly break in a predominantly residential land-use pattern.

In addition, such establishments generate a subtle multiplier effect that benefits local business. Their employees are well paid, which produces sales opportunities for restaurants, cocktail lounges, foreign car lots, and novelty stores. Also, these newly arrived businesses create advantages for local typewriter and office machine salesmen, print shops, plumbing supply houses, and the like. As their business receipts increase in a local boom-town economy, so does the value of their property, an effect soon discovered by an alert assessor. Meanwhile, the political economy of the central city continues to suffer as it loses its office buildings and light industry. Its tax base shrinks, but its problems grow.

To be sure, business dispersion to suburbs does produce some dilemmas for local officials. Whenever there is talk of raising property taxes, the industries, sales offices, and insurance firms begin hinting a move to a more benign business climate. More often than not, they are joined by elderly local statesmen on the executive board of the local chamber of commerce. They fretfully point up the difficulty of luring new business to a jurisdiction where taxes are punitive; a Robin Hood taxation policy will never work. To meet the competition of other locales, the cost of doing business has to be pared to the bone.

There is good reason to suppose that the firms are bluffing, and that their local allies have been taken in. For one thing, it would take very low taxes to compensate firms for the expenses of business at an unfavorable location, and it is never easy to assemble a new skilled labor supply. In any case, there are likely to be nonrecoverable costs sunk in the present site. Once taxes are raised, the capitalized value of property diminishes, making it extraordinarily difficult to unload the building unless effective tax rates in all suitable locales are approximately equal.

The arrangement of market forces and incentives is markedly different in older industrial suburbs. No matter how great their fiscal productivity, steel mills and auto assembly plants are eyesores. They also consume a great deal of land, not only for the plant itself but also for parking lots for workers' cars. As a result, residential neighborhoods nearby are downgraded in the consumers' perspective; plant workers prefer to live in modest residential suburbs located within driving distance of the worksite. Thus, workers labor in one suburb but have to educate their children in another with a less lucrative tax base.[a]

---

[a]School districts covering adjacent communities may help in adjusting the imbalance between need and capacity. An industrial suburb with low net residential densities and relatively small numbers of school-age children can be compelled to transfer funds to nearby suburbs where its working-force resides.

The Case of Cleveland

The dynamic tension between revenues and expenditure patterns may be seen in metropolitan areas all over the country. In the following pages, we seek to illustrate these patterns with case studies of major cities.

In the half-century between Appomattox and World War I, Cleveland's population grew as a result of domestic and foreign immigration, natural population growth, and annexation of suburban hamlets just over the city line. Shortly before the war, population began to trickle out of the city to ten villages and nineteen townships outside Cleveland. As the exodus grew, suburbs applied for and received charters of incorporation; with each new incorporation, rural townships decreased in population, territory, and importance. In 1910, nine of every ten people living in the metropolitan region lived in Cleveland; by 1960 more than half lived in its suburbs.

As a result, the line between city and suburb became less distinct. Industry followed population out to suburbs, shifting to advantageous locations along transportation rights-of-way. Around them huddled the suburbs, some occupied by suburban industrial workers and others by white-collar commuters. The end result was a collection of suburbs clearly differentiated by economic base. Clinging closely to Cleveland's border, some suburbs struck a rough balance between industry and commerce. Dormitory suburbs, each more or less homogeneous in income level, were found throughout the metropolis, with the most prosperous in a broad band east of the central city.

Hellmuth and Sachs, in a careful multivariate analysis done during the fifties, demonstrated how closely total taxable wealth conformed to differences in demographic composition and economic base. The average assessed valuation per capita barely exceeded $3,000, but the spread on either side of the mean was enormous. Oakwood's came to $1,307 per person, just over forty percent of the regional average, but Cuyahoga Heights's was over $122,000 per person, or forty times the mean. Suburbs with high averages generally consisted of two sharply distinguishable types: the industrial enclave and the affluent commuter colonies housing the top white-collar echelons.[6]

The fiscal imbalance among communities was partially reflected in their levels of municipal service. Some expenditures were unavoidable; residents had to be provided with education, streets, and sanitation. Smaller and poorer suburbs could pay for fewer governmental functions than larger and wealthier communities, e.g., full-time fire protection or regular refuse collection and disposal. Like sought like; low-expenditure suburbs tended to bunch together geographically, as did more prosperous communities with appreciably higher levels of public services. Generally, larger populations enabled public authorities to attain economies of scale in these services; except for industrial enclaves, sheer population size best accounted for variations in expenditure levels.[7]

However, growth in population and taxable wealth do not automatically produce a rising balance between income and outlay. Expenditure decisions are conscious choices. After all, the city council might decide that consumer satisfactions are better maximized by letting households use their discretionary income to purchase goods and services in private rather than in collective markets. A firm tax base is at most a necessary condition for stepping up public expenditures; it is not a sufficient one.[8]

Happily for the social scientist, many expenditures in Cuyahoga County are enacted by public plebiscite, which tell us much about voter preferences for public services. Thus, Uyeki examined voting patterns in county-wide referenda from 1940 to 1960; including tax levies for welfare (N=12); such physical additions as roads, sewers and a zoo (N=22); and "good government" issues, such as creating a state board of education or using voting machines (N=17). Using the Shevky-Bell social rank index, Uyeki found that variations in the social rank of suburbs correlated positively with a tendency to approve increased public expenditures and endorse "good government" proposals. He concluded:

> ... what we have operating in the metropolitan area of greater Cleveland over the two-decade period is a dominant social consensus which is generated by residents of the higher socio-economic suburbs identifying with the larger good of the community and voting in large proportions for welfare levies, bonds to improve the physical plant of the community, and even extending to support measures for metropolitan government which might entail giving up some of their sovereignty. This ... occurs regardless of differences in family status or ethnic composition.[9]

Much the same profile is found when we correlate social rank with expenditure patterns of *individual* suburban municipalities. Suburbs ranking high on total operating expenditures also ranked high on socioeconomic status (r=.64). The same relationship held when outlays for specific functions were considered: expenditures for fire protection (.70), refuse and sewage disposal (.63), police (.62), general government (.58), and street and highways (.52). Total operating expenditure is of course a composite of all these separate outlays, but the small range of the coefficients for the separate functions suggests that prosperous suburbs insisted on uniformly high expenditure levels.

The issue of metropolitan government has probably had a longer and more turbulent career in Cleveland than in any other metropolitan area in the nation. From 1933 to 1959, some ten referenda were conducted on this issue. In seven of these, the suburbs supported metropolitan reform more enthusiastically than Cleveland residents. A finer analysis of voting patterns demonstrates considerable variation among suburban communities, as well as among different neighborhoods in Cleveland. By and large, as Norton has shown, affluent suburbs were ranged more strongly in support of reform than their less prosperous neighbors. Suburbs reacting most favorably to metropolitan reform contained the best educated and most affluent populations of all. In the city, the relationship was reversed for a time; the largest margins in favor of reform proposals were cast in black wards of Cleveland, here as elsewhere, low both in income and education. Norton concluded:

Indeed, if one were matching municipalities in wards of the central city with suburbs in the metropolitan area by their voting behavior on referenda issues, he would bring together the greatest social divergencies in wealth and education; and we would also match the wards which are most heavily Negro with [suburban] municipalities which have never welcomed the Negro.[10]

But each succeeding referendum encountered increased opposition from black precincts. As their numbers increased and as white families forsook the central city for suburban communities, the percentage of black voters in Cleveland's electorate swelled dramatically. Concentrated in the core city, blacks increasingly recognized that they would be swamped by white suburban votes in a merged government. They also feared that metropolitan decision makers would be insensitive to black demands for better housing and the alleviation of poverty and civil rights, preferring instead to promote policy goals more finely attuned to preferences of affluent white citizens.[11]

The Philadelphia Story

Philadelphia lies at the core of the oldest metropolitan land masses in the United States. With their origins deep in colonial history, Philadelphia's suburbs now sprawl across three states. An analysis of its four Pennsylvania suburban counties (Bucks, Chester, Delaware, and Montgomery) revealed that few suburbs were exactly alike.[12] The older suburbs lining the shores of the Delaware River were manufacturing centers, legacies of an older era when bulky goods had to travel over water. Their populations in 1960 were overwhelmingly lower status. Upland, strung along Philadelphia's Main Line, was a tier of mellow residential suburbs. Apart from high residential densities, in only one other respect did they resemble manufacturing centers along the river shores; their people were decidedly elderly, with relatively few young adults in their childbearing years. Socioeconomically, their population was markedly upper status compared with the poorer blue collars in the suburban bottomlands. Spread out in an irregular band somewhat further away from downtown Philadelphia were newer municipalities which had experienced a spurt of population growth during the fifties. Even so, they had not filled up to the congested densities characteristic of older Main Line suburbs and packed industrial towns. A large number of families here were headed by prosperous, well-educated young adults on their way up in the world.

Hence all the variables one might use to differentiate suburbs crosshatched in a bewildering variety of combinations:

The pattern of variation is one of extreme complexity. Few of the variables that contribute to the pattern of differentiation vary from community to community in a consistent fashion. Community characteristics appear to be independent of one another. Although social rank, wealth and some of the property characteristics are correlated, the intermunicipal variation among them is far from congruent.[13]

Much variation in volume and type of expenditure could be expressed in terms of complex interactions among three key variables: economic base, density, and social rank. Despite the generally low status of their inhabitants, industrial municipalities burdened themselves with consistently high expenditures for public housekeeping services, an anomaly explained by lucrative assessments levied against industrial real estate and by high costs involved in servicing aging physical facilities. Older and more thickly populated residential suburbs made uniformly lower per capita outlays for all governmental functions except libraries and refuse removal. Among high density suburbs, the more prosperous along the Main Line generally spent more on services than those housing factory workers. Compared with lower density residential suburbs at the fringe of the region, more thickly populated suburbs had larger per capita outlays for all functions, except for streets and planning.

More densely populated suburbs also shied away from planning because there was so little left to plan. Newer suburbs hugging outer limits of the urban fringe still had vast undeveloped land within their borders. Unwilling to let land-use patterns be regulated by the marketplace and at the same time recognizing the benefits of new industrial and commercial development, they hired planners to help shield them against adverse consequences of strictly laissez-faire policies.[14]

For most public expenditures, the fiscal capacity of the autonomous suburb formed the dominant constraint of the local political economy. The burden of financing a new public library, playground or more frequent garbage pickup fell squarely on the resources of the individual town. Unless improvements could be financed from natural growth in the revenue base, the suburb had to decide whether the stream of satisfactions produced by the public good was worth the higher taxes it entailed.

Public education constituted a significant (and intended) exception. Because of state subsidies allocated to each school district, financial support of public education in Philadelphia's suburbs was less tightly circumscribed by their fiscal ability. The state formula allocated funds in direct proportion to the number of students enrolled in the district, and in inverse proportion to the calculated market value of its real property. Apart from encouraging formation of consolidated school districts, state policy weakened the tendency of the local resource base to be the prime determinant of the total money spent on educating children in public schools. More impecunious districts with relatively large numbers of enrolled children received larger subsidies for each child than did more affluent jurisdictions with fewer children.

With differences in resource levels more or less evened out by the state's equalization formula, evaluations as to the intrinsic worth of schooling emerged as the most significant factor in accounting for variations in educational expenditures. Analysis demonstrated clearly that higher social rank communities spent more on educating each child than those further down the scale, indirect evidence of the importance white collars assign to schooling their children. Low-status suburbs invariably spent more on the provision of other municipal services than education, a pattern reversed in places of high social rank. Even when education was made less expensive by a policy that explicitly transferred wealth from rich to poor jurisdictions, low status suburbs still preferred to invest more heavily in municipal housekeeping services than in education.[15]

It is important to stress that both revenue and expenditure decisions do not mechanically respond to differences in density, assets and economic base; they flow from conscious political judgments. At any point in time, citizens and their officials have to decide whether to spend a little bit more or less, provide more for sewers and less for schools, exclude industry or entice it, or reject a proposed bond issue rather than plunge further into debt. Public budgeting cannot escape the political process of translating resources, opportunities, preferences, and impulses into goals and programs.

How well did the budgetary judgments of elected officials in Philadelphia's suburbs reflect their constituents' values? A comparison showed that the distribution of preferences *among* communities coincided with their social rank and that elected officials mirrored preferences of their constituents with great accuracy. Although there were exceptions at every status level, upper status suburbanites and their councilmen thought their governments should fund a wide range of amenities, even if they could be financed only by higher taxes. People in less well-to-do suburbs were more concerned with holding the line on further taxation, even at the sacrifice of improved public services and other amenities. Recognizing that taxes on commercial and industrial property were partial substitutes for levies on residential real estate, they were also more receptive than suburbanites in upper-status communities to the idea of importing industry. Citizens and officials in high-ranking communities expected the government to protect property values and maintain the "quality" of its residents. Lower-status suburban residents were less concerned with property values than in using the coercive powers of government to exclude "undesirables."

When the strands are drawn together, two separate conceptions of the public interest emerge. Whatever upper-status suburbanites may have thought of "socialism" in the abstract, they saw their local government as a collective instrument for providing a reliable flow of quality services to help make life comfortable and pleasant and to conserve values that made their suburban haven a nice living place. Lower-class suburbanites were more ready to tolerate, or even to prefer, a frugal government, one that would hold taxes down even at the cost of depleted public services.[16]

The Limitations of Budgetary Analysis

Analysis of revenue and expenditure patterns enables us to see how readily measurable community characteristics—status, density, the prevailing mix in land-use patterns—help mediate the process of transforming limited resources into policy outcomes.[17] Budgets are informative in telling us something about goals a suburb chooses to pursue and the way it distributes the burden among those who pay its bills. Nonetheless, they possess severe limitations as a basic data source, some technical and some theoretical.

First, budgetary categories are not readily comparable. One jurisdiction may file its expenses for snow removal under "maintenance of roads and streets," another may log the same expenses elsewhere; and if it is located in an especially benign climate like Southern California's it may have no expenses whatever for snow removal. Schools furnish another example. A jurisdiction unable or unwilling to achieve economies of scale through consolidation has to reflect all costs of educating its children as a charge against its own budget. In another, many of these same expenditures will appear on the books of a school district with independent taxing authority. Then, too, not all children are educated in public schools. Where a significantly large minority of parents can afford private schooling, a substantial fraction of actual educational expenditures will appear only on ledgers of private households.

Great within a state, problems of comparability magnify as one crosses state lines. Charters and statutes afford municipalities in some states greater latitude in exploiting revenue sources than they do in others. Because of differences in formulas which states use to apportion grants-in-aid to their local communities, the impact of state subsidies vary sharply.[18] The uneven effect of different state norms and practices holds true on the expenditure side as well. Although municipalities in all states are required by law to support at least some programs, performance standards and hence aggregate expenditures change from one to another.[19]

Adding further to incomparability is the fact that no two suburbs face exactly the same price schedules for capital and labor. Depending upon prevailing wage rates in the local construction industry, costs of land and materials, and the interest a suburb pays on its bonds, the same school building or fire station can cost one suburb much more to build than another. Where alternative opportunities are thin, suburban planners, teachers, and policemen may be compelled to work for a pittance. In other locations, the comparative advantage shifts from buyer to seller. If other governments and private firms bid against one another for their services, these employees are likely to find the strenuous competition reflected in a more generous salary schedule. For these reasons, it cannot be lightly assumed that the same dollar spent in different suburban jurisdictions will buy equivalent units of service.

Nor do the limitations stop there. Some significant variations in policy goals may not be reflected at all in budgetary statements. Large outlays for public housing are equivocal. They signify only that a community has decided to side-step private market constraints in assembling housing stock for its poorer citizens. Without further examination it is impossible to decide whether the subsidized housing is integrated or segregated, or whether it is sprinkled throughout middle-class neighborhoods rather than being concentrated in poorer wards of the city. And, as is well known, budget makers have very little freedom in "allocating" resources. Most commitments are inherited from previous administrations; they are literally "uncontrollable" because frozen into routines. These are all severe impediments in using taxes and expenditures as a proxy measures of decisional outcomes.[20]

It is equally difficult to obtain standardized measures of independent variables one might use in explaining variations in these outcomes. Governmental forms and electoral rules furnish two telling examples. Even assuming that one was able to "measure" outputs and thus pinpoint variations in policy outcomes, it is problematical whether they could explain very much variation in suburbs. First, nonpartisan elections are the rule in an overwhelming proportion of city manager suburbs, making it difficult to disentangle the consequences of electoral rules from structural forms.[21] More important is the fact that both labels pulverize significant variations in the operating political structure of the communities that have them. Some energetic city managers tour the civic associations drumming up support for proposals and options they intend to lay before the city council. "God bless all civic associations," Wood quotes one astute manager, "they are the city manager's ward machines."[22] Other managers feel more comfortable in city hall where they can monitor and guide the municipal bureaucracy. Even so, they do not stay completely aloof from politics. The most abstemious city managers find that they must prepare the agenda for the city council on a wide variety of issues and supply it with pertinent information.

In similar fashion, we will show in the next chapter how the "nonpartisan" tag homogenizes much variation in the actual conduct of nominations and elections; it is naive to accept the label at face value. As one observer put it, "The Chicago Council consists of forty-seven nonpartisan Democrats and three nonpartisan Republicans." Wilson stresses the point we are making:

... the study of a single institution or organization almost invariably leads the research deeper and deeper into the organization and farther and farther away from those *gross* characteristics of the organization that distinguish it from others in the same community or *indicate its similarity to comparable organizations in other communities.*[23]

As Wilson suggests, the alternative is to forget all the sermons extolling the virtues of statistical analysis of a large number of observations and instead study a small number of communities intensively. In his view, variables that can be

routinely extracted from standard data collections are too ambiguous to generate unequivocal conclusions, no matter how great the level of statistical refine-
ment. Trading the mechanical correlation of uninformative variables for in-depth
studies rich in local anthropological detail, Wilson recommends, is a way to
"learn what the 'outcomes' are, how they may be measured (if at all), and what
factors seem to be causally related to them."[24]

There are problems connected with this strategy, too. For one thing, it is very
expensive. Getting data on the socioeconomic composition of municipalities or
their constitutionally prescribed governing structures is not cheap either, but
most of the costs are borne by taxpayers and foundations. Then, too, unless one
is lucky enough to have a properly constructed sample of all American suburbs,
he has no hope of estimating the relevant parameters for the entire universe. All
one can legitimately do is describe relationships within a single suburb or a small
collection.

There are some clear advantages, too. Routine multiple correlation analysis
often fails to take account of possible interactions among socioeconomic and
structural measures that constitute their sample of independent variables, leaving
open the possibility that additivity does not hold. In accounting for variance, it
may be entirely possible that joint effects of any pair of independent variables
may be considerably greater than their simple arithmetic sum.[b] Whenever they
are found, interaction effects cause chagrin and consternation because they mini-
mize the prospects for broad generalizations. A comment by Peterson explains
why:

His findings are most perplexing: each time he introduces another explanatory
variable he finds variance explained by the interaction term. Thus, with each
level of sophistication in the explanatory variables, he is pushed away from
global explanations toward unique descriptions. For an example, a given variable
might contribute to civic pluralism only in a special class of cities such as New
England towns, founded on textile production between 1830 and 1945 and using English-speaking immigrant labor.[25]

Interaction effects therefore confront social scientists with an uncomfortable
dilemma. Ignoring them produces pseudogeneralizations; however, the greater
the proportion of variation they explain, the greater the probability of concluding that suburbs are more unique than they are alike. Between these traps of the
spurious and the special the next chapters seek to illuminate the commonalities
and varieties of suburban politics and policy.

---

[b]For example, suppose that a correlation analysis shows that residential suburbs make smaller per capita outlays for public housing than do industrial suburbs, and that suburbs with
tiny percentages of blacks also make smaller outlays for public housing than those with
more blacks. Closer analysis shows, however, that nearly all the residential suburbs with a
small percentage of black households make comparatively large outlays for public housing,
perhaps to keep them concentrated in an inconspicuous corner of the community. That is a
specimen of an interaction effect.

To Insure Domestic Tranquility

If suburban studies have suffered from hasty generalization, the fault lies partly in the questionable sampling and uninformative measures once used and in a failure to exploit survey and aggregate data. In this volume, we have sought to develop larger and more adequate samples of suburbs and suburbanites as a basis for our conclusions. Yet macroanalysis alone has its limitations, also, for it obscures the nuances of suburban political processes. In the following chapters we turn to a set of case studies to help illuminate suburban variety. This chapter pulls together material on electoral politics in a small number of American suburbs. The next deals with disputes over public education and land-use controls, two areas of decision making that stimulate considerable suburban political conflict.

These materials include a variety of case studies, both published and unpublished. Fortunately, some of the published analyses are comparative in focus, giving us opportunities to explain variations among at least some suburbs. The unpublished sources consist primarily of student reports on various aspects of political life in a number of suburbs. The "sample" of suburbs is obviously adventitious and opportunistic. It adheres to none of the statistical recipes for choosing units from a population whose significant parameters are known.[a] Therefore, except where the factual base is especially rich and firm, we shall be cautious in coaxing conclusions from limited data.

Representation

It is not surprising that suburban councilmen reflect the socioeconomic composition of their communities. In a study of 37 suburbs within St. Louis County, Downes discovered that the immediate social context helped set the status level of elected representatives. Using a special index of social rank, he found that increases in municipal social rank were regularly associated with increases in the average status of councilmen. High-status municipalities recruited councilmen with at least a bachelor's degree who were employed in the upper white-collar echelons. Suburbs further down the status hierarchy by and large chose council-

---

[a]Our procedure is not wildly heterodox. Our sampling strategy is no more adventitious than Dahl's choice of New Haven, Kaplan's of Newark, or, for that matter, Hunter's selection of Atlanta (Regional City). They were in each case chosen because the scholars happened to be on the scene. This is also true of the case studies which follow.

men of working-class occupations and fewer years of formal education. In the lowest category of all, well over half the councilmen had not completed high school, and an additional 16 percent possessed no more than a high school diploma.[1]

Williams and his colleagues found much the same in Philadelphia suburbs. Among councilmen in high-status suburbs, almost 80 percent had at least entered college. By contrast, not a single councilman in a low-status suburb had any college education at all. Educational levels were regularly associated with occupational attainment, so much so that one was a good surrogate for the other. Somewhat less than 10 percent of the councilmen in the low-status suburbs worked at white-collar occupations; in the most prestigious suburbs, more than nine in every ten councilmen were white collars. Moreover, the gross differences between the two types of suburbs were even more pronounced in the biographies of their elected representatives. The elected officials in the high-status suburbs had even higher social ranks than their constituents. In the low-status suburbs, the councilmen had even fewer years of schooling and a higher proportion of workers employed in the less prestigious occupations.[2]

Yet such homogeneity in social background does not always produce similar preferences. Downes found that more than 40 percent of the councilmen reported factional splits on the council, with the percentages even higher in the communities experiencing rapid growth.[3] Parallel findings emerge from another comparative analysis of bloc formation in nonpartisan city councils. Of 82 suburban councils in the suburbs ringing San Francisco Bay, Eulau discovered that almost a quarter exhibited relatively durable divisions between two readily identifiable council factions. Another third split into momentary coalitions which tended to dissolve once the vote was taken. Small cliques of councilmen voted with one another in irregular patterns displaying little stability from one issue to the next. Only the remainder exhibited the strain towards unanimity purportedly typical of suburban legislative bodies. As might be expected, there was an association between the ferocity of debate and backstairs politicking on the one hand, and the propensity of the councils to split into factions on the other; the greater the level of oppositional activity, the greater the probability of permanent council factions.[4]

Most studies of representation deal with patterns of recruitment or with behavior of representatives once elected; comparatively few concentrate on why legislators at any level of government decline to seek reelection. In their analysis of suburban San Francisco city councils, Prewitt and Eulau demonstrated that over half of all councilmen left office voluntarily. Moreover, statistical analysis could not isolate any demographic factors which would help explain the incidence of voluntary retirement; so even were the rates from one community to another that they conclude, "It is a very permanent, even institutionalized, feature of nonpartisan politics in the Bay Area."[5]

Turning to the effects of competitive elections on turnover in office, these authors discovered that most of the seats were as safe as they are in the one-party baronies of the rural South. Overall, only 20 percent of the incumbents failed in their bids to seek reelection. In fully a quarter of the suburbs, no incumbent office-holder was ever defeated at the polls. Electoral competition was fierce in only a handful of jurisdictions; in only four of 82 suburbs were as many as half the contestants seeking reelection ousted from office.[6]

Kirlin has conducted a parallel analysis in 66 Los Angeles suburbs.[7] He also found that councilmen were able to hold their seats in successive elections. Between 1960 and 1970, incumbents were reelected in 72 percent of the races, a rate only marginally smaller than the 80 percent Prewitt and Eulau recorded. However, Kirlin looked at races where two or three incumbents ran for office simultaneously, offering the electorate the opportunity of endorsing or rejecting either a sizable minority or an absolute majority of the council. Half the cities experienced at least one election in which two or three incumbents were simultaneously turned out of office. In half of these (one-sixth of the total), incumbents were turned out of office twice in the decade. A stepwise regression analysis showed significant differences between safe suburbs and those with high turnover rates. More than half (53 percent) of the variance between low and high electoral conflict cities could be explained by demographic variables.

Kirlin's findings cast doubt on the traditional hypothesis that smaller political jurisdictions dampen political conflict. The sheer size of the suburban population growth was *negatively* related to the simultaneous ousting of two or three of the incumbents seeking reelection. In addition, it has been argued that demographic heterogeneity operates to increase political conflict by splitting the electorate along the lines of race, class or nativity. Kirlin's analysis shows that three of the four census measures routinely used as surrogates for social heterogeneity (foreign and mixed parentage, households earning less than $3,000 per year, and non-white) were *inversely* associated with failures of incumbent councilmen to renew their hold on office.[8] Only the share of resident population actually born abroad makes a positive contribution. Variables most frequently thought to account for divisive political conflict failed to register. Instead of diverse and rapidly growing cities experiencing convulsive turnover, the phenomenon occurred in the more socially homogeneous and relatively stable communities.

The ethos of nonpartisan government holds that every contestant is to run on his own, in a sort of free-for-all. In this context of invisible parties, the election process is much like the start of those long-distance races; everybody is on his own, eyes straight ahead, with considerable jostling in the pack. Without the integrative functions of the party, candidates must raise their own funds, rarely coalesce with other candidates on a slate, but strive earnestly to reach across party and status lines in a scramble for votes. Under these conditions, the impression provided the voter is best characterized by the local practice of slapping one's posters on buildings, fences and poles—or at anything that does not slap back. On election day, the city walls provide a kaleidoscope of jarring and confusing posters. So, too, may be the results of the election for the voter.

But, even in the most simon-pure city, running for office requires scarce resources. Flybills have to be printed and left on doorsteps or handed to commuters as they disembark from the 5:19. One must confer with civic associations and see that publicity releases get to local editorial offices on time. Then, too, councilmanic candidates welcome journalistic endorsement and expressed approval of the blue-ribbon civic associations untainted by any intimations of partisanship. All these activities demand money and labor. Even though unknowns sometimes surprise by winning an election, on the whole candidates are better off having some dependable help in boosting their efforts.

Adrian has sketched some of the major dimensions delineating how such elections are actually conducted. In some cities, Chicago for example, nonpartisanship is transparent hypocrisy. Candidates run with acknowledged support of regular party politicians and encounter no significant opposition from other social organizations. In others, the party forms more or less covert alliances with other groups, under such names as "Good Government League" or "Committee of Concerned Citizens," designed to conceal the actual makeup of the coalition. In a third group, other social organizations play a dominant role, and party personnel never appear at all. These organizations may persist from one election to another, or they may dissolve the morning after the ballots are counted. Some are headed by local business firms, often with the assistance of the local newspaper editor. In the fourth type, prevalent in smaller cities, candidates form a personal organization composed of friends and neighbors.[9]

Given this variety, it would be a mistake to assume that all "nonpartisan" elections are alike. Rather, it is with such a gross category in hand that one can usefully turn to the case study to illuminate the dynamics of suburban politics. Little has been published so far about the way avowedly nonpartisan organizations respond to social change, which always tests the ability of homegrown structures to muffle, roll with, or crack under shock. The remainder of this chapter offers such case studies as illumination of the proposition that "nonpartisanship" does not sufficiently describe suburban local politics.

Case Studies in Suburban Nonpartisanship

Nonpartisanship in Gray View

Gray View is a suburb nestled against the eastern borders of a large midwestern city.[10] Physically, it is not impressive with its tract subdivisions interleaved among the older neighborhoods. The dominant architectural style is a story-and-a-half shingle perched on a square lot, and most of the trees have disappeared under the bulldozer blade or are withering from Dutch Elm disease. In the shopping center, younger customers inquire about price and quality in English; older ones talk to clerks in a motley of Slavic dialects. The Adamskis, Zdanowiczes and Chognackes appearing on the high school graduation program provide further indication that over a third of the population is of foreign or mixed parentage. Gray View is a resolutely Democratic suburb. Only twice since 1932 has it voted for Republicans, a gubernatorial candidate in 1940, and a congressman six years later.

Until 1956, the regular party organizations sponsored candidates for local offices. In a special election that year, its citizens adopted a municipal charter that abolished party designations on local election ballots. Though the charter stripped party names from the ballots, Gray View's parties did not shrivel up; they simply went underground. Candidates for office still came from party ranks; they still enlisted party workers to canvass neighborhoods and speak to organizations in a search for votes; and they still raided party treasuries to pay for advertisements in *The Gray View Outlook*.

A perennial underdog in all local elections, the Republicans discovered new allies among migrants streaming into Gray View. Many younger families who moved out to Gray View were regular Democrats in state and national elections. But those who sought to participate in the local Democratic party were outraged by the alleged "corrupt" and "dictatorial" tactics of Judge Stan Stefanski, its leader for over two decades. So, younger Democrats formed an Independent Democratic party, which they described as a group of "good men interested in good, honest government."

Stefanski's power lay in the older residents of Gray View, the "Bohemians," as newer Democrats called the old-timers, who voted for all Democratic nominees—and the judge chose the nominees. Stefanski spoke the old-timers' language, worshipped where they worshipped, and ate the foreign dishes they relished. Before the passage of the charter, Stefanski was able to dictate nominations on the strength of these tribal loyalties. If he had to, he could divert the flow of municipal jobs and services to benefit his grateful kinsmen.

Incensed, newer migrants coalesced with the beleaguered Republicans to pass the new charter in 1956. It did not rid Gray View of the evil effects of partisan loyalties, nor did it demolish Stefanski's machine. What it did accomplish was to deprive a chieftain of his patent to a scarce and valued political resource—a familiar brand-name and the loyalties attached to it. With party designations sheared off the ballot, the judge could no longer be sure that the old-timers would vote for the candidates he handpicked, as it was hard to tell who they were. He had now to expend his resources in telling the voters who bore his endorsement.

He was not conspicuously successful. In the 1957 primary elections for mayor, the two top vote-getters were Stefanski and George Fowler, a real estate operator and local Republican leader. John Frierson, favored by the Independent Democratic faction, finished a distant third. The Independent Democrats thereafter endorsed Fowler, who won the general election by a slender mar-

gin. Any voter reading *The Gray View Outlook* knew about the coalition, because Independent Democrats, along with the Chamber of Commerce, took out
advertisements supporting Fowler. Two years later, the same pattern emerged.
After Frierson came in third in the primaries, Independent Democrats once more
endorsed Fowler who won the general elections with 50.1 percent of the vote.
The sequence was somewhat different in 1961. Fowler lost the primary amidst
accusations he was tampering with the zoning code in an effort to lure industry
to Gray View, a charge made more plausible by Fowler's occupation. Upon his
defeat, Fowler urged his Republican supporters to vote for Frierson in the general election, and he rode into office with that support.

The sequence of events suggests that alignments established during the charter
struggle have persisted long afterwards. The overriding impulse to weaken the
Stefanski organization drove dissident Democrats and regular Republicans into a
precarious alliance. The rules of the road decreed that both organizations should
band together behind the candidate running second in the primary. As older residents die off or grow weary, the common adversary will probably begin to disappear. In a broader sense, the events illustrate the cleavage between newcomers
and old settlers with opposed conceptions of what the public interest demands.
It also suggests how the ethos of nonpartisan elections can be destroyed even
though the forms remain intact.

Nonpartisanship in River View

River View and Gray View have the same last name; both are suburbs of the
same core city, and both have been inundated by massive immigration.[11] The
resemblance ends there. No proletarian village, River View is a suburb of well-
kept homes, and its nearly 17,000 residents aim to keep it that way. Census
statistics only confirm what the eye can easily see—River View is a prosperous
suburb. In 1960, the median family income topped $11,000, and almost 85 per-
cent of all the housing was in single-family dwellings. Wealthy as it is, River View
is nonetheless crowded. Houses are set upon small plots of land, liberating residents from the seasonal drudgeries of mowing lawns and raking leaves. Population density is high, about 8,500 per square mile, nearly double that of Gray
View. To make the land go further, a number of apartment buildings have been
built as buffers between other residential areas and four large shopping centers
whose shops offer customers everything from jewelled trinkets all the way up to
$250 couturier suits from the most fashionable houses in the world.

At one time, River View was a cozy suburb for 2,200 Protestants, but no
longer. When Newman University decided to flee downtown for a suburban location, it cashed in an option it held to buy land in River View. The Catholics who
subsequently followed the college out to the suburb put up a church, a parochial
school, and a nunnery. But numerically and politically the most important sub-

urban immigrants have been Jewish. After World War II, many Jews deserted the core city for its affluent suburbs, including River View. Now it is a transformed village, shaped by currents of an urban affluence that kept first-generation Americans in the city while their offspring rushed to the suburbs.

The sheer numerical preponderance of the Jewish population has flavored politics in River View. The newcomers to Gray View had to instigate alliances with established centers of power in order to wear down an entrenched local oligarchy. Not so in River View, where the suburban movement was far too vigorous to depend on the treacherous vagaries of political coalitions. The changes were all fashioned within the framework of an existing charter passed in 1941 before immigration accelerated population growth. This new constitution banned primary elections entirely and required candidates to run without partisan identification. It required that elections for the seven-man council and mayor be held in odd-numbered years, so as to dampen the presumed coattail effect of state and national elections. To shield the council against transient impulsive majorities, only half the offices are contested in any single election.

Jeffrey Crews, one of the founders of the village, sat in the mayor's chair from the incorporation of the suburb until 1939. To symbolize the seclusion of local affairs from divisive currents of partisan passion, Crews ran for mayor as an Independent, generally without opposition. In 1939, he relinquished his office to James Franklin, who held office until his retirement in 1965. Franklin had become what might well be the case elsewhere, an old settler who fell casualty to the social change he witnessed but could not control.

In many ways, Franklin's biography encapsulates the history of River View. Many of the councilmen were his personal friends, and some were his neighbors. The office—or at least his civic colleagues—sought out the man, conscripting his energy and talents for one more worthwhile civic concern. Some men were asked to run by Franklin himself; others were coaxed to run by officers of various civic associations after the mayor dropped word that the prospective candidate had demonstrated his mettle by heading up a charity drive. Nomination for council office was surplus income earned from gathering recognition elsewhere; men accepted it as a civic duty. Franklin presided over an informal Good Government caucus of luminaries in business and civic organizations. Once proposed for office, the candidate was almost sure to be elected.

The various groups knitted into this governing clique acted as Franklin's mobilizing agents; few strong mayors in machine-run cities have ever secured such an overwhelming centralization of actual political control. The few insurgent candidates who ran in every election were largely invisible, for they had not served out their civic apprenticeship. Unlike their counterparts in Gray View, they could not hitch their aspirations to a political party hungry for power. They picked up only the votes of friends, neighbors, and a few disgruntled voters.

Glimmers of ethnic politics soon began to poke through the placid surface of municipal politics. In 1943, in the first election after charter passage, Samuel Gordon won a seat on the city council, receiving an especially heavy vote in precincts newly settled by Jews. He replaced a Protestant incumbent whose votes were thinly spread across the entire community. Jewish representation on the council thereafter kept pace with the population pouring into River View from the core city's wards. Eight years later, only two gentile councilmen remained. Two years after that, the old settler minority dwindled to one.

In that election, four incumbents, two of them Jews, ran as a slate. The pair of gentile incumbents recognized that electoral success depended upon winning Jewish votes, not upon gaining the endorsement of local businessmen. So they cut themselves loose from their old moorings and joined the Jewish candidates. The Jews were elected; the gentiles were not. When interviewed, both gentiles felt that their Jewish allies on the slate had tried to live up to the terms of the contract, but there were simply more Jews than Catholics, and more Catholics than Protestants.

The winning Jewish candidates were especially embarrassed by the outcome. As one put it, he was sorry he had been "associated with any kind of a ghetto system," where every man "puts an 'X' by the name of one of his own." So heady and irresistible was the spirit of political ecumenism that two of the Jewish councilmen approached the Catholic lawyer one had beaten to "express their shame" and offer him their support in the 1961 elections. He again failed, but his perseverance prevailed four years and two elections later, making him the council's sole gentile.

Franklin found the Jewish councilmen hard to deal with. Power was not his by default, as it had been with the earlier councils composed of friends and neighbors. His judgment was challenged as it had never been before on minor administrative details, more significant as tests of strength than for their intrinsic content. Piece by piece, the vigilant council withdrew the autonomy ceded Franklin by its predecessors. When he sought to act without getting council approval beforehand, the council trimmed his salary.

In 1965, Franklin called it quits. He had won the previous election only because opposition votes were divided among four other candidates. A Jewish realtor running for council had actually outpolled him by 1,200 votes. Irritated by the friction between mayor and council, councilmen warned him they would unite behind a single candidate if Franklin had the temerity to place his name on the ballot. He chose not to run. The roster of the Republican party in River View presently lists Harvey Franklin as ward leader. Harvey is James' son. Already shut out of local politics, he presides over an organization in a suburb which state party leaders have written off.[b]

---

[b]With good reason. In 1952, Eisenhower led Stevenson by 18 percent; four years later, Stevenson got 56.5 percent of the vote; Kennedy picked up another 10 percent in 1960; and Goldwater was massacred by a margin of four to one. Even in 1968, Humphrey drew almost 71 percent. Since the vast bulk of the suburban immigration was Jewish, it is difficult to

Both Gray View and River View operated under charters that prohibited partisan elections. If we mistake the symbol for the reality, we have already said everything about public elections that deserves mention. But different political forms can develop under the same constitutional cloak. Newcomers to Gray View were as Democratic in state and national elections as old-timers. But the similarity in their partisan identifications did not win them equal status as partners in local politics. So long as they chose to infiltrate the regular Democratic party, differences in ethnicity and political ethics both conspired against the newcomers. When they chose instead to grind away at the machine by combining with Republicans, they began to win. The insurgents first changed the charter to trammel their opposition. Then they reaped electoral benefits by violating the spirit if not the letter of the charter they had helped pass. In Gray View, the one-party machine was transformed into a factional system, with a style of competition that transcended party lines without abolishing them. The transfer of power in River View was more orderly. The Good Government caucus of local businessmen was not decimated by infiltration or outflanked by a coalition. Knowing that their numbers would eventually prevail, the newcomers simply bypassed it in their quest for office and power.

Nonpartisanship in Oaklawn

A somewhat different pattern is displayed in Oaklawn.[12] One of the most prosperous suburbs of New York City, it is a village of detached one-family houses standing on wide lots. No manufacturing is permitted in Oaklawn, and only one public restaurant is licensed to serve liquor. The 1960 census showed that 90 percent of the adults had at least a bachelor's degree, and 95 percent of the youngsters did not stop with a high school diploma. Many of the residents are top executives in New York City; others are prominent professionals—lawyers, doctors, accountants, and engineers. Both men and women assume much civic responsibility in cultural, philanthropic, and educational organizations, leading many of its citizens to complain that the town is "somewhat over-organized."

The most prestigious and inclusive organization is the Civic Club. Founded in 1904, it is an organization of about 1,200 men, whose purpose is "to promote concerted and intelligent action on all matters affecting the welfare of Oaklawn [and] to procure accurate information thereon for discussion and dissemination in order to assist in the formation of public judgment." To become a member, one needs to show an interest in civic affairs. Upon written certification of

---

avoid the conclusion that they carried their political convictions with them to River View. For further evidence of the effects of religious affiliation in attenuating the normally high correlation between socioeconomic status and Republican votes, see Benjamin Walter and Frederick M. Wirt, "Social and Political Dimensions of American Suburbs," in Brian Berry (ed.), *Classification of Cities: New Methods and Alternate Uses* (New York: John Wiley, 1972).

"good character and interest," admission is automatic. The club has fifteen committees to study and report on local affairs. The president of the club automatically serves as chairman of the Voters' League, whose job is to select the slate of nominees for mayor, village trustees, and Board of Education. The slate appears on three ballots (Republican, Democratic, and Independent Citizens) in an uncontested election. Because election results are a foregone conclusion, voting turnout is small, seldom as much as 10 percent of the electorate.[13]

The Voters' League generally selects a ticket of seven which consists of:

1. Six men and one woman.
2. Six gentiles and one Jew.
3. One CPA or financial expert to assist the village treasurer.
4. One engineer to help the hired city manager, and
5. Five Republicans and two Democrats.

An unwritten requirement is that all officials belong to the Civic Club; it has never been broken. It is also considered desirable to spread representation among Oaklawn's eleven districts. Sometimes it has proved impossible for the Voters' League to fill all these requirements simultaneously. On some occasions, there have been no women on the council; on others, no Jews. Occasionally, some election districts have had no representatives on the Council for as many as three consecutive elections.

The Voters' League leadership consists of the president of the Civic Club; the chairlady of the local Woman's Club; a representative chosen by neighborhood associations throughout the city; and two invited members, one man and one woman. The other 44 members of the League are selected by these five from the candidates chosen by each election district. Chairman of the Republican and Democratic Town Committees also sit on the League as nonvoting members.

Since an increasing number of Democrats have begun to settle in Oaklawn, that party's chairman no longer feels that traditional arrangements for sharing elective office are entirely satisfactory. To an interviewer, he confided, ". . . the slate method of nomination is undemocratic. The Civic Club bosses and runs Oaklawn. It is a self-chosen and self-perpetuating nucleus that leads the town." The running of the town, he complained, is based too much on personality and the need to impress village elders. As he phrased it,

. . . nonpartisan government has gone far enough. Men running for public office should present their views to the public and have the issues decided on their merits. Politicians are as good as nonpartisan leaders. The Council is not responsive to the wishes of the residents. It is inactive and doesn't know what is going on because the Manager runs the administrative area.

For his part, the Republican leader felt that partisan elections might "enliven things," but that the Democrats would wind up "with less representation than their present 5-2 ratio; they might be blanked out completely."[14]

Nonpartisanship in Emerson Hills

The events in Oaklawn duplicate patterns already observed in River View. Before the influx of migrants with different party identifications and ethnicity, a Good Government caucus dominated public office. As many scholars remarked before, immigration generates conflicting planes of social identification which eventually results in the development of a rival political organization seeking to depose the established leadership.[15]

Comparison with another case study hints that this might be the case. In Emerson Hills, a suburb of Chicago, almost 70 percent of the population are professionals, proprietors, or clerical workers—salesmen, the three principal components of the white-collar corps.[16] Although the population has increased, its composition has remained stable. Almost 90 percent of the population is native-born; more important, all the churches are Protestant. It has always voted Republican in state and national elections by a steady margin of about 4 to 1.

Election to local office is accomplished by means of a caucus system. The governing caucus is composed of 44 delegates from eleven districts, selected in sparsely attended neighborhood conventions. Local informants remark that only about 2 percent of the eligible citizens show up for neighborhood meetings, a description borne out by actual observation. Another 76 are selected by such organizations as the League of Women Voters, American Legion, and charitable associations. In turn, the caucus chooses a twelve-man nominating committee which interviews prospective candidates. Those who pass muster are presented as a single slate to the entire village.

Over a thirty-year period, slate candidates have won every election. In the last election, an "Independent" slate ran for office. It lost all but one race. Protesting caucus domination, one "concerned home owner" wrote, "I do not know which candidates would receive my vote unless I know for what they stand. How about a word from the candidates on the following issues . . . ?" The leader of the caucus responded, "You don't want a campaign over issues because there are none." Another, a former councilman said, "It would cause breaks in friendship, strife and enemies. . . . Small towns would be torn apart." A third suggested, "Nearly all these five men the Caucus nominates would not run if they had to campaign; they are willing to work at the job as a community service but are not interested in fighting." Another, less restrained, called the insurgent candidates "stinkers" for running.

However, with the disclosure that the leader of the insurgent group had been convicted of conspiracy to murder some years before, the rival faction collapsed. In addition, leaders of the established caucus let it be known that some Independents had unsuccessfully presented their credentials to the caucus some years before, further discrediting the rival group. The Independent group ran candidates in the next election, but all lost to caucus nominees. For their part, Independent leaders have dispiritedly given up on the idea of openly contesting elections. They calculate their best chance is to secure nomination by the caucus, once the dust has settled and old grievances have softened.

The evidence indicates that the insurgents failed because they lacked any sort of enduring social and economic base to serve as foundation for a permanent opposition. They were all Protestant Republicans in a suburb made up of Protestant Republicans, and the lack of any sizable concentrations of poor people guaranteed.that conflict could not develop along class lines.

Nonpartisanship in Bluefield Park

In at least some suburbs, "nonpartisan" organizations are interchangeable with regular political parties. Only the names differ. Part of Armstrong Township in Baker County, Bluefield Park is a suburb immediately adjacent to Ichiban, a large midwestern city.[17] Incorporated in 1914, Bluefield Park's population in 1920 was only about 1,400. Seven years later, a realtor put up more than a thousand brick bungalows on brushlands lining the eastern borders of Bluefield Park. By 1930, the population shot up to more than 11,000, and that number more than doubled over the next thirty years. The 1960 census disclosed that the adults in Bluefield Park had a median education of 10.8 years, slightly more than half its household were headed by white-collar workers, and the median family income was $8,500. Older neighborhoods filled up with families descended from Scandinavian or Irish stock; those more recently settled are of predominantly Italian ancestry.

Bluefield Park has a formally nonpartisan city council, whose six members are elected at large for staggered two-year terms. Half the council is elected every two years, while the village president is elected every four. Competition for elected office has been institutionalized for many years. Two groups regularly slate and run candidates for all positions. Because of state law requiring that "continuing party organizations" hold primary elections, the groups prudently change their names with each election to avoid the uncertainties of a wide-open primary. In one year, the Liberty party confronts the Peoples' Voice party. The next time around, the New Liberty party opposes the Peoples' Choice party; two years later, the Liberty party once more takes on the Peoples' Voice party. Circumscribing state law in this way enables stable caucuses of leaders to slate candidates for elective public office, and the similarity in labels insures that few voters will be taken in by the ruse. Under whatever name is chosen, the Liberty pary is governed by Republican leaders. The opposition is made up of Democrats, the minority party in Bluefield Park but the majority party in Armstrong Township.

The acknowledged leader of the Liberty party is Guido Montarelli, son of a skilled artisan, born and raised in Bluefield Park. Able to attend college for only two years, he returned home to enter politics. At twenty-nine he was elected to the city council and four years later was chosen village president. A story circulated around Bluefield Park claims that he had to borrow a suit for the installation ceremony. By the time Montarelli reached his forty-fifth birthday in 1965, he was village president, local liquor commissioner, Armstrong Township committeeman for the Republican party, president of the Bluefield Park Savings and Loan Association, director of the largest bank in town, president of a construction firm, and member of the Baker County Republican party central committee. He had also been a state representative for three consecutive terms.

Since 1943, when Montarelli became village president, the Liberty party has never lost an election. In 1965, the council consisted of six men, all Republicans active in party affairs. John Carlson was a former precinct captain, township committeeman, and officer in Montarelli's savings and loan association. George Peters, then president of the local Chamber of Commerce, had at one time been a precinct committeeman, and Jay Celler had been president of the Armstrong Township Young Republicans Club and was currently a precinct committeeman. Joseph Pringnano was a precinct captain and treasurer of the Armstrong Township Republican organization; and Geoffrey Brockton, also a precinct committeeman, had just finished his term as vice-president of the Bluefield Park Young Republicans.

It was not always so. Before 1949, J.M. Mueller, a Democrat with firm connections to the Democratic machine in nearby Ichiban, had been alternately village president and councilman. Democratic strength in local elections grew from large numbers of county and state workers who regularly voted for Democrats in local elections. His eye set on higher office, Mueller evidently did not place a high premium on winning local elections. Informants claim that he "let" Republicans win occasionally to co-opt them into the leadership structure and to discipline Democrats currently out of favor. Republicans concerned with "doing something for Bluefield Park" calculated they would do better by accepting Mueller's terms than by confronting him openly.

After Mueller resigned the village presidency to move into Armstrong Township politics, Republicans began contesting local politics seriously. Pledging to end "corruption" and "mismanagement," they gained a foothold in the 1949 local races with the election of Montarelli. They gained two more seats on the council in the next election and by 1953 had won all the elected offices.

When Mueller left this suburb's political life, control over local party affairs passed to the township leader, who was more concerned with township elections and distribution of county patronage than he was with local affairs in Bluefield Park. Local Democrats complained that the township organization was completely disinterested in Bluefield Park. One grumbled that it took ten years for a "Peoples' Voice" representative to call on him after he moved into town, but only five minutes for a Republican-Liberty party worker to ring his doorbell.

Although the overlap was not perfect, the Liberty party enrolled many of the same personnel who worked for the Republican party in state and national elections. All twenty-five precincts had captains and cocaptains, and about half, particularly those located in the Italian sector of Bluefield Park, had block captains as well Republicans benefitted from the weakness of party identifications at the local level. One councilman estimated that about half the registered Democrats voted for Liberty party candidates, and John Schultz, a Democratic township committeeman, conceded the prevalence of "side-switching" in local elections. An examination of electoral data hints that his surmise is correct. The Liberty party's margin in local elections is consistently greater than the Republican party's lead in national and state elections.

Campaign rhetoric revolved about the Democratic party. Liberty party campaign material stressed that it will "keep Ichiban politics out of our town," and urged voters to "Vote for your neighbor who refuses to be regimented by a political machine." For its part, the Peoples' Choice party refused to acknowledge any connection with the Democratic party of Armstrong Township, much less with Mayor Reilley's party in Ichiban. Instead, it preferred to talk about the gambling that presumably has flowered with the connivance of Montarelli's Liberty party, and to suggest that "one-party rule will lead to complacency."

At the time interviews were completed, Democrats were disheartened. Even though their control of township office was firm, they saw little possibility of dislodging the Liberty party in Bluefield Park. Robert McDonald, a Peoples' Voice candidate for council in 1963, said that Montarelli "can sell things" and grudgingly conceded that he had done a good job while in office. Another compared him with Ichiban's Mayor Reilley; "Both are political bosses; I don't know about Reilley, but Montarelli's word is as good as gold." In any case, Democrats felt they had more to gain by holding on to township offices and patronage jobs they could distribute than by squandering their resources in a vain effort to unseat the Liberty party.

From one point of view, the conduct of public elections was either risible or contemptible, a clear case of hypocrisy run rampant. From another, the elaborate masquerade testified to the extraordinary vitality of the nonpartisan ethos. Though endorsement and recruitment patterns indisputably worked to the advantage of the Republican-Liberty party, at no time did Democrats publically label them a sham. They preferred instead to contest elections within the symbolic constraints of nonpartisanship.

Summary

The study of nonpartisan elections has a long way to go. It would be desirable to discriminate among all the variants of nonpartisan elections and conduct a full-blown multivariate analysis to determine the social contexts most hospitable to each type. Unfortunately, it is currently impossible to decide the relative frequency of each separate variety. The empirical foundation does not exist, and it would be extraordinarily expensive to develop it. Our tentative notion is that the Caucus of Civic Notables is likely to be most prevalent in homogeneous, middle-class communities which offer little opportunity for social differentiation along class, religious or ethnic lines. In a preponderant majority of these suburbs, the incumbent caucus will most probably be a peak association of local businessmen and leaders of prestigious civic organizations with a solid reputation for probity and good deeds.

The events in River View, Oaklawn, and Emerson Hills hint what may happen when a caucus-ridden suburb is swamped by migrants. If they differ in ethnicity and partisanship from the incumbents, they are likely to try to displace the dominant association of local notables in their drive for power. On the other hand, if the host and alien population are alike on both these dimensions, insurgent factions composed of newcomers are likely to fail in any overt assault on the caucus of the incumbents. Where one national party or another is dominant, caucus leaders will probably not shun the help of local party personnel so long as elections themselves appear scrupulously nonpartisan. Where national parties have about equal strength, party leaders are likely to be frozen out of any *overt* role in local elections.

12 Settling Disputes

Over a decade ago, Wood lamented the paucity of evidence on suburban political disputes. Sketching out the possibilities, he constructed an ideal type, a homogeneous community where the conduct of public affairs has been reduced to settled routine. In the "vacuous" suburb, nonpartisan elections and professionalized management work the way reformers intended. Trash is collected on schedule, zoning codes are scrupulously enforced, and qualified teachers staff the public schools under watchful eyes of a seasoned superintendent. Once set in motion, governmental institutions work smoothly, without rancor or error. Should the garbage truck miss a pickup, a telephone call will get a polite apology, and a work order will find its way down the ladder of control. Attempts to rally people out of sorts with settled routines will be met with abhorrence. Dissidents are gently but firmly reminded that it is considered improper to "grind axes in public" or to "tear the community apart" for self-seeking reasons.[1]

Despite the consensual ideology that tends to muffle conflict, convulsive disputes do erupt from competing demands which resist graceful negotiation with elected officials and professional managers. We have already suggested that established electoral modes can be overturned by newcomers, particularly those who differ ethnically and occupationally from old settlers. Conflicts may also arise *between* elections. Whether these disputes are episodic or enduring, they constitute important occasions in the life of the community.

The Politics of Education

One such arena of conflict is public education. It is not difficult to appreciate the salience of school politics in suburbs. People decide to move to suburbs for many reasons. One important motivation, sociologists have found, is to secure better education for children.[2] Suburban parents prize smaller classes and more individualized instruction, modern school buildings with the latest in educational hardware, and a generous array of extracurricular activities. However, this education is expensive; public school expenditures per child run consistently higher in suburbs than in congested wards of the city, sometimes by as much as $100 per child.[3]

Limited by an inadequate tax base, suburbs improvise expedients for narrowing the gap between income and outlay. In some states, intergovernmental transfer payments help lighten the load. In squeezing money from state coffers, sub-

161

urbs and their school districts do better than cities they surround. Sacks and Ranney calculate that in 1960 state aid for each suburban schoolchild averaged $165, forty dollars more than the mean amount for core city schools. When large federal funds became available for American schools in the late sixties, core cities got a larger share than their suburbs but still not large enough to overcome a differential which had reached $100 in major states.[4] Many suburbs have learned to stretch the tax dollar by forcing developers to bear part of costs of streets, sewers, and curbstones in new subdivisions; taxes saved here can be diverted to schools. However, all these devices—together with nuisance taxes, user charges, and revenue from renting parking spaces—seldom cover costs. Once these alternatives have been exhausted, all that remains is to boost the property tax rate, the mainstay of American local governments.[5]

Even when the revenues are earmarked for education, hiking the tax rate stirs impassioned opposition. After all, public expenditures consume resources that could be devoted to private uses. In the classical theory of public finance, shifting resources from private to public uses is justified when *indivisible* benefits are produced. National defense provides the standard example. Everyone gains from national defense; nobody can be excluded from enjoying its benefits, no matter how much or how little he pays to secure them.

However, the free market is woefully inefficient in supplying such indivisible goods. Although all consumers benefit, each will seek an excuse to transfer the costs to others and enjoy a free ride. Since every member of society will make the same calculation, no resources will be forthcoming and everyone will be worse off. Therefore, government must supplant the operations of voluntary markets and compel all citizens to pay for such collective goods.[6]

The trouble is that it is practically impossible to find such indivisibilities, even in the area of national defense. As Walter put it:

I disagree with [the] contention that national defense is an example of a *pure* public or indivisible good. It is not indivisible; some benefit more than others. People employed in the missile industry benefit more than the people who produce bayonets. For militant pacifists, national defense is not a merit want at all. Even if the production of national defense consumed no scarce resources at all—a sheer absurdity—it would still be socially harmful, as seen from the ethical perspectives of a pacifist. For one thing, it encourages the formation of a militaristic culture and causes people to become jingoistic and bellicose, which makes pacifists unhappy. And, of course, in the real world, producing guns and battleships consumes resources that could have been used in building homes and hospitals.[7]

Similarly, as a collective good, public education also contains important divisibilities; that is, access to the good cannot be equally distributed. In particular, groups such as bachelors, spinsters, childless couples, parents with children in private or parochial schools, and married couples with grown children draw smaller benefits from school expenditures than do parents with children currently in public school. True, all citizens gain from having a well-educated electorate, and employers are happy to see some costs of training employees borne by taxpayers in general. But these benefits are remote and diffuse, while the tax burden is immediate, a point which helps to account for the reluctance of many taxpayers to support expensive public education. Some cases will illuminate these general propositions.

Conflict in Old Harbor and Levittown

In "Old Harbor," a pseudonym for a New England village, Dobriner furnishes an example of rifts that can occur in socially heterogeneous suburbs.[8] For 300 years a sleepy and isolated community, Old Harbor has been radically transformed during the past forty years. First, the automobile opened Old Harbor to tourists and vacationers. Having a tough time making ends meet, owners of large estates saw an advantage in carving up their property into small plots for bungalows to rent or sell to summer residents who returned to the city after Labor Day. Next, a permanent assault began on the town after World War II. Old Harbor became more than a pleasant place for families to ride out a hot summer; it was transformed into permanent quarters for people earning livelihoods in the nearby city. New and expensive housing curled away from the heart of the old village along bay promontories and over inland hills and valleys. Old Harbor was no longer a secluded village; it was swamped with new inhabitants who differed in many important respects from old-timers. Most of the latter were locally employed as retailers and small businessmen; newcomers worked in the city or in an adjoining county. Rather more elderly than new arrivals, old-timers were less likely to have children currently in school. Though hardly impoverished, their median annual incomes were some $3,000 less than the $9,700 a year recorded for suburban migrants.

The cleavage between the status and values of older and newer residents was amply reflected in battles over financing schools. With most of their children already grown, old-timers were reluctant to subsidize education of other people's offspring. Not that they were opposed to all school expenditures; it was just that they could not see the need for all the "extravagances" demanded by more affluent newcomers. In Dobriner's words, old settlers saw:

a good education as including the basic skills taught by a dedicated but maidenly teacher in a plain school building. The suburbanites, on the other hand, are educational radicals; they are irrepressible spenders and cult-like in their dedication to the cause of modern education.[9]

They also believed that new settlers judged quality by expense; "the more costly a pending proposition is the more the newcomers will take to it," and as Dobriner remarks, "They are not entirely wrong."[10]

In Old Harbor, this dispute was thrust upon the school board. In an atmosphere shaped by traditions of New England town meetings, each citizen had a chance to speak his mind. Except for extremists, nobody was alarmed by the necessity to blend opposing points of view into an agreeable compromise. By settling for a smaller gymnasium here and for one less guidance counsellor there, the schism between all but the most intransigent could be narrowed. Participation in making educational decisions was personal and direct; no semi-permanent corps of leaders intervened between citizens and officials.

In other jurisdictions, citizens form into more or less stable groups to promote their conception of the public interest. Levittown, New York, is one such community.[11] Like Old Harbor, Levittown's school enrollments have swelled since the end of World War II. In 1947, the one school had forty students and two teachers. By 1960, there were fifteen schools, attended by more than 18,000 children. To absorb the cost of building more than one new schoolhouse every year and expanding the faculty to 678, the property tax rate had increased almost ninefold, 73¢ in 1947 to $6.45 per $100 of assessed valuation in 1960. With no industry and few commercial establishments, the financial burden necessarily fell on homeowners.

Moreover, the class structure of Levittown had undergone a gradual but thorough change since 1947. The first settlers were predominantly middle class. There were few wealthy people and comparatively few blue collars. As their incomes rose, many of the earliest residents sold their Cape Cods and moved further out on Long Island. More likely than not, their places were taken by blue collars, who constituted almost half of Levittown's 1960 population. The median adult education had dropped almost a full year since 1950, during a decade when the average education of all Americans had markedly increased. Catholics, many born to immigrant families, were slightly dominant among blue collars, while Protestants and Jews were overwhelmingly so among white collars.

The school board had to run hard just to stay in place. Each school building became overcrowded a year or two after it was built. Once more alarmed by the pressure of enrollments upon facilities, the school board in 1958 proposed putting up two new grade schools and adding fifty-nine classrooms to existing elementary schools. This was immediately opposed by a committee composed primarily of Catholics grumbling about further tax rate increases. Like the old-timers in Old Harbor, this committee took the view that larger classes were preferable to building additional schools. More inclined to accept the professional judgment that leaner student-teacher ratios result in better education, two other groups, one consisting mainly of Jews, supported the majority on the school board. In a public referendum, the proposals failed to get the two-thirds majority required by law.

School Conflict as Status Conflict

More than a set of isolated case studies support the reality of status polarization in educational politics. Minar's comparative analysis of forty-eight suburban elementary school districts in Cook County, Illinois, illuminates the strong association between social rank and support for public schools.[12] Two measures of affluence (share of labor force in professional and managerial occupations and proportion of all households with annual incomes over $10,000) displayed robust negative correlations with participation (-.49) and dissent (-.66) in school board elections.[13] Though marginally more likely to vote in school bond and tax levy referenda than lower rank suburbs, the residents of affluent suburbs generally cast larger affirmative votes. Moreover, higher status suburbs were more prone to select school boards by a caucus procedure. As might be expected from our earlier discussion of councilmanic elections in Oaklawn and Emerson Hills, nominating caucuses consist of downtown merchants, civic associations, and, most important of all, local Parent-Teachers Associations and Leagues of Women Voters. Caucus sponsorship had been reduced to a familiar routine: nomination, interview, and certification. Nominees were chosen with an eye for preserving areal and sex balance so that every identifiable interest would be assured of at least symbolic representation on the school board. To insure smooth working relationships, there was pre-endorsement consultation with the incumbent board and administration on nominees' qualifications. Most often, candidates ran unopposed.

In less affluent suburbs, caucuses were infrequently used and electoral conflict was rather intense. School boards here were more quarrelsome than those in consensual suburbs. In more affluent suburbs, school boards saw finance and capital development as their most important tasks and hence were prone to surrender authority over curriculum and personnel to the superintendent and his staff, regarding them as matters better left to disinterested professional expertise. In low-status, high-conflict suburbs, board members were more inclined to see momentous issues in every administrative detail and therefore resisted ceding autonomy to professionals. In short, they refused to "take education out of politics," preferring instead to pit their judgment against the accumulated wisdom of technicians.

As a general rule, the dolorous postmortem on the defeat of a school bond or tax will pin the blame on voter ignorance, obstinacy or perversity. Whatever the truth of these indictments, they almost certainly overstate the case. One need not be an utter skeptic to question claims of professional educators and their civic group allies. As disciples of "school betterment," they always proclaim that smaller teacher-student ratios, better equipped schoolrooms, and higher teacher salaries will invariably usher in better education.[a] As for chronic issues of per-

[a]Dye's analysis of spending patterns in sixty-seven urban school systems suggests that their enthusiasm may be misplaced. Expenditures per pupil showed the highest correlation with teachers' salaries (.63) but none (.02) with teacher turnover. If teachers are incompetent, it is difficult to see how paying them more money will make them any better. That is, while it is argued that higher teacher salaries will entice better teachers to apply for jobs, the absence of any association between expenditures and turnover indicates that the predicted effect does not take place. It is more plausible that increased salaries merely reduce incentives for less committed teachers to leave the work force. See Thomas R. Dye, "Government Structure, Urban Environment and Educational Policy," *Midwest Journal of Political Science*, 11 (1967), 372.

sonnel and curricular change, they argue that such matters are to be decided according to professional criteria. Lay "interference" in these arenas of decision is bound to be mischievous, no matter how well-intentioned are those who sit on the school board. When pressed for reasons, advocates refer to "the application of approved professional standards," a justification which often carries more weight with college-educated people than it does with distrustful blue collars. (They are particularly hard to convince if they discover that the school superintendent's most enthusiastic allies send their children to private school.)

Underneath all the clamor raised against "extravagances" in Old Harbor and Levittown lay a shrewd calculation that weighed promised benefits against immediate costs. Elderly residents of Old Harbor stood to gain little from increased educational expenditures in any case, and had much to lose from an additional tax burden imposed on their already strained budgets. In a somewhat different sense, these considerations were also paramount for blue collars in Levittown. Less concerned than white collars with sending their children to prestigious universities, they felt justified in their reluctance to finance the outlay demanded by white collar neighbors.

Scattered evidence suggests that blue-collar suburbs can be just as warm in their devotion to education as white-collar ones if they can find a way to shift the burden forward to industrial and commercial rate-payers. In Gray View, a school bond issue had to be presented to voters three times before it was finally passed in 1961,[14] a phenomenon which became widespread in suburbs in the late sixties. However, in a neighboring suburb of roughly equivalent social status, not a single one of seven school bond issues failed between 1949 and 1958. Although both suburbs spent almost the same for education per capita, the median vote in favor of bond issues was distinctly lower in Gray View—52.1 percent to 70.5 percent. The difference lay in the fact that Gray View was zoned against light industry, while its neighbor was not. Although those in the industrial suburb had smaller disposable incomes than people in Gray View, assessed valuation per square mile was larger—$10,967 to $8,741—and hence the yield of the property tax in the industrial suburb was $400 more per capita.

The Politics of Zoning

No matter how firm their abstract dedication to "the inviolability of private property rights," suburbanites are doctrinaire socialists when it comes to local zoning and subdivision controls. Zoning codes are the means that suburban governments employ to counteract the marketplace, where land-use patterns result from thousands of unregulated transactions between buyer and seller. In a free market, once these two agree on a price, the new owner is free to do what he wants with his parcel of land. But where zoning codes are in force, government becomes a silent partner to any sales agreement. When he subscribes to the zoning code, the landowner tacitly promises the government that he will not put the land to a use the code considers noxious.

Quite apart from price, zoning regulations constitute an important constraint on land-use patterns. In a broader sense, they help shape social and economic environments of a community by outlawing "undesirable" land uses. Restrictions on minimum lot size will shield suburbs against unwelcome effects of low-cost, high-density tract developments. By permitting apartment houses only around borders of industrial parks, suburbs create architectural buffers between the factory and dispersed housing. Often, zoning regulations grow out of conscious calculations of alternatives foregone; Gray View decided to do without increased expenditures for education rather than permit development of light industry. In most cases, zoning enforcement is delegated to a local planning commission and an appeals board. On some occasions, the configuration of political forces can be so overwhelming that the decision to alter or enforce the existing codes is made by the city council. Again, we can better illuminate these aspects of suburban politics by reference to case studies.

Zoning Conflict in La Piedra, Les Champs, and Shawnee Hills

This first study is of La Piedra, a suburb of San Francisco.[15] Chartered around the turn of the century, it soon earned an unsavory reputation for gambling and prostitution. After World War II, it became the new home of returning veterans who wanted to do away with La Piedra's randy reputation as the "Sin Capital" of the Bay Region. Organized in 1946, the Citizens' League for Good Government set about to fumigate La Piedra. It successfully backed two candidates for the city council, overwhelming the incumbents through sheer force of numbers. Five weeks later, the three remaining councilmen were removed by a recall initiated by the League. To make a clean sweep, the council adopted a council-city manager plan two years later.

At that time, Santa Isabel Avenue, La Piedra's major commercial thoroughfare, was lined with small shops selling food, clothing, and hardware. But that was no longer the case in the late sixties. Many store windows had been boarded up, some older shops had sold out to neon-lit "convenience stores" which sold groceries and beer until midnight, while only a few seedy holdovers remained from an earlier day—one a theater marquee boasting of "bosoms galore." The decline in this kind of economy stemmed from a major change in this suburb's zoning.

In 1957, a syndicate of developers approached the city council with a scheme to erect a large shopping plaza close to a major highway. This plaza needed approval of the council on two major points: (1) to relax the zoning code, which reserved a portion of the land sought by the syndicate as a historical site, and

(2) to service the area with wider gauge water pipe, street lights on access roads, and the like. Contending that the proposed plaza would bankrupt them, small storekeepers along Santa Isabel Avenue fought it through their mutual protective association, the chamber of commerce. They were no match for the newcomers. The councilmen maintained that the plaza would substantially broaden the tax base, desperately needed to hold down the tax rate at a time when population pressures were grinding against limited school and municipal facilities. Besides, councilmen argued, the plaza would be built on the site of La Piedra's dog track, the last major vestige of a bawdy era. In addition, councilmen expected new merchants to settle in La Piedra, adding further residential values to its tax base. For these reasons, the variance was granted and the plaza built.

La Piedra is no unique case. Other suburbs have had to face up to competition between shopping centers and the Main Street merchants' previous crossroads monopoly. With spreading highways and the advent of the two-car family, retailers along the main stem have discovered that their location close to residential areas no longer confers precious advantages of easy access. Measured by travel time, outlying plazas are no less convenient than Main Street. In addition, parking a car on a huge expanse of asphalt is considerably less wearing than an anxious cruising of Main Street in search of parking space, which is generally across the street.

In Les Champs, a midwestern suburb, local merchants short of curbstone parking persuaded the city council to build off-street lots near Main Street stores. Also at their behest, the council authorized "Free Parking Days" to lure shoppers away from the huge plaza outside town.[16] In La Piedra, the governing caucus brushed aside claims of downtown merchants who were legacies of a tawdry era it was trying to forget. The chamber of commerce in Les Champs, however, enjoyed greater access to officials because of their social standing and respectability.[17] Indeed, the chamber was part of the governing caucus that sponsored candidates in Les Champs' nonpartisan elections for city council.

The summary of these two case studies rubs against the easy generalization that "businessmen run things." Taken in the round, the "businessman" is as spongy an analytic concept as "the college professor." It fails to allow for the clearcut differences of interest that may divide businessmen on individual issues. In these two cases, Main Street merchants had little in common with proprietors of shopping centers; what helped one would hurt the other. It is also a mistake to assert that all businessmen are endowed with equal esteem and social approbation; the bawdy-house proprietor and the owner of La Piedra's dog track were "businessmen." But both enjoyed significantly less prestige than retail merchants in La Piedra's new plaza or Les Champs' Main Street.

Merchants are not the only group involved in zoning politics. Neighborhood associations may also be politically activated by proposed changes in zoning codes, as we may see in Shawnee Hills. Here, a big-city department store sought to have an undeveloped area outside town rezoned from residential to commercial.[18] Arguing that the land could not possibly support more homes, store architects submitted plans that would "complement" the residential character of adjoining areas. The architects were immediately countered by a neighborhood association of nearby homeowners. They argued that the store's location would benefit surrounding areas more than it would Shawnee Hills. In addition, they claimed, traffic and congestion would disrupt the quiet character of the neighborhood. After four years and two separate hearings by the state supreme court, the commissioners agreed to rezoning of the area.

Once they sensed that alterations in zoning codes were likely to be decided by a state tribunal rather than a local council, other interests sought to trade on this judicial precedent. A syndicate of merchants entered a motion to have a neighborhood shopping center on the other side of town rezoned as commercial. There were limits on the floor space of stores in neighborhood shopping areas that prevented large stores from bidding for locations. The impending change in neighborhood tone once more stimulated formation of a local association in Bluestone Manor, the very prosperous area adjacent to the proposed shopping center. It was joined by the developer of Bluestone Manor, worried by adverse effects of the center on the value of his few remaining lots. Together, they raised enough money to battle the syndicate all the way to the state supreme court. Faithful to its own precedent, the court directed township commissioners to grant the variance. Shortly afterwards, property-owners in Bluestone Manor heard the clanking of bulldozers beginning to clear land for the new center.

A parallel case suggests how a different outcome may result if the power of legal decision resides in the local city council rather than with a more remote judicial body. The Primrose is the major thoroughfare in the hill region of La Piedra. Compatible with its rustic setting, The Primrose is unbounded by sidewalks, while on either side stand the most costly, elegant homes in La Piedra, widely valued for their sweeping vistas of the Bay Area. In 1965, the price for new homes overlooking the bay ranged between $80,000 and $90,000. Also, La Piedra's sole country club leads off The Primrose, as do a large park and a recreation center.

In 1960, the planning commission proposed that setback regulations be eased to permit widening of The Primrose and the installation of sidewalks on either side. Aroused, occupants of palatial manors along The Primrose formed a homeowner's association to fight the proposal. In council elections that year, three incumbents were replaced by candidates endorsed by the association. Knowing it would not win, the planning commission diplomatically withdrew its request for a change in the zoning code.[19]

Social and Political Changes:
An Overview

In the 1830s, the amazingly prescient Alexis de Tocqueville underscored the importance for America of voluntary organizations:

In no country of the world has the principle of association been more successfully used, or more unsparingly applied to a multitude of different objects, than in America. Besides the permanent associations which are established by law under the names of townships, cities, and counties, a vast number of others are formed and maintained by the agency of private individuals.[20]

When values they cherished were threatened by the plans of others, wealthy residents of both La Piedra and Shawnee Hills spontaneously formed mutual protective associations to fend off perceived danger. Outcomes of the controversies varied because of interactions among the resources disputants brought to bear in promoting their own interests. In Shawnee Hills, homeowners failed when their opponents found they could shift the controversy to a distant state judicial body insulated from any threat of local retaliation at the polls. In La Piedra, the same dispute was locally decided. Hillside residents were thus able to trade on their prestige in stimulating an electoral alliance which effectively fended off their opposition.

Rather than form new associations, Main Street merchants in both La Piedra and Les Champs exploited existing organizations. In Les Champs, shopkeepers used both their high social standing and traditional representation in the governing caucus to get their way. Recognizing that they alone could not finance new parking space, they parlayed these assets into a successful effort to have the city do the task for them. Potent in Les Champs, the chamber of commerce was ineffectual in La Piedra. In both suburbs, Main Street merchants were the chamber's mainstays, but in La Piedra they suffered from two disabilities. They were not part of the new governing coalition, for the sheer numerical weight of newcomers had allowed them to brush aside the chamber in their quest for political power. Too, as proprietors of marginal businesses, local merchants lacked the esteem accorded shopkeepers in Les Champs.

Detailed narratives of all the disputes that arose in the communities we investigated would run to many hundreds of pages. Even so, we found, as did Martin's survey of suburban schools, that the most remarkable feature of these conflicts is their relative infrequency.[21] For the most part, energies of elected officials and appointed administrators alike were absorbed by housekeeping chores. Attentive to grumblings of individual citizens, they prodded the public works department to be more punctual in collecting trash and filling chuckholes on suburban streets. Backed by parent-teachers associations, teachers and superintendents maneuvered to get better facilities for schools. Virtually unchallenged in its authority, the governing caucus of local businessmen and their auxiliaries from various civic associations presided over the allocation of elected political offices. Once this was accomplished, components of the dominant alliance retreated to their civic associations and business enterprises. Having little inclination to run the suburb, they were content with a presumptive veto over any proposed action which would adversely affect their constituencies. For the most part, conflicts that did erupt were episodic rather than cumulative. Though tempers flared during the controversy, the losing side never sought to end the hegemony of the ruling alliance.

Simplifying drastically, we can say that controversies developed in a matrix of low-tension pluralistic conflict. Disputes began as plans of actors collided. Against a background of massive public indifference, protagonists amassed the resources readily at hand—social standing, time, group cohesion, control over information, and, occasionally, sentiments of righteous indignation. By and large, public officials sidestepped the conflict in the hope that antagonists would find an acceptable compromise on their own. They intervened only when a prolonged stalemate seemed to be developing. Often joined by leaders of more active civic associations, they then invited contenders to sit down and bargain, hoping they would arrive at a satisfactory division of the stakes. Even so, political officials hesitated to impose a settlement on contending parties. Instead, they preferred to play the role of broker, knowing that any attempt to force an agreement would leave them vulnerable to the accusation that they were "playing politics." Once disputes were settled, enmities receded and officials returned to their accustomed and uneventful job of supervising routine civic housekeeping.

However, it is a mistake to assume that all suburban political systems are as completely unalterable as those of remote rural villages, where prevailing distributions of political influence can persist for decades. In such sleepy communities as Vidich and Bensman's Springdale, there were chronic inequalities in abilities of different citizens to influence decisions of their local governments.[22] So persistent and clear-cut were these inequalities that it was possible for Vidich and Bensman to distinguish between policy makers and ordinary citizens. Old Harbor, River View, Gray View, La Piedra, Levittown, and Bluefield Park—all were suburbs in stasis until they were assaulted by waves of newcomers with markedly different policy goals and political ambitions. Their more or less sudden arrival in massive numbers endangered the hegemony of old-timers. When they started to plumb the dimensions of local political life, they discovered that they were blocked by customary mechanisms of slating and electing candidates for public office. They also found that they could not attain educational objectives they treasured for their children within the network of constraints and suppositions that formed normal procedures for allocating resources to public schools. Unwilling to bend to the consensually sanctioned scheme, they sought to challenge the existing political order.

Severe and continuous conflict was inevitable. Newcomers organized to press their demands, but as they did so, old-timers stiffened their resistance. With one exception, there was no way open for the vanishing rear guard to blunt the cutting edge of intergroup strife. Only in Old Harbor did the town meeting permit antagonists to search out some broader area of agreement in the controversy over funding public schools. Since each side was prepared to yield a little in the short run rather than permanently polarize the community between old-timer and newcomer, each side retreated from its most preferred position in the search for a viable compromise. Later, though, Old Harbor's old-timers would lose all power, if that suburb followed the pattern elsewhere.

The fight over schools produced one permanent expectation; it established the right of newcomers to be heard. Dobriner comments,

Though the suburbanites are circumscribed in their interests, they are nonetheless organized, and can marshal massive political displeasure at the polls. As a consequence, the villager politicians must somehow walk a tightrope, balancing the political expediency of pleasing the newcomers against their own desire to keep the village what it was.[23]

The school dispute alerted city fathers to the necessity of placating the new arrivals.

In all other cases, cleavage between established residents and eager new suburbanites grew more sharp and bitter over time. Insulated from feedback, managers of governing caucuses in Grey View and River View made no effort to absorb new arrivals into the governing stratum. They had enjoyed monopolistic exercise of political power for so long that they were unwilling to relinquish or share it. Thwarted in their ambitions to win political office, newcomers capitalized on their political resources in a successful campaign to alter prevailing distributions of political power. Once they developed political organizations for mobilizing voters, they were bound to swamp the old villagers. In both communities, an old guard was displaced and new elite installed within the letter of a nonpartisan city charter. Wilier than the established political stratum in Grey View and River View, Democratic leaders in Bluefield Park abandoned the village entirely and retreated to their township stronghold. Only in La Piedra were changes formalized in a written document attesting to the political dominance of newcomers.

It is only a small exaggeration to call the succession of elites in these communities a "revolution," for the outcome of the conflict was to disestablish a ruling coalition grown secure in its long hegemony. Massive immigration is the key to the circulation of elites. As was true in Dahl's study of New Haven and Gans' study of Levittown, Penna., the inundation of newcomers triggered an extended sequence of political conflict between old settlers and recent migrants.[24] On a larger scale, studies of many school districts in Southern California found that changes in population composition led to increased conflict over school policy, then defeat of incumbents, followed by removal of superintendents, and finally the development of a new policy profile.[25]

Summary

In other studies, then, as well as our own, we see enough to infer a process of conflict and resolution which is more than a string of episodic contests between old-timers and newcomers. Rather, we are witnessing status conflict projected on the political realm; at issue are differences in values, life styles, and aspirations for self and community. The conflict is intense, even bitter, in most cases, but most often newcomers eventually exercise their dominance over office, issue, and the basic orientation of local government. This broad sequence of social change can be sensed in old hamlets and rural townships, once isolated on the far reaches of the central city. They have been assaulted by migrants. The white clapboard schoolhouse has been replaced by a school complex, outfitted with the latest educational technology. The suburban village has been tied into the life of the entire region by the freeways that have pierced the slumbering countryside. Blue- or white-collar migrants—all "city folk" to the rural old guard no matter what distinctions the Census Bureau finds—spill all over the rural corners whose major source of excitement used to be the annual county fair.

The sequence of change is patterned. As Sokolow noted in a careful study of three townships near Lansing, a broad process of political and governmental change accompanies the social transition from rural to suburban. "Local governments have moved from regulatory to facilitative programs, from minimum to maximum levels of finance and administration, and from stable to changing formal structures."[26] The political chronicles we have presented in the last pair of chapters are consistent with a rough theory of suburban community change. It cannot be said that the instances we have enumerated constitute a fair test of the theory. As always, a definitive appraisal must await a broader sampling of suburban communities.

The first stage occurs when newcomers arrive in large numbers. Finding the old-timers thoroughly in command of the governmental machinery, they nonetheless place new demands on the local political system. They may seek political office, only to be rebuffed by the dominant incumbent coalition. Or they may strive for new or expanded governmental services, which the old-timers regard either as "new fangled" (contrary to regime norms) or "extravagant" (redistributing governmental resources in a way the incumbents find repellent). Massive immigration is a necessary condition for regime transformation, not a sufficient one. If the suburb continues to absorb newcomers who prize the same goals the incumbents cherish, conflict between host and alien is not likely to develop. If it does break out, it is likely to be contained by co-opting the most ambitious new arrivals in the existing structure. Then, too, old settlers can ingeniously manipulate the legal authority vested in the autonomous suburb to retard or arrest the pace of in-migration, as well as to bar the most troublesome newcomers from entering at all. Zoning and taxing controls are formidable weapons that lay at the disposal of the incumbents; with good reason they can be termed little immigration laws.

In the second stage, the newcomers are able to attain a rough parity of political and electoral strength with the old-timers. As this occurs, their representatives on city council or in town meeting criticize received criteria for conducting public affairs or for allocating community resources. They may even question the equity of the procedures traditionally employed in distributing elected office. Constrained by the goal of moderating potentially severe conflict, factions may drift away from both host and alien society to frame compromises. This pattern of accommodation was visible in both Old Harbor and River View, but not in La Piedra or Gray View, where hostilities were too broad and intense to be plastered over.

In the third stage, newcomers surpass old-timers in political resources. They gain in number and organization, finally displacing the declining remnants of the old guard from political office. Their tenure in office gives them the legal authority they need to control the production and allocation of governmental services. In this stage, the transformation has been completed. The insurgent newcomers constitute a new governing coalition, a phenomenon which occurred virtually overnight in La Piedra and over a longer stretch of time in River View. Dispirited, the old settlers withdraw from public life and transfer their energies to their private clubs and associations.

It is this "principle of association" which impressed de Tocqueville and which we urge here as a powerful analytic tool to study the inner political life of suburban communities undergoing rapid population turnover. Status differentials appear as the basic force underlying the formation of political interest groups, one set trying to hang on to the power and privilege it has enjoyed and the other trying to seize those prerogatives. These differentials seem to be the cause of suburban political cleavage today as much as they were in the days when Madison depicted interest groups as the basic energizing force of democratic politics. It has been the thrust of much of this book that status cleavage is an important variable in accounting for suburban political life, despite the wish of some observers to see only anomic men and women in dreary suburban locales. With Donaldson, we agree that such visions tell us more about the critic than they do about the criticized dimensions of life in the suburbs.[27]

The variety which our analysis of voting and attitudes have attested to challenges any shallow perception of suburban Americans. Rather, they are as diverse as the citizens of city neighborhoods and rural hamlets from which they are but one or two steps removed. What they perceive their community to be, what they expect of its governing, what they do with its democratic processes, including the most basic, the ballot—all show marks of a diverse people. In that regard, then, they are of a piece with their ancestors who sailed over here, "went West," fled the farm—or stayed behind. Resistant to blacks as were their ancestors, possessed of differing and changeable minds about party candidates, not always clear what their "community" means to them—they are the new Americans—who share much with the old.

Part 5
National Policy Problems

13 The Search for National Suburban Policy

If suburbs are as varied as this volume attests, then public policy which seeks to guide urban fringe development effectively must take such diversity into account. It is a curious fact of American political life, however, that although public policy makers have held and cited the statistics of suburban variety perhaps longer than novelists and journalists have promoted the myth of suburban homogeneity, the former have seldom acted as if the facts were true.

The United States does not now have a national urban policy, nor does it possess a reasoned or even compiled national policy toward suburbs. Indeed, due to fragmentation of suburban interests and their lack of involvement in Washington affairs, national suburban "policy" tends to have even less coherence than national urban policy. But there are a great number of federal programs which affect suburbs. In addition, in large part as the result of the evolution of national urban policy, an effort has begun to guide suburban growth toward public objectives. With knowledge of what suburbs are actually like, we are now better able to assess the conceptualization of suburbia implicit in these programs and the likely impact of these views on national suburban policies.

The Evolution of National Suburban Policy

The federal establishment has relied on four different views of suburbia in developing its policies affecting suburbia. Each tells us much about how perceptions shape behavior which produce a "program" that has as much rationale as a box of loose type.

The first is a non-view, involving programs with important but hidden consequences for the life of suburbs, which those who formulated and implemented these programs did not see. The second view might be called the philosophy of agrarianism in reverse.[1] Americans traditionally fear urbanization and glorify the rural life. The belief that rural virtues are higher has a double edge today. It produces public paeans to the countryside and also notions that the city is where thorny problems exist and where federal attention should be engaged. Thus policies for suburbs were developed within the context of a process geared to urban programs.

The third view is that of the urban "system." This policy approach arises from a view of the metropolis as a totality, so that solutions to urban ills de-

177

mand regional approaches. In this perspective, suburban policies should not be distinguished from urban policies, for suburban development cannot be separated from that of the metropolis. The fourth view is less well developed. Involving rediscovery of suburban pathologies, it responds to the notion expressed by anthropologist Margaret Mead that the suburban housing boom is one of the greatest disasters in American history. In this view "the suburbs are an outrage [because] all the problems that people moved to the suburbs to avoid . . . crime, defective schools, and now drug addiction . . . have followed them from the cities into the suburbs."[2] Policy response to this view of suburbia involves a search for ways to move beyond suburban patterns to develop new types of ex-urban growth.

Hidden Suburban Policies

During the twentieth century Washington has had an implicit pro-suburban bias hidden within some policies designed to do other things. This unwitting promotion of suburban development evolved from fear of population overconcentration in big cities and from housing preferences of Americans for the single-family home. As a result, the federal government, attempting to overcome the inability of people to obtain financing to buy housing, also acted to move housing out of the big city.

Beginning in the early thirties with the President's Conference on Homebuilding and Home Ownership, federal policies encouraged homeownership through amortized long-term mortgages, federal insurance of home mortgages, encouragement of large-scale developments of single family homes, and guidance of the supply of longer-term credit for housing. Franklin D. Roosevelt obtained passage of a whole series of acts—the Federal Home Loan Bank system in 1932, the Home Owner's Loan Corporation of 1933, and the National Housing Act of 1934 setting up the Federal Housing Administration—designed to develop new low density communities and to facilitate homeownership for nonfarm population.

Up to the fifties, most FHA-backed purchases were made in suburbs. This developed because its loan underwriting standards used to evaluate homes rested on criteria which favored single-family dwellings, new properties, and notions of neighborhood "viability" (absence of smog and fog, harmoniousness of race and nationality relations) and neighborhood "appeal." As noted in earlier chapters, this land-extensive focus could work better in suburbs than in cities. Thus from 1937 to 1967, while the federal government constructed 700,000 public housing units, mostly in central cities, and helped put 235,000 families in multifamily housing units, FHA in contrast issued mortgage guarantees for nine million suburban homes and allowed some 28 million families to secure low-cost home improvement loans.[3]

The federal Interestate and Defense Highway system begun in 1956 is also said to have helped to suburbanize America. By facilitating intra-metropolitan travel, this program eased the commuting associated with the suburban life style. As an example of the spread of the federal transportation budget, for the 1967 fiscal year only 30 percent of the funds allocated for local transportation went to core city programs. Of the remainder for inter-urban expenditures, 90 percent was for highways and only 10 percent for public mass transit. Federal transportation policy thus emphasized commuting and particularly commuting by automobile. However, mass transit ridership had already begun to level off a generation before the impact of suburban living began to be felt.[4]

While the availability of federal aid for highways that could go to suburbs could be compensated for by federal programs to support public transit systems of benefit largely to central city dwellers, available data suggest that recent public transit support also favors the commuting suburbanite.[5] For example, to the extent that federal funds are used in construction of San Francisco's new rapid transit system (BART) or Washington's new Metropolitan Transit Authority (WMATA) system, hidden subsidies to suburban commuters appear because the bulk of the line mileage and stations will be in suburbs. BART will have a total of 75 miles of line and 37 stations but less than 8 miles and only 11 stations in San Francisco, with the remainder spread out to East Bay suburbs. Though this may aid the economy of San Francisco, the expenditures are supportive of the suburban traveler, not the inner city poor directly. WMATA is a 98 mile system extending into Maryland and Virginia with the same bias in favor of suburban commuters, although the costs are not so distributed.[6]

A third set of programs for federally assisted sewage and treatment plants also is in aid of suburban life. In addition, in some states suburbs receive more than central cities in education aid, but this is as a product largely of state rather than federal aid formulas. Indeed, the Elementary and Secondary Education Act of 1965 has begun to redistribute funds for education into the central cities, although the amount of aid provided is relatively small. As Table 13-1 shows from a recent Ford study, redistribution formulas produce no clear picture of city-suburb advantage in these federal funds; in California suburbs do better than cities, in Texas about the same, and elsewhere rather poorly. The important element of this Act is that it was designed to assist education of the poor, most of whom were thought to be in the cities. But as Table 13-1 and other studies show, suburbs benefit also, sometimes even well-off suburbs.[7]

Agrarianism in Reverse

During the sixties, concern for urban problems grew sharply. The consensus that emerged—that Washington had a general responsibility to the cities—eventuated in a variety of programs aimed at city problems. In 1965 many of these were

Table 13-1

Federal Aid and Total Revenue By Central City, Outside Central City, and Non-metropolitan Areas, 1967

State	Fed. Aid	Total Revenue	% Fed. Aid
California			
Central City	$39	$684	5.8
Outside Central City	40	817	4.8
Nonmetro	54	641	8.4
New York			
Central City	68	876	7.7
Outside Central City	31	1037	3.0
Nonmetro	31	923	3.4
Texas			
Central City	38	479	7.9
Outside Central City	36	485	7.4
Nonmetro	63	535	11.8
Michigan			
Central City	29	683	4.2
Outside Central City	17	666	2.5
Nonmetro	30	629	4.8
Massachusetts			
Central City	69	675	10.2
Outside Central City	38	779	4.8
Nonmetro	n.a.	n.a.	n.a.

Source: Joel S. Berke, et al., *Federal Aid to Public Education: Who Benefits?* (Syracuse: Syracuse University Research Corporation, 1971), 57.

brought together in establishment of the Department of Housing and Urban Development.[8] At this point, national policy did not officially recognize suburbia as a distinctive location for American urbanization. To the extent suburban problems were treated, it was because most central city development programs were discretionary and became in fact usable in suburbs as well. Overt discussion of policies swirled around the core's problems, however, for it was the previous prejudice against cities and in favor of suburbs which HUD was organized to overcome.

Three patterns of national-suburban programing developed. First, programs designed for central cities and passed in Congress with rural backing were used in suburban communities. Since federal grant-in-aid statistics are reported by municipal size and not jurisdictional categories, it is difficult to specify precisely how much of this type of cross usage occurs. However, if we can assume roughly that jurisdictions below 50,000 have a higher likelihood of being suburban in fact or outlook,[9] we have a useful measure.

Thus, Washington provided $167 million in aid to communities *under* 50,000 in 1968-69, or $3.14 per capita, and $977 million to those *over* 50,000, or from $7.27 to $31.18 per capita.[10] In the 1964 summaries of urban renewal activities, 70 percent of 800 jurisdictions with such federal assistance had populations under 50,000.[11] In 1968, only 8 percent of the jurisdictions with low-rent public housing were cities over 50,000, though these contained 67 percent of the units built.[12] Similarly, of the first 63 communities in the Model Cities program, nine were under 10,000. Receiving funds from the 1970 Model Cities program were such suburbs as Compton, Pittsburgh, and Richmond, California; East St. Louis, Illinois; Highland Park, Michigan; Plainfield, New Jersey; and Cohoes, New York. The most specific urban program aid to suburbs probably goes to those over 50,000. In 1968-69, for example, of 23 reporting suburbs over 50,000 in California, 12 received federal aid (program unspecified) of $3,570,364.[13]

Second, there are programs developed with cities in mind which are likely to become largely suburban because of difficulties in implementing them in the existing urban context. For example, the 1968 Housing and Urban Development Act was designed in part to help the poor buy homes through long-term interest subsidies. Mainly because of land costs in inner cities, the program will operate heavily, if at all, in suburbs. Though two established low-income housing programs—public housing and rent supplements—have not to date been used actively in suburbs because of the objections of local jurisdictions, the new program does not require concurrence of suburban governments.

What normally occurs, however, when programs designed for cities are converted for suburban use, is that program goals begin to shift, too. In this particular case:

... there is a strong and disconcerting possibility that the program will not serve minority groups as well as it will serve whites. The surest way to serve black families would be to offer low cost ownership housing in or near areas where black families are already established, so that new homeowners are not required to take on the additional burden of serving as pioneers. Such areas today, however, are located primarily in the central cities, where there is little land available ... Patterns of discrimination are well established in the housing market, and unless federal fair housing regulations are enforced aggressively, developers and mortgage lenders may well favor white families. In this event, the program would probably serve mainly to help the lower middle-income whites still in the old neighborhoods follow the more affluent middle class to suburbia.[14]

Third, within the public context of mounting concern for central cities, some programs were devised which, although available to all towns, were particularly attractive to suburbs. Thus there are programs designed to bring some cohesion to suburban growth. These principally employed incentives for better planning

(Section 701 of the Housing Act of 1954) and later included aid for mass transit, open space, and public works. Of 5,533 public-works planning advances made by 1962, only 430 were to jurisdictions over 50,000, which are mainly cities.[15] The most popular suburban program is for water and sewer grants, the fourth largest and fastest growing item in the 1970 urban development package. Much of the pressure for continuous expansion of this program is congressional. In fiscal year 1971, for example, $100 million was added to the budget requests of HUD by the leading Republican on urban legislation, William J. Widnall (R-NJ).

Despite failure to recognize officially the existence of suburban variety, an implicit recognition of differences among types of suburbs appears in administration of these programs advertised for core cities. A general picture of suburban participation in existing programs is found from a sample of HUD grants for urban development from mid-1968 through 1970.[16] Fewer grants and less money went to suburbs than to central cities. More interesting, there were marked differences in suburbs participating in different programs. Table 13-2

Table 13-2
HUD Allocations to Suburbs, 1968-1970

Demography of Receiving Suburbs	Total Allocations to Suburbs[a]	Suburbs in Central City Programs[b]	Suburbs in Metropolitan Programs[c]
More nonwhite[d]	40%	40%	0
Less nonwhite	25	19	5
More income	9	3	5
Less income	56	56	0
More poor	0	0	0
More rich	8	3	5
More sound units	26	20	5
Less sound units	39	39	0

[a]The demographic data are from the 1960 Census and are available only for jurisdictions over 25,000, so the percentage does not sum 100.

[b]The programs are urban renewal, model cities, interim assistance to blighted areas, neighborhood facilities, demolition, code enforcement, urban beautification, historic preservation, urban property insurance, and urban parks.

[c]The programs include public facilities loans, open space land, water and sewer facilities, parks and recreation, advance land acquisition, land development, new communities, small town services, flood insurance, and community development training. A third category of programs, the planning grants (comprehensive planning assistance, public works planning, planned areawide development, urban mass transportation planning, and social planning) also exists, but no grants from these fall into the sample.

[d]These characteristics were compared to national statistics, as follows: nonwhite, national average of 11.4 percent; median family income, national average of $5560; poverty, national percentage of families with income under $3000 or over $10,000; sound units, more or less than the national average of 74 percent. Drawn from *County and City Data Book* (Washington, D.C.: Government Printing Office, 1967).

presents the results. In those programs HUD regards as aimed at central city development, suburbs receiving grants tended to be relatively less well off than the national average, while in the so-called metropolitan programs, more funds went to suburbs with higher incomes, fewer nonwhites, and fewer unsound housing units than the national average.

The best symbolic manifestation of policies arising from reverse agrarianism is provided by President Johnson's appointment of the Task Force on Suburban Problems in 1967. This was two months after the president had set up several major commissions—the much-heralded Commission on Civil Disorder in the wake of city riots in 1967, the National Commission on Urban Problems chaired by Paul Douglas, and the blue ribbon panel on Urban Housing.[17] The suburban task force, with only one government official, was kept secret because President Johnson did not wish to distract public attention from poverty, slum, and rehabilitation programs, then being studied for the urban core.

The Urban System

In the closing years of the Johnson Administration, systems analysis became the dominant approach for developing solutions to urban problems. As applied to the metropolitan area, the systems approach led to the view that the federal government ought not to deal with the problems of suburbs alone, because to do so implies that they can logically and practically be distinguished from the metropolitan whole. The first stirrings of discontent with the prior emphasis on the city or suburb alone took the form of enthusiasm for regional planning. Congress, starting in 1967, had imposed areawide planning requirements on grants popular in the suburbs for the use of federal water and sewer, open space, mass transportation, and, later, law enforcement assistance funds. Unless an areal comprehensive plan is devised, no federal funds will be forthcoming for these public works.[18]

Such requirements caused an institutional revolution in suburbia. First, hundreds of interjurisdictional agreements for functional programs were made among suburbs. Then, suburbs joined the numerous Councils of Government or Regional Planning Agencies organized to satisfy areal planning requirements of federal law. Today only six SMSAs do not have areawide general planning bodies, and over 6,000 applications for federal assistance have been received and reviewed by SMSAs with such bodies. The goals of these planners' requirements were to bring more coherence to management of metropolitan areas, and to readjust local decision-making to emphasize metropolitan considerations rather than those of single jurisdictions.

Failure to deal adequately with suburban problems and with spillovers to central cities from suburban patterns were later attributed to the weakness of these new metropolitan institutions, particularly in land development, financing, and social problems. Thus, the President's Task Force on Suburban Problems worked from the notion that "suburban problems are an indivisible part of the urban crisis" and that help to the suburbs must heal the whole city.[19] Hence it recommended improving the metropolitan base by increasing financing available to local governments through an urban development bank (URBANK) modeled after the World Bank.[20] The choice of URBANK as the key to improving the entire urban system was in part a matter of political pragmatism, the assumption being that any attempt to force suburbs to make changes was unfeasible. But such a cautious judgment may have been risky, for a Republican HUD secretary then proposed a bolder notion of the urban system—that suburbs are places that do not solve but add to urban problems. Orr describes this view well:

To describe suburban life styles is to encourage a political climate in which the middle class can more easily divorce its own interests from those of the wider population. For pragmatic reasons, we ought to refuse to carve the metropolis into competitive parts, each warring for its own advantage. The myth of the urban organism encourages us [to see] the suburbs as a place that contributes to urban problems but as yet supplies few answers.[21]

The most politically explosive effort of Washington to intervene in suburban development arose from this view. It involved steps to implement a policy which would disperse low income and minority groups now concentrated in the central city into the suburbs.

Dispersal as a Suburban Policy

Dispersal policies arise more from analyses of city than of suburban life. Their premises are that the chief urban crisis today is the poverty and isolation of minority groups in the large ghettoes of the core. One major determinant of this poverty is the spatial distribution of employment. Over the last decade there has been a national trend for suburbanization of jobs in metropolitan areas. In Washington's efforts to influence these employment patterns, there are three possible strategies. First, it might move jobs to the poor. But, moving jobs from suburbs to cities is not only expensive but bucks the current trend of job growth in suburbs, particularly since it is the low- and semi-skilled jobs which appear to be moving fastest out of the city.

Thus, efforts to "gild the ghetto" by spending programs aimed at building the economy of the central city are less likely to be effective than a second strategy—moving people where jobs are going.[22] Dispersal to suburbs is then a possible alternative, or at least a supplement, to more familiar programs to improve the quality of life in central city. It provides an alternative to urban renewal, efforts to spur black capitalism, neighborhood development corporations, and other essentially inner city enrichment efforts.[23] A third alternative is simply to improve transportation between poor and jobs, but leave both in locations they now occupy.

The earliest dispersal effort involved the notion that public housing might be built in suburbs. But local hostility has been so virulent that in California and other states, existing laws allow voters in communities affected to veto acceptance of public housing through referendums. Such laws were upheld by the U.S. Supreme Court in mid-1971 as not violative of equal protection of the laws.[24] Nevertheless, the Kerner Commission had argued forcefully that an integrationist or metropolitan strategy would in the long run be the most fruitful solution, not because of abstract virtues of integration but because it would be the easiest way to provide blacks as well as whites with better education, housing, and jobs. And, those blacks likely to wish to shift to suburbs would be those who were young and moving up, rather than established families, as in the case of white veterans after World War II.

The Housing and Urban Development Act of 1968 indicated implicit adoption of a similar view in requiring that metropolitan planning, a condition for receiving categorical grants, include a housing element as part of comprehensive land-use plans. This requirement was said to mean "that consideration was to be given to the projection of zoning, community facilities, and population growth trends, so that the housing needs of all classes of the population, at different prices and rentals, both of the region and of the individual local communities, should be adequately covered."[25] Aggressive implementation of Title VIII (Fair Housing) of the Civil Rights Act of 1968 was urged. For example, the then general counsel of HUD, Sherman Unger, interpreted the act as giving the HUD secretary power to subpoena offenders and hold public hearings in cases where suburbs acted to foment minority race concentration.[26] And, in February, 1970, President Nixon signed Executive Order #11512 which required an agency to obtain General Services Administration approval before locating a federal facility, also advising GSA to consider availability of low- and moderate-income housing as a factor in the location decision.

The Nixon Administration
Tries Dispersal

In 1970, HUD Secretary George Romney concluded that none of these postures was adequate to change suburban development. While metropolitan planning bodies were providing forums to facilitate informal consultation and diffusion of information among suburbs and cities, they did not seem to be imposing an area-wide balancing of metropolitan priorities on controversial matters.[27]

Romney was also influenced by HUD's experience in 1969 with Operation Breakthrough, a demonstration program aimed at encouraging better and cheaper means of producing housing. The program ran into stiff public resistance on six of eleven demonstration sites where local authorities were pressed by residents who viewed it as a low-income housing program and hence feared massive economic and racial integration. Two sites, near Wilmington, Delaware, and Houston, Texas, were eliminated as a result of their unwillingness to waive building and zoning codes to allow introduction of prototype housing. Although officials of Operation Breakthrough tried to change its image as a program for low-income housing, HUD officials also concluded that operation of zoning ordinances in the suburbs, not housing costs alone, was the key to restrictive development. Such ordinances are creating "great white belts around the cities that hold ethnic minorities encircled while the suburban community residents say, 'We want it that way'," said one HUD official.[28] In chapter 4, we have shown evidence of this constriction.

A tougher HUD posture was then adopted. The first and most stringent mechanism for enforcing suburban dispersal was to cut off funds to suburbs that pursued a policy of racial discrimination in housing or failed to implement a plan providing low-cost housing on scattered sites. The most famous case of such effort to enforce dispersal policy occurred in Warren, Michigan, an industrial suburb of Detroit with about 180,000 people. Detroit is 40 percent black, and while about 40 percent of Warren's work force is black, only 28 nonwhite families live there, 22 at a federal installation. In May, 1970, HUD cut off Warren's urban renewal funds on grounds that the suburb was racially discriminating in housing. Warren's residents collected 14,800 signatures on a petition for outlawing the renewal program.[29] The incident also damaged the Senate campaign of Secretary Romney's wife. HUD gave up on Warren but continued to press for use of federal programs to promote low-income housing. It urged that the Department of Justice intervene in a housing case in Blackjack, Missouri, where a moderate-income public housing project was rezoned out of existence, allegedly for racially discriminatory reasons.

HUD otherwise tried to soften its approach by creating a priority system for parcelling out new funds (particularly for water and sewers) in which openness determined the likelihood of obtaining grants. In October, 1970, HUD issued regulations in which a community received a score on a 25-point base to rate its application for aid. Nine of the 25 points are related to community activity in the low-income housing field and to the percentage of housing accessible to those with low and moderate income.

In 1971 some communities accepted plans which disperse federally subsidized low-income housing throughout white suburbs. Suburbs of Dayton, Ohio,[a] with the social range demonstrated earlier in this book, agreed to a plan in which each

---

[a]Dayton is an industrial city of 250,000. All its 3,350 low-cost units to date have been constructed in the city. The integrated plan followed rejection by HUD of an application by the suburb of Kettering, south of Dayton, to obtain $65,000 for public parks, because the suburb had restrained its human relations commission from seeking housing for black families.

community was assigned a share of some 14,000 units, many in public housing, expected to be built in the area over four years. The reasons for agreement are as diverse as the suburbs involved: Trotwood approved the plan because it is in the path of an expanding black community leaving the central city; Kettering, a middle-income suburb, accepted the plan to obtain a park grant from HUD; Oakwood, a community of mansions and middle-income housing, accepted the principle that no community has the right to exclude potential residents on class grounds alone, but still took issue with the quota it had been assigned.

The view of suburbia underlying this program is that suburbs are where the money is. Vice-president Spiro Agnew stated this assumption most boldly, saying he rejected the idea that because problems of race and poverty are found in the ghettos, the solutions are there.

These ghetto oriented programs tend to ignore the geographical distribution of resources throughout the metropolitan region. Resources needed to solve the urban poverty problem—land, money, and jobs—are presently in scarce supply in the inner cities. They exist in substantial supply in suburban areas, but are not being sufficiently utilized in solving inner city problems.[30]

Although there is little doubt that pressure for opening suburbs will continue,[31] most discussion of dispersal today concerns the real utility of such a change for ghetto residents, who could be abandoning a central city power base they might increasingly control. In this view, dispersal is suspect as a scheme for destroying black power with its concentration in the core and for excusing a decrease in funds to alleviate core city problems. In addition, consideration skepticism has been expressed in Congress as to whether HUD has sufficient strength—in such dispersal tools as site and tenant selection and new, low-income housing criteria for urban development programs to move black residents into white suburbia. And, there has been a very effective attack on the notion that Washington should use punitive procedures in an area heretofore a matter of local policy choice.

President Nixon in December, 1970, declared that what he termed "forced integration" of suburbs was not in the national public interest. Secretary Romney later also deplored the term, and HUD has officially moved away from its original dispersal aim.[32] In June, 1971, Nixon declared in a major statement on housing that while his Administration would encourage towns to provide subsidized housing in areas where it is needed, and would move against instances of racial discrimination, it would not force such projects on those not wanting federally assisted housing, or penalize them by withholding other federal funds. This statement, based on an intensive investigation by the Civil Rights subcommittee of President Nixon's Domestic Affairs Council, emphasizes both that "in choosing among the various applications for Federal aid, consideration should be given to their impact on patterns of racial concentration" and also that the "kinds of land use questions involved in housing site selection are essentially local in nature."[33]

A few days after the message, GSA and HUD agreed that whenever a federal facility is built, they would develop an affirmative plan to assure federal personnel access to low-income housing.[34] A suit was also brought against Blackjack, Missouri. At the same time, HUD emphasized that its guidelines did not require communities to accept low-income housing, or to forfeit federal aid if they refuse. Thus, it is somewhat cloudy what will come out of the president's stance. From the suburban perspective, however, it seems quite clear that with this statement the view has moved from the systems position that suburban and urban policy are unitary, to return to the earlier notion that two separate worlds coexist. The president's federal policies relative to equal housing opportunity ratify that at least this kind of separation will continue to exist for metropolitan America.

The New Communities Alternative

The dispersal program relies on the view that suburbia is a place to which people aspire and should be helped to move. A different view pervades the thrust for the most popular program affecting suburbia today—*creation of new communities.* A broad assembly of public and private interests sees federal participation in development of exurban new towns as the best all-purpose answer to problems of population growth and congestion.

The notion of suburia underlying the new communities' effort is that suburbia, far from being desirable, is unsatisfactory as it has currently evolved. The President's Task Force on Suburban Problems pointed out that in suburbs Americans were looking for space, private homes, better education for their children, social status, local ties, manageability in an age of bigness, and freedom from city problems such as crime. It then documented the extent to which they have *not* escaped such problems by moving to suburbia. By starting afresh, the task force concluded, "a new option of organizing patterns of life can often be given people now limited to variations of suburban sprawl." Other proponents of new communities believe that federal facilities and their jobs have to be located so as to aid balanced growth. This means creation of new jobs outside major metropolitan areas and also away from suburbs where housing is restricted. Bypassing suburbs via growth in new towns is thus also a political strategy for improving the status of the poor.[35]

This multipurpose notion of new communities has given it a powerful thrust in national politics. In 1968, President Johnson proposed support of private investment in development of so-called "new towns," such as Reston, Virginia, and Columbia, Maryland. Hence, Title IV of the Housing and Urban Development Act of 1968 offered loan guarantees up to $250 million to private developers building total communities, plus supplemental grants for water and sewer facilities and open space acquisition. While Republicans originally opposed this, claiming it would expose the Treasury to financial risk from doubtful ventures, considerable sentiment for expanding the program developed under President Nixon. Secretary Romney pressed Nixon to recommend that Congress vastly expand the government's authority to help create new communities. The topic took on further partisan tones when the 1971 housing bill reported by a House committee pained the administration, in part because it usurped the work of its task force by including provision for expanded aid for new communities, and in part because it was sponsored by leading Democrats. The administration ultimately backed off from presenting a program because of cost concerns, but Congress passed an expanded new communities program anyway.[36]

Despite such political wrangling during two administrations, by November, 1970, three plans for new communities had received approval, the first being Jonathan, Minnesota. Since the 1960 census found only 22,223 blacks in Minnesota, racial balance is probably not a key social goal in this community. The second application approved was for St. Charles, south of Washington, D.C., where 80 percent of the housing is to be low- or moderate-income, single-family units. The third community was Park Forest South, Illinois, an appendage to the community of Whyte's *The Organization Man*. The existing base on which housing will be developed is a strong blue-collar area. Developers of these new communities talk less of racial balance and solutions to inner city problems than of the need for improvements on suburbia. Some emphasize the need for a more communal atmosphere, others for spatial planning to allow a life free from the ordeal of intra-metropolitan transportation, and others the need for more rational land development.[37]

The image of suburbia presented by this effort is, despite rhetoric about integration, one of dissatisfaction with suburban life. The vision is of whites, who once shaped metropolis by their retreat from the spreading blight of the city, now finding the good schools, countrified atmosphere, and grass roots government of suburbia lost because of fragmented development. Across the country, angry suburbanites are indeed turning down proposals to increase funds for municipal activities—even for public education. They are disgusted with rising costs of land and public services and the vanishing of recreational space in swamps of suburban sprawl. New towns are said to offer the hope that a clean slate will permit the creation of the suburbia once hoped for, albeit with a somewhat more heterogeneous group of people imposed by federal regulations.

Revenue Sharing

The most recent thrust of federal urban policy suggests a declining federal interest in suburbs. The aim of President Nixon's domestic policy with regard to cities is now to reduce the dependence of both urban and suburban governments on the property tax by giving them funds from other sources, chiefly the federal income tax. Critics say that revenue sharing under the proposed distribution formula, which emphasizes revenue *effort*, would aid wealthy suburbs at the expense of core cities. In fact, however, many cities make a better effort than surrounding suburbs, although the output is less.[b] Revenue sharing might change suburban direction also, if it led suburbanites to worry less about their tax rates and thus be less likely to bar the poor.[38] Alternatively, non-categorical distributions of funds might remove opportunities for either changing the current system by subsidy incentives or for promoting ameliorative programs, like the construction of mass transit systems which enable city dwellers to obtain suburban jobs without necessarily living in the suburbs. However, the Nixon administration's statements about revenue sharing, as well as its emphasis on standardization and development of national offices, grant consolidation, and reorganization of manpower and welfare programs, suggest less a concern with impacts on polarization of class and race in communities than with eliminating conflicting federal programs and proliferating requirements in current grant-in-aid programs.[39] The underlying reason for declining interest in cities may be that until early 1971 the administration had to deal with 31 Republican governors, but relatively few Republican mayors of large cities. Thus, its constituency provides a political basis for the view that metropolitan problems can today be resolved at the state level.[40]

[b]Some comparisons on effort include: Baltimore $225 vs. Montgomery County $212; Boston $262 vs. Brockton $215 and Cambridge $237.50; Chicago $160 vs. Evanston $79; Cleveland $101 vs. Cleveland Heights $67 and Lakewood $32; Detroit $127 vs. Ann Arbor, $101.

14 The National Politics of Suburban Policy Making

How can we explain the variety of assumptions and hence programs through which the federal government affects suburban development? Contrary to the common sense notion that such policies are a result of the power of suburban interests, as contrasted to the relative weakness of central city poor, we believe rather that they reflect the disorganization of suburban political influence in the national arena. That is, programs affecting suburbia are a response to different sets of pressures, on which no overriding suburban "interest" is imposed.

Actors and Process in Suburban Policy Making

Among the sets of programs we have discussed in the last chapter, there are several different kinds of political histories. At the initiation stage, the federal government, more than any group, was the significant initiator of change in matters of dispersal, new towns, and metropolitan planning. Here, initiative for new policies came from what Wood has called "intervening elites"—task forces, White House, academics in and out of government. The process of getting legislation through and affecting HUD's administration of it varies, however.

In the new towns case, when President Johnson, as a result of task force advice, advocated new community support from 1964 to 1966, mayors and homebuilders opposed it. Not until their backing was acquired in 1968, by expanding the program to include assistance for new towns *within* cities, and by encouraging small homebuilders to participate, did Congress act favorably. Since 1968, planners, and politicians of both parties have tried to outbid each other for the right to prescribe the agenda for new community development. Despite the fact that the administration ultimately backed off because of its concerns for inflation, causing a struggle over the new communities' title, the legislation became mainly a matter of arbitration among competing claims of affected actors, and not a matter of overcoming organized opposition.

Implementation of the program will be heavily affected by the claims of investment bankers and private developers. Since HUD cannot itself directly construct new towns, and has only limited financial support for them (initially even the waste and water programs of the Department of Agriculture, listed as supplementary grants for new towns, were not funded), and since few states have yet created public development corporations to build new towns, the future of this program depends on which builders are selected and how guidelines are imposed. Builder applicants for many new communities grants are organizations which have previously participated in Operation Breakthrough, an experiment in innovative housing construction, which foundered on conflicts with local zoning ordinances.

Dispersal policy, like new towns, arose through the impetus of the intervenors—in this case the Douglas Commission, presidential advisor Daniel Moynihan, and then the two black assistant secretaries at HUD. But here, HUD began to act within the administrative process, converting existing programs without seeking legislative approval of new authority. Interest groups stayed well clear of the debate because of earlier noted intense racial overtones of the issue, though many had taken prior positions on it. Congressmen at first reacted to administrative initiatives with positions ranging from support to opposition, but their main concern was that local jurisdictions participate in implementing any dispersal plans. Perhaps it is precisely because dispersal was a redistributional policy without backing of any interest group-Congressional alliance that it was such a weak reed. But it foundered also because the president was opposed.[1]

The metropolitan planning notion in its earliest conception was a rational outsider's response to the complexity of federal metropolitan grants-in-aid process. Senator Edmund Muskie gave the idea early support, but unlike the new towns program, this approach never picked up major interest group backing. It had support from only minor leagues like professional associations, such as the American Society of Planning Officials, whose tax exempt status keeps them somewhat quiet in Congress, and like functional groups of regional officials whose positions were created by the program. Indeed, so puny was the legislative backing that one section could be passed only in tandem with the model cities program, and a companion section authorizing supplementary grants was never funded. Punitive administration of the program—including withdrawal of funds from jurisdictions whose programs did not conform to metropolitan plans—also has proved very difficult.[2]

But rational outsiders continue to keep the idea and the program alive. After consulting with some thirty academics and professionals in the urban development field, the majority members of the Housing Subcommittee of the House of Representatives in 1971 moved to introduce a bill requiring that all states be given three years to enact legislation establishing metropolitan housing agencies to serve major housing market areas. If such a program is not developed, neither the state nor its political subdivisions would receive federal housing or community development funds. Presumably this is an effort to increase the potential for constructing low- and moderate-income housing in suburbs, an approach which views the problem in a metropolitan context.

The urban programs in which suburbs participate are products of an entirely different process. Here there are relationships among fairly well defined interest groups, including the U.S. Conference of Mayors, National Housing Conference,

National Association of Housing and Redevelopment Officials, National Association of Home builders, along with HUD and the Housing Subcommittee.[3] Dominated by big city concerns, most of these groups, mayors in particular, are not very interested in the FHA mortgage insurance program, on which most early pro-suburban policies turned. They are also potential opponents of the comprehensive development planning concept in metropolitan programs. These programs threaten control of the mayor or involve the possibility of long delays which would deny him visible credit for results. The mayors have favored area-wide planning only for air and water pollution, which they would not ordinarily control in any case.

Finally, the hidden pro-suburban policies noted in the last chapter were produced through yet another set of interactions, that of the standard tripartite alliance among interest groups, congressional committees, and federal bureaus. These essentially functional alliances are in most instances much stronger than the geographic alliances of either urban or suburban units.[4] Nothing is more characteristic of the very real autonomy of linked administrative, functional, and interest groups than the successful fight by an alliance of mortgage and savings and loan groups, housing industry and real estate boards to keep FHA a separate entity within HUD. The National Association of Real Estate Boards and most mortgage bankers are opposed to such efforts as dispersal which seek to house low- and moderate-income people in suburbia.

The Non-Expression of Suburban Interest

In this buzz and confusion, is there an overriding suburban view of policy? One possibility is that such a view might be seen in organized citizen pressures from suburbs. But, the evidence of such politicking in the national arena is not that it is powerful but that it is virtually nonexistent. The suburbanite is said to own a home financed by federal mortgages, drive to work on federally aided highways, and have his wastes processed at federally assisted treatment plants. But there has seldom been pronounced concern for suburban programs expressed by suburbanites in national politics.

Several scholars have noted this curious silence. Hacker found that suburbanites had been extremely diffident about their serious underrepresentation at the federal level arising out of malapportionment. Indeed, he comments, "Suburbanites are relatively unconcerned about the [national] government's role in their continued existences."[5] In a similar vein, Danielson indicates that transportation policy for suburbs is a product of their restricted joint resources, lack of federal lobbyists, limited contacts with federal officialdom, and infrequent involvement in issues at the national level as a defined territorial interest group.[6] In consequence, lacking alternative means of access, suburbs use durable and traditional congressional channels as their main pathway for influence. As a result, suburban policies, including hidden pro-suburban programs and suburban benefits existing within urban grant programs, more frequently bear the imprint of functional alliances and pork-barrel tactics than of a comprehensive or even crisis plan.

Suburbs confirm this view of themselves as being distant from federal executive agencies in a recent survey of the degree to which different jurisdictions found other levels of government helpful. Most cities, except those in the northeast, found Washington more helpful than their states. But suburbs indicated much more negative response than other jurisdictions. Thirty-four percent of the suburbs, as opposed to 14 percent of the central cities, claimed that neither government was helpful, although they much favored working with the states.[7]

If suburban influence on policy making is a matter mainly of congressional position, then does a suburban congressional bloc provide a force for coherence? The numerical majority for such a bloc has not really existed in the past. In the 90th Congress, 115 of the 435 congressmen came from cities of over 50,000 and 223 from rural or small town districts. Only 75 districts were more suburban than urban in character, while 22 were mixed. The roll call records of suburban congressmen during the Johnson administration also suggest the absence of a uniform suburban directive; rather, there were differences among suburban congressmen mainly traceable to party affiliation. If suburban representatives were cohesive, their votes would be alike; if not, other factors, such as party, should be shown more significant in shaping such votes.

In Table 14-1, the difference between party votes of 46 suburban congressmen on 18 Great Society issues is indicated. In ten (56 percent) of these bills, suburban congressmen divided sharply in terms of their party by as much as 70 percentage points. In only one out of six bills did party make little difference; in two (voting rights and presidential continuity) no suburban interest is detectable. Viewed in another way, the 22 members of the Democratic suburban delegation were in support of Great Society programs 81 percent of the time, while the 24 Republican cohorts were in support only 45 percent. The gap between the two delegations was even larger for 43 issues in foreign policy during the 89th Congress, 96 percent for the Democrats and 52 percent for the Republicans.[8]

The importance of party rather than locale is not just a product of position on Great Society issues. Table 14-2 shows that in all regions and jurisdictions in 1961, Democrats were supportive of a larger federal role and opposed to the conservative coalition. Party superseded locale on such diverse issues as food stamps (Table 14-3) and water pollution control (Table 14-4).

Some finer distinctions are possible, however, according to spatial location in the SMSA. As Sharkansky's analysis demonstrates, moving from congressional districts entirely within the core city outwards to those partly and then entirely in suburbia, there was during the mid- and early sixties a distinctive progression in the vote. There was decreasing support of municipal issues and of a large fed-

Table 14-1

Analysis of 18 Great Society Issues and the Suburban Vote by Party Differences 89th Congress, 1st Session

Range of Party Differences	N	%	Bill
90-100%	3	17	Defeat of GOP Proposal on Medicare Rent Supplements Authorization Anti-Poverty Program
80-89	2	11	Creation of HUD Rent Supplements Financing
70-79	5	28	House Rules Committee Change Appalachia Assistance Program Defeat of GOP Amendment on Foreign Aid Right to Work Provision Farm Program
60-69	0	0	—
50-59	3	17	Aid to Education Arts & Humanities Foundation District of Columbia Home Rule
40-49	2	11	Medicare Program Highway Beautification
30-39	0	0	—
20-29	0	0	—
10-19	1	6	Voting Rights
0-9	2	11	Immigration Revisions Presidential Continuity Amendment

Source: Calculated from *Congressional Quarterly Weekly*, 22 (August 21, 1964), 1787-98; and Ibid., 23 (October 29, 1965), 2179.

Table 14-2

Congressmen's Support of Larger Federal Role on 10 Issues, 1961, and Support of Conservative Coalition, by Region, Locale, and Party

	Urban		Suburban		Rural	
	R	D	R	D	R	D
	A. % Support of Larger Federal Role					
East	23	96	24	93	20	83
South	0	64	10	75	14	55
Midwest	4	99	5	97	5	91
West	8	99	0	98	20	97
	B. % Support of Conservative Coalition					
East	57	7	60	12	68	20
South	84	57	83	51	79	62
Midwest	83	10	80	12	83	27
West	74	10	87	12	65	15

Source: *Congressional Quarterly Weekly Report*, 20 (Feb. 21, 1962), 155.

Table 14-3
Congressmen's Support of Food Stamp Bill, 1963, By Locale and Party

	No. Reps.	% Pro Food Stamp (Final Passage)
Democrats		
Urban	94	90.4
Suburban	28	96.4
Rural	20	86.7
Republicans		
Urban	34	11.8
Suburban	35	11.4
Rural	107	74.7

Source: Frederick N. Cleveland, ed., *Congress and Urban Problems* (Washington, D.C.: The Brookings Institution, 1969), 305.

Table 14-4
Congressmen's Support of Water Pollution Control on Related House Roll Calls by Locale and Party

		Democrats			Republicans		
	Roll Calls	Rural	Sub	Urban	Rural	Sub	Urban
1959	Recommittal	85	100	93	9	21	0
1959	Passage	86	100	91	16	43	6
1960	Veto Override	85	93	96	11	15	6
1961	Recommittal	87	100	97	16	17	6
1961	Passage	86	100	97	50	53	33

eral role and an increasing support of the conservative congressional coalition.[9] This also appears to be the case with respect to the mass transit issue, where pro-transit votes decline sharply once outside metropolis, as seen in Table 14-5. In this case, the strongest Republican support did come from the suburbs; half the 30 suburban Republicans voted their "commuter" interests. But 17 of 18 Democrats did also, and in every other constituency overwhelmingly backed the bill. Suburbanites also represented the deviants from Republican ranks in supporting a larger federal role in juvenile delinquency control.[10] While it is evident that the suburbs do not emerge as a distinct general voting bloc, in selected instances of issues of special concern to suburbanites there is some specialization. However, as most analysis shows, party is the more important predictor of roll call behavior, although constituency does play a role in explaining deviant voting.[11]

Table 14-5
Congressmen's Support of House Transit Bill, 1963, By Locale and Party

Constituency	Democrats		Republicans	
	% Pro	All Ds	% Pro	All Rs
Urban	88.6	79	26.3	19
Mixed, Urban-Suburban	86.1	36	20.0	40
Suburban	94.2	18	50.0	30
Rural	61.2	103	6.3	79
Total	83.8	236	19.6	168

Source: Frederic N. Cleaveland, ed., *Congress and Urban Problems* (Washington, D.C.: The Brookings Institution, 1969), 345.

Many observers of suburban voting in Congress predict that the picture is likely to be different after 1972. Assuming the population estimates from the 1970 census bring about shifts in congressional representation, suburban congressmen will become the largest geographical group in the U.S. House of Representatives. One projection estimates that 129 representatives will come from suburbs, 62 from mixed urban-suburban districts, 100 from central cities and 144 from rural areas. If the mixed districts split evenly between core and rim, suburban congressmen will outnumber both those from cities and rural districts for the first time.

What does the changing size of suburban representation mean for national policy for the suburbs? Gerald Pomper argues that the shift in population will benefit conservative politicians; Richard Lehne asserts that suburban representatives will stand closer to their more liberal central city colleagues than to more conservative rural representatives on many issues.[12] As his data, shown in Table 14-6 indicates, looking at issues alone may suggest liberalism. Congress could be nudged away from recalcitrance on those liberal programs of particular concern to the suburbs, such as inter-city transportation, aid to education and in the future, air pollution control and perhaps congressional structural reform. But note the drop off in support for the Voting Rights Act recorded here, and, more important, the omission of controls for party. Suburbs may weigh heavily on specific issues, but party will in general be controlling, causing the overall record to defy any easy categorization of movements toward "liberalism" or "conservatism" in the Congress.

Of course, voting is not the only mechanism for expressing a unified interest. Organization is another. To the extent that suburbia is represented in the national arena beyond its congressional members, the role falls to the National League of Cities, which represents small and medium-sized cities. But the NLC has serious limits as a vehicle for interest articulation. It includes nonsuburban as well as suburban jurisdictions; its members are not mayors of cities but representatives of leagues of municipalities in different states; and, as a response to the influence

Table 14-6

Selected Role Call Votes After 1968, by Spatial Location

Bill	Central City	Outside Central City	Rural
		(Proportion in Favor)	
Housing and Urban Development Act (1968)	82%	65%	52%
Unspecified Food Stamp Funds	75	54	46
Cut Office of Economic Opportunity Funds	23	32	66
Family Assistance Program	80	77	33
Cut Mass Transit Funds	31	39	86
Freedom of Choice Busing	30	34	68
Voting Rights Act (1970)	80	65	34
Approval of Gun Control	82	83	25
Extend Farm Support Program	51	29	66
Limit Agricultural Payments	80	85	37

Source: Richard Lehne, "Warming Up for 1972," *Trans-Action*, Sept. 1971; p. 78.

of large cities, it has recently merged its staff with the U.S. Conference of Mayors.

The picture of action without coordination is slightly modified by the fact that there is, of course, some overlap in the different political groupings for making and administering policies which affect suburbs. Individuals are sometimes active in a variety of arenas. For example, Hugh Mields has served with the HHFA, the National Association of Housing and Redevelopment Officials, the NLC, the U.S. Conference of Mayors, and acted as chief consultant to Rep. Thomas Ashley (D-Ohio) in developing the new towns legislation in 1970. And, while suburbanites have shown little interest in positive federal action, many policies favorably affecting them are initiated by functional groups with specific interests in special programs. Here suburban interests are reflected in policy because they are paralleled by the concerns of important functional groups which in turn have influence in decision-making centers. When the passage of bills through Congress is at issue, the suburbanite is also protected by his congressmen to the extent that constituents feel threatened by federal action. But this influence is largely negative and reactive.

In sum, the federal role in suburbs is varied and contradictory because it arises from a number of separate sources, each with a life of its own. This is why Congress can enact areawide planning requirements, assist in growth policy, and also promote highway programs, FHA activities, and negotiated dispersal. What, then, is the result?

An Evaluation of National
Suburban Policy

There are very little reliable data on the consequences of various federal suburban programs. We shall endeavor here to trace some common understandings about these effects and then offer interpretations of how assumptions about suburbia have impact on federal policies. Finally, we shall try to specify the probable consequences of continuing the present line as opposed to alternatives based on recognition of suburban variety.

Consequences of Suburban Programs

Among possible criteria for evaluating suburban programs are Washington's own rationales for them. The overall national goal in this area is said to be provision of a "steadily improving environment which will permit the individual to maximize his choice of a decent dwelling, in a neighborhood of his choice, near economic opportunities he seeks and with equal opportunity to enjoy the educational, cultural and social services and amenities, which these parts of America's urban community may offer," according to the President's Task Force on Suburban Problems. From this perspective, the record of suburban programs is very mixed.

The most discussed impact of federal policy are indirect outcomes which have led to the very "creation" of the suburban pattern. While most accounts attribute a causal role to FHA,[13] it is difficult actually to prove that FHA and the Veterans Administration accelerated suburbanization *beyond what would have occurred as the product of other forces*. That is, FHA's role seems to be feeble in stimulating demand for suburban housing above the level established for boom periods without mortgage insurance.

For example, the National Bureau of Economic Research, studying the effects of FHA insurance on stimulating housing demand from 1934-1941 and 1948-1950, concluded that effects before the war were modest and after the war not evident. "The somewhat greater relative increase in mortgage debt in the post-World War II boom than in the expansion of the Twenties . . . suggests that the primary manifestation of the credit liberalization programs is found in construction costs and housing prices."[14] In addition, important as credit was to home buying, it was clearly not the only factor supporting the increased capability to buy single-family homes. Prosperity, lowering age of marriage, bias toward homeownership by the middle class and against holding of idle land by the wealthy contained in income tax provisions—all were apparently factors.[15]

A similar case can be made with respect to the interstate highway program.

Since it was enacted in 1956 and intercity routes were constructed first, it is hard to see how a program which began urban operation only in 1962 could "cause" the suburban boom. In addition, the current impact of the highway program is to cut wide concrete swaths in some suburbs. Nevertheless, it can be argued that at its initiation the highway program and the FHA underwrote suburban development, and that next to encouragement of homeownership, other federal thrusts were relatively minor.

If the impact of FHA on the ability of individuals to buy their own homes is difficult to assess, the impact on the "equal opportunity" goal sought by the task force is less so. Criticism has been constant of FHA as promoter of residential racial segregation between city and suburb. At the very least, its passive attitude toward directing the private housing and home finance industry away from policies which contribute to segregation continues to help a dual housing market persist. The U.S. Commission on Civil Rights charged in 1971 that FHA's administration of the two-year-old Section 235 housing program continued this trend. Section 235 provides subsidies for mortgage interest payments for good, dispersed housing for low- and moderate-income families. By April, 1971, 110,000 minority families had bought homes under the program. However black buyers are directed under administration of Section 235 into black neighborhoods, while "white buyers get the new 235 housing in the white suburbs," the Commission reported.[16]

It should be emphasized that such policies have permitted some individuals to maximize their choices of dwelling type and neighborhood. The overwhelming preference of the American family in housing is the single-family home, preferably self-owned and detached. To the extent that FHA has facilitated building such homes, it might get high marks despite its record on not making this life-style fully accessible to minorities. The most valid criticisms of suburban policy are thus its effect on racial and class polarization and the weakness of programs to deal with the resulting imbalances.

A sharp and crucial distinction is apparent between policies to promote suburban growth and current activities directed to control effects of such growth. Strategies for metropolitanization have relied almost exclusively on planning and creation of institutions. Thus, metropolitan aspects of the family of urban planning grants, and the review requirements that are largely responsible for the creation of areawide planning agencies and Councils of Government (COG) of local officials, virtually exhaust federal means to pursue metropolitan objectives. The one exception, the 205 program providing financial incentives for cooperative programing by suburban jurisdictions, has never been funded. In contrast, programs aimed at growth rely on direct benefits through grants to local jurisdictions. Thus there are the ever-popular grants for water and sewer construction, park and recreation development, and acquisition of open space. While planning is intended to control physical development of suburbs, stronger tools now actually serve to encourage further and uncoordinated growth.

Conflicting programs are not necessarily fatal, but in this case the crucial link-ing device—a metropolitanwide review of local jurisdiction applications for feder-al grants by an areawide agency fomented by HUD—has not overcome the pro-gram tension. While federal agencies report themselves satisfied with the 204 process, outside evaluators say that most areawide agencies do not effectively review applications—they simply assure their conformity to federal require-ments. In addition, the fields in which the most numerous review agencies—the COGs—concentrate their attention and the manner in which they make decisions mean that mainly short-range and noncontroversial projects are generated.[17] Thus, although there has been some attention to centralized police training by COGs to attack growing suburban crime problems, other problems have been ignored: important environmental conditions like noise pollution by aircraft, ref-use disposal and waste management, leveling tactics of land developers, and in-adequacies of recreational and open space preservation on the metropolitan edge. Land is the suburb's major resource, but the COGs have not been powerful enough to withstand pressure from urban investors, developers, and speculators to scar it. Indeed, the Suburban Task Force, whose chairman is an architect of the metropolitan planning legislation, recommended a new public corporation to attack the land problem because of the immediacy of pressures on land and the weakness of the COGs to protect it.[a] While federal policy has thus encouraged the rush to provide facilities that suburban citizens wanted, it has not prevented, either by regulation of private use or by incentive grants, suburban land from being "cut too fine and built too thick." The Suburban Task Force maintained that in the process we have destroyed the "sense of community" in suburbia as well as the environment.

Other federal programs noted in the preceding chapter have other conse-quences. Both the dispersal program and the new communities legislation are efforts to speak to problems which federal policy actually helped to create. Dis-persal is an effort to right the wrongs of spatial income and ethnic segregation. The new communities program is in part an attempt to realign land planning to overcome the ecological hazards of piecemeal building. But effort is not the same as result, and in these programs there are "miles to go and promises to

[a]The task force recommended a federal demonstration program of grants and long-term, moderate-interest loans to assist in the creation of State Land Development Corporations which would acquire land at key locations adjacent to tax supported improvements like highway interchanges, and prepare a unified plan for such high intensity uses as community centers or high-rise apartments. Sale or leasing of these high activity centers would remain in public hands. Although this is a departure from the usual public role in land development, several states had moved in this direction, even before the task force made its recommenda-tions. Maine has preempted zoning of all major industrial and commercial installations, Hawaii has a strong land-use law passed in 1961, and Wisconsin has established limited con-trol over private land development. State power over land development has also been as-serted in Massachusetts and Washington, but most strongly in the creation of the New York State Urban Development Corporation. New Jersey has attacked land problems in the Mead-owlands Commission Act. The task force also recommended a Federal Urban Parklands Cor-poration as a mechanism to acquire one million acres of land and water around urban areas.

keep." Both programs are receiving little support in the executive branch. Nor can it be safely predicted that they would actually serve to alter the current pattern. The simple removal of exclusionary restrictions will not provide low-income housing for blacks in the suburbs. The role of new communities in providing housing for the poor is also questionable. Derthick has observed:

Because the cost of new construction is high, because Congress is unwilling to supply large enough subsidies, because local governments give public housing low priority and because local citizen opposition often blocks acquisition of sites or construction, American governments have not managed to build much new housing for the poor . . . Building housing for the poor is no less of a problem because it is to be built as part of a new town.[18]

Another justification for new communities outside the central core is to improve the environment of the already better-off by changing the scale of suburban land planning. But, large-scale land development is not necessarily good development in suburbia. Enormous acreage is currently being developed by large nationwide corporations now appearing in the housing market building on the urban fringe in southwestern and western states where land is still cheap and plentiful. They often give little attention to the soundness of infrastructure, open space preservation or ecological balance, and less to social issues.[19] The large appliance conglomerate which invests in subdivisions looks on new houses as "cheap boxes in which to enclose appliances," yet these are the very companies most likely to develop federally supported new communities.[20] Therefore even if we disallow the stated equal opportunity goals of suburban housing policies as rhetoric which will allow practices favorable to suburban whites to proceed without opposition, the results for white suburbanites do not leave us sanguine.

The Impact of Assumptions: Suburban Myths and Policy Positions

Stereotypes of the American suburb we have identified as implicit in federal policy undoubtedly touch reality in some important dimensions of suburban experience. These stereotypes' fault is not so much in commission as in omission, for they cause us to ignore other dimensions, whose acknowledgement more fully describes suburban America. The most important omission concerns the fate of the poor in communities in *64* metropolitan areas where there is as much hardship in the *suburbs* as in the *city*—e.g., places around Pittsburg where in 1960 there were more substandard dwellings in suburbs than in the city, and communities around Los Angeles where there were more poor families in suburbs than in the core. That there is already a need for public action to help families living in older suburbs has so far received almost no attention. In part this is because relatively few *black* families are resident in suburbia in comparison with central cities—the Douglas Commission estimated the black population in the suburbs at 2.8 million, and projected it would jump to 6.8 million by 1985 but be lost in a sea of additions to white suburban population.[21] We have noted in chapter 4 the lack of change in the proportion of northern black suburbanites over a seventy year period, so this projection seems very reasonable. But the myopia about suburban poverty is not only a matter of numbers and race. It is also due to the difficulty of perceiving the conditions of those poor who do reside in suburbia in the face of the usual picture of wealthy white suburbanites.

Striking statistics on housing, employment, and income reveal that conditions are worse in suburbs where blacks do live than in central cities.[22] Even where in general these conditions do not hold, blacks in wealthy suburbs tend to be poorly integrated into networks of services and opportunities. A study of Nassau County, New York, recently found its poor residents disadvantaged by their isolation in neighborhoods far from public services, transportation, and information on how to negotiate the complex institutional environment.[23] Even as companion to—and not replacement for—aid to central cities, federal assistance to suburbs in meeting service costs arising from programs aiding low-income residents, or schemes to employ federal credit to protect homeowners against feared dangers of black neighbors,[24] are very difficult to grasp if one has only the view that all suburbs are rich and white.

Oversimplified notions of suburbia also may provide a basis on which even the best intentioned policies will soon be perverted. There is good reason for Washington to move against territorial divisions of races within urban areas. But given the controversial nature of dispersal strategies, weakness of executive support for dispersal programs, and difficulties of courts in devising adequate remedies for enforcing removal of exclusionary restrictions,[25] these efforts to spur opening suburbs to blacks and poor will mostly spur movement of blacks into *older* suburbs. That possibility requires clarification.

The number of such places is small but growing. In California, Compton is the classic example, but Richmond, Pasadena, Inglewood, Pomona, and Vallejo also have black populations growing faster than their net growth rate. What is striking about them is that they are beginning to take on the characteristics of core cities. That is, they have problems that cannot be resolved with their limited economic and physical capacities, and they are tending to be segregated much like the cities near them.[26] To the extent that such black suburbs can mobilize to apply for federal funds,[b] they may compete to participate in programs designed for central cities, as other poor suburbs have before them. But there is

---

[b]The first request for federal aid in Compton was not made until 1966, although its need for assistance was marked before that. The 1969 population of Compton was 78,000 of which 70 percent was black, as compared to a 1959 population of 48,000 of which 40 percent was black.

also a strong case for more positive government action in these older suburbs, to which poorer blacks and whites leaving central cities may migrate. The suburban stereotype tends to efface existence of these suburbs and thus the need for such assistance. But without it, one basic issue of the eighties may involve an effort to reduce disadvantages created by an accelerated movement of poor or black people to a suburbia in which they will find neither greater equality between races nor a chance for marked changes in social and economic status.

If, instead of the stereotype, we accept a more varietal view it becomes apparent that a number of different kinds of suburban problems coexist:

1. In some suburbs, bars to equal opportunity and access for all citizens arise from efforts to determine residential settlement patterns. These efforts are clearly at the expense of the well-being of residents in the central city of their metropolitan area.
2. In some suburbs, poverty, social isolation and segregation of suburban poor, as well as attendant overburdening of the "minority" suburbs, is already a reality.
3. In some suburbs, accommodation to population growth and spread has come at the cost of misuse of open land and fouling of air and water.
4. In some suburbs, distinctive or new problems are appearing, particularly juvenile crime and high costs of transportation in areas of low density and large space.

We may wish to rank these problems as more or less important, but we ought not, by emphasizing one, to deny that the others also exist.

Toward a National Suburban Policy?

Despite indirect benefits commonly associated with the federal suburban relationship, over time it appears that Washington's role has been not so much that of helpful partner as bumbling associate. In adopting a variety of contradictory assumptions about suburbs, the federal government has created public works programs which cut up suburban land and structural reforms which institutionalize the stalemate already existing in metropolitan regions, engendered little obedience to laws seeking to alter the segregated distribution of space, and little attention to the plight of the suburban poor.

It is likely that we need not wring our hands too hard over some of these problems. To the extent that distinctive suburban problems, particularly those involving misuse of natural resources, are recognized before it is too late to ameliorate them, urban state legislatures may well act. After years of submission to rural representatives, suburbanites have gained numerical power in such states as Illinois, New York, California, Pennsylvania, Michigan, and New Jersey. States may well respond to demands for protection of the land. And, to the extent that some suburbs actually do share problems with central cities, movements to promote programs to help simultaneously close-in suburbs as well as cities may begin to occur. Where suburban variety in state party affiliation exists and is related to variations in demographic conditions, a suburb-city alliance as well as a suburb-rural alliance are possible. Indeed, this seems already to be occurring in suburbs of New York, where Democratic candidates now commonly win legislative contests in Nassau and Westchester county districts. Interviews with political leaders there on their willingness to provide jobs and housing for inner city poor found them pointing instead to their own poverty problems and calling for aid for housing, transportation, welfare, and medical aid for the suburban poor.[27] Pleas for a national program of assistance are already emerging from suburbs which have never sought help from the federal government before. As one survey of suburbia noted in mid-1971:

The Nixon Administration has been pressing hard for decentralization and local solutions to the nation's troubles. But from Baltimore county to Cleveland's inner and outer cities, from Orange County to Houston and the Atlanta suburbs, mayors, county officials, planners, poverty workers and urbanologists all sounded the same note: without strong federal leadership and financial assistance, no dent can be made in a multitude of problems ranging from poverty, housing, and integration to sewers, pollution control, and population dispersal.[28]

What role should the federal government then play in the suburban world?[29] Given obvious inconsistencies among policies, one possibility would be to move toward *grant consolidation*. It can be argued that the specialized nature of each program with a suburban impact makes it difficult to provide balanced federal policy for such communities. Therefore, suburban programs should be reshaped into a few basic programs,[30] in which the impact of functional grants on jurisdictions is carefully assessed from an areal perspective. While a comprehensive look at the impact of federal policies on suburban areas has merit, efforts to consolidate programs may in the end not be worth the costs they would engender. The constituencies of each special program would resist collapsing their set of operations into a general scheme. Moreover, many inconsistencies identified in present programs result from the fact that they have been designed to work toward quite different objectives: increasing availability of single-family housing, providing assistance for suburban expansion, checking negative aspects of suburban sprawl, and providing housing opportunities for low-income families in suburbs. These objectives are often in conflict. Any program that tried to achieve all of them at the same time would probably rest on some very unstable compromises. The existence of programs with opposing goals and differing assumptions about what suburbia is like is, after all, not an inaccurate perspective on demographic and political variations in suburbia. Consolidation might eliminate some gaps in suburban-affecting programs, but it would probably not mark a fundamental change from the disaggregated federal approach to suburban policy.

Alternatively, a case can be made that grants-in-aid and tax rebate powers should be used by Washington to redraw local boundaries better to reflect the socioeconomic limits of city and suburb alike. It has been repeatedly urged that the federal government deal with suburbs as designations of place mainly by presiding over the destruction of their boundaries. In the fifties many political scientists advocated *metropolitan government* on grounds not dissimilar to that used to support the urban systems approach to national policy and dispersal programs. While recognizing that institutional changes do not provide easy answers for metropolitan problems, many still advocate some kind of metropolitan administrative unit and the use of federal programs to catalyze their creation.[31] The most widely discussed proposal for redesigning the present structure involves a two-level system in which some functions would be assigned in their entirety to an areawide government, others to a neighborhood unit, and others shared between the two. In this creation, municipal governments as they exist today could have little or no role if they did not encompass articulated communities. Suburban jurisdictions might do better than existing central city jurisdictions in retaining their identity, since they frequently represent the kind of community control for which city subgroups are clamoring, but the area as a whole would also be governed by a centralized unit.[32] Other advocates of revised structures for governance of metropolitan areas have suggested redrawn "metropolitan states," or at a minimum, organization of some functional programs on a metropolitan basis, such as those for housing.[33]

As we noted in earlier chapters, numerous studies of metropolitan reform efforts in the past have indicated metropolitan consolidation is politically unpopular at the local level. Given such local resistance, federal programs to promote metropolitanization will probably not produce great changes in the way things get done, unless the rewards and penalties of noncompliance are very great. The fate of programs mounted by the Office of Economic Opportunity and the Model Cities Administration, which sought to operate within boundaries other than the traditional municipal jurisdictions, is instructive. In one way or another these have been converted over time so that they fall under municipal officials' control. This casts further doubt on the political feasibility of programs which would tend to weaken municipalities at the behest of new metropolitan or neighborhood units.

It can also be argued that the kind of metropolitan decentralization in existence represents the way people in fact wish to live and that Washington has no right to manipulate programs to "force" change, be it to metropolitan jurisdictions or integrated communities. While much of the debate about what "force" implies is a cover for racial or class biases—and some ignorance—there is considerable doubt that Congress could pass direct legislation restricting zoning, revising outward the areal scope of municipal jurisdictions or compelling racial integration for all communities. Thus, despite the fact that many cooperative ventures among suburbs or between suburbs and central cities are now creating *de jure* metropolitan systems, the prospects for resolving inconsistencies in federal policy by encouraging them to be worked out at a metropolitan level in different areas are politically poor.

Given the protectiveness and insularity associated with the more accurately stereotyped suburbs, programs which *leave jurisdictional boundaries alone but attempt to affect life within them* appear more promising in the short run. The numbers of programs which have been proposed under this rubric defy complete listing. Examples include programs for: improving mobility in suburbia by developing special transportation systems to serve low- and moderate-density areas; assisting the move to suburbs by both homeownership assistance and rate subsidies to jurisdictions which accept such groups as the elderly, blacks, low-income families or Vietnam veterans; and insuring homeowners against losses in housing resale value due to racial integration. The most far reaching proposals leave boundaries alone but attempt to change key functions and styles associated with boundary maintenance. Such are proposals that Congress authorize federal preemption of local zoning where such action is necessary to provide sites for federally subsidized housing, or that Congress revise tax laws to expand tax advantages of homeownership to multiple unit dwellers in suburbs. Arguments about what function is most crucial and what scheme best alters it have raged for the last decade; reports of presidential commissions are replete with proposals along these lines.

If consolidation seems substantively unrealistic and metropolitan government politically infeasible, manipulative tinkering as described above totters on an expected failure of will. Programs aiming to alter key behaviors cannot be assumed automatically to help those they are supposed to assist. In the case of suburban programs, one reason is that these communities are not very dependent on federal grants. Thus, threats of withholding federal funds, unless the jurisdiction takes a particular action, are simply not credible.[34] Communities accept program grants mainly for things they wish to do and hence reject those which impose unacceptable costs. Congress has never offered enough bonus money or made conditions of noncooperation harsh enough to generate action. There is thus some doubt that we mean it in talking about altering behavior while leaving jurisdictional boundaries intact. This ambivalence is probably the death of such programs.

Two recent suggestions for federal programs attempt to get around this in different ways. One approach is to make funds available to suburbs of specific types. Such characterized a 1971 bill which referred to all municipalities but provided them community development grants according to their population, poverty, and overcrowding. Presumably poor suburbs would be favored over rich suburbs in such a grant system.[35] It is significant that in reports on the proposal,

Republicans objected to folding water and sewer grants into this package; as we noted in Table 13-2, these now go largely to wealthier communities. Alternatively, programs have been proposed which provide aid for functions not now well thought about or planned for in suburbs but nevertheless attractive to them. Thus, municipal efforts to suppress air traffic noise have been singled out as an area in which incentives to municipalities are needed but which would not require any more centralized governmental jurisdiction. This obviates the problem of ineffectiveness of the federal stick when lightly applied, but leaves open the question of what to do about actions that suburbs do not wish to undertake but which may nevertheless be deemed in the national interest.

At present, the most popular way out of this dilemma centers on a fourth stance. The federal government is urged to recognize that because suburbs are varied, interests of localities are less a matter of place than of group or individual interests and characteristics. The implication is that *federal programs should not be geared to jurisdictions but to groups or individuals, wherever they may reside.* Instead of funds being diverted to pay local administrative expenses, programs should put money directly into pockets of the people to be affected. This was the starting philosophy of the Nixon assistance program in the welfare field; it also lies behind proposals which would remove requirements for local government approval for using rent supplements. In addition, to the extent that specific problem areas for national action by such direct grants cannot be identified, communities would also receive shared revenues from Washington with no strings attached to aid them in pursuing local goals.[36] This proposal speaks to the very real financial plight of local units. It also is an attempt to restore the influence of geographical governmental jurisdictions (municipalities and states) and to decrease the role of functional "subgovernments," clusters of agencies and interest groups with common, specialized, programatic interests at the national, state, and local levels.

The impact of such proposals—divorcing the federal government from prescribing amenity levels for local jurisdictions or setting detailed unit costs and income limits and returning it to making fundamental decisions—would be salutary. But how many problems can or will be declared "national?" How many can actually be affected by direct subsidy? How well will even the somewhat invigorated geographical governments fare in controlling their fates when functional alliances continue to exist in many fields? And, in a system of national programing plus unrestricted revenue sharing, might we not in fact end with Washington relinquishing its national responsibilities, particularly in regard to integration of minorities?

Our view of what should be done is premised on our central theme, i.e., that the term "suburb" encompasses an enormous variety of jurisdictional types. Within this vast and varied world on the city's rim, federal activities should be selectively directed. Policy should be less focused on functional programs for those suburbs undergoing expansion and more on key social problems. This means less emphasis on assuring clean water and hygienic sewers and more on the status of the suburban poor, on service needs of poor suburbs, and on problems encountered in achieving interjurisdictional mobility for individuals.

One potentially important step has recently been taken toward meeting the service needs of poor suburbs in a California Supreme Court decision.[37] This averred that the state's public school financing system, which depends on local property taxes and leads to wide disparities in school revenues between jurisdictions (as in other states), violated the equal protection clause. The court's reasoning was that this funding scheme discriminates against the poor when it makes the quality of a child's education a function of the wealth of his parents and neighbors. In California, Beverly Hills could spend $975 per pupil for education, but Baldwin Park could afford only $522. Fundamental interests, such as the right to education in public school, may not be conditioned by jurisdictional wealth, the court declared. Six weeks later, a federal district court came to the same decision about Minnesota schools and their financing. Several other states will soon face similar litigation.

The states must now move to wipe out these disparities in financing, providing in some way for equal funds in poor and rich cities and suburbs. Remedial policy may move in the direction of a statewide property tax adjustment device; the property tax, more radical observers have suggested, might be abandoned entirely for its historical purpose and be replaced by industrial or business taxes. Clearly this raises problems of political feasibility in securing such changes.

There are a number of uncertainties in construing these recent decisions. One is the view of the U.S. Supreme Court on the matter and the extension of this principle to other states. Another is the impact of equal financing in actually equalizing educational opportunities and their products among and within districts with differing needs. A third looks even farther—under what conditions might this principle be extended to other governmental services?[c] Nevertheless, the case provides a beginning in the process of arriving at a system which will equalize financing for services among jurisdictions without unifying them or homogenizing life styles in all communities. Certainly the federal role in inducing such change should grow, at least for schools. Presently providing around 7 percent of the budget of American school districts, federal monies will be under pressures to increase. Revenue sharing may be the future course, or we may see some program modeled on the social security system, where federal funds reward state effort to meet national goals.

Helping poor suburbs is not the same as helping all the suburban poor, however. City service experiences indicate that areas and people within one governmental jurisdiction are frequently dissimilarly affected by "uniform" or citywide

[c]The Court intimates no views on other services but notes a decision by the Fifth Circuit Court of Appeals which forbids a town to discriminate racially in providing municipal services and suggests that wealth discrimination in providing all such services might also be invalid.

programs. Thus, the degree to which the federal government provides direct aid to individuals, particularly to low- and moderate-income households, is crucial for the future status of individuals with suburban addresses but without suburban images.

Individual mobility is the most difficult issue. Downs and others have suggested numerous tactics to "open up" the suburbs. These include the weakening of the power of small local units to block federally assisted housing by empowering areawide or state agencies to operate in the suburbs. The Housing Subcommittee of the U.S. House of Representatives has already adopted this strategy in part in its proposed legislation. We do not believe, however, that the federal government has the will either to directly right the inequities in mobility or even to make a substantial contribution to programs which would address the reasons for bottling up of low-income families; nor would it, at this time, commit the resources needed to overcome current growth patterns. Thus, in an ironic way, the chief nexus of a suburban policy which seeks to take the spotlight off the new expanding suburbs will probably be in just those places. It must at least be made certain that all the money to be spent for new construction outside central cities in the seventies and thereafter helps reduce, not magnify, the racial and economic segregation of metropolitan areas.

These policy references point up what is perhaps the major problem raised in this book. Scholars attest to a fact of suburban variety, but policy makers are either unaware of it or fail to reflect on its consequences. Such reflection, however, unless it be fragmentary and *ad hoc*, requires the use of a tested model of what urban-suburban change and stability mean. In the growing contact between the specialist, with his knowledge of urban life and change, and the policy maker, with his responsibility for reacting to demands for social change, there is some hope. But, as this book so clearly attests, the specialist's lack of an appropriate model for explaining his knowledge provides even more pessimism. It is no longer enough for both specialist and policy maker to know that there is variety both within and outside the city. Both must now confront the central issue of redefining that large and fast growing portion of the metropolis loosely called "suburbia" in a way which will help to change the conditions of life for its citizens.

Notes

Notes

Notes to Chapter 1

1. For a detailed presentation of the rules the Census Bureau uses in delineating these areas, see U.S. Bureau of the Census, *County and City Data Book, 1962* (Washington, D.C.: Government Printing Office, 1962), xi-xiii.

2. Jeffrey K. Hadden and Edgar F. Borgatta, *American Cities: Their Social Characteristics* (Chicago: Rand McNally, 1965), App. III.

3. John Sirjamaki, *The Sociology of Cities* (New York: Random House, 1964), 21, 35, 52; Eric Hoffer, *First Things, Last Things* (New York: Harper & Row, 1971), 81.

4. J.W. Thompson, *Economic and Social History of Europe in the Later Middle Ages* (New York: Century, 1931), 603.

5. Lewis Mumford, *The Culture of Cities* (New York: Harcourt, Brace and Co., 1938), 16; Alvin Boskoff, *The Sociology of Urban Regions* (New York: Appleton-Century-Crofts, 1962), 23.

6. Jean Gottman, *Megalopolis: The Urbanized Northeastern Seaboard of the United States* (New York: The Twentieth Century Fund, 1961), 168.

7. Carl Bridenbaugh, *Cities in the Wilderness: The First Century of Urban Life in America, 1625-1742* (New York: Ronald Press, 1938), 32-33.

8. Ibid., 118.

9. Ibid., 9, 98, 255.

10. Ibid., 24.

11. Ibid.

12. Gottman, op. cit., p. 211.

13. Bridenbaugh, op. cit., 305.

14. Ibid.

15. Edward C. Banfield, *The Unheavenly City* (Boston: Little, Brown, 1968), 25-26.

16. Ralph Weld, *Brooklyn Village, 1816-1834* (New York: Columbia University Press, 1938), 28, cited in Anselm L. Strauss, *Images of the American City* (New York: Free Press, 1961), 231.

17. Sam B. Warner, Jr., *Streetcar Suburbs: The Process of Growth in Boston, 1870-1900* (Cambridge: Harvard University Press, 1962), 18-19.

18. Richard C. Wade, *The Urban Frontier: Pioneer Life in Early Pittsburgh, Cincinnati, Lexington, Louisville, and St. Louis* (Chicago: University of Chicago Press, 1959), 22.

19. Ibid., 305.

20. The following references to Cincinnati, Louisville, St. Louis, Lexington are from ibid., 305-07.

21. Warner, loc. cit.

22. Christopher Tunnard and Henry H. Reed, *American Skyline* (Boston: Houghton-Mifflin, 1955), 169-71; and Warner, op. cit., 58.

23. Graham R. Taylor, *Satellite Cities* (New York and London: D. Appleton and Co., 1915) examines the early industrial suburbs, as does H. Paul Douglass, *The Suburban Trend* (London: Century Co., 1925). For a pungent description of Homestead and other Pittsburgh suburban milltowns, see Tunnard and Reed, op. cit., 165-66.

Notes to Chapter 2

1. There is an extensive literature on this conflict, ranging from the research of W.I. Thomas and F. Znaniecki, *The Polish Peasant in Europe and America* (Boston: Badger, 1918-1920), 5 vols., to the more concise Maldwyn A. Jones, *American Immigration* (Chicago: University of Chicago, 1960) or the more passionate Oscar Handlin, *The Uprooted* (New York: Gossett & Dunlap, 1951). The focus may be upon the individual, as in E.V. Stonequist, *The Marginal Man* (New York: Scribner's Sons, 1937), and in innumerable novels; or it may be upon the group, as in W. Lloyd Warner and L. Srole, *The Social Systems of American Ethnic Groups* (New Haven: Yale University Press, 1945), or Stephen Birmingham, *Our Crowd* (New York: Harper & Row, 1967), which we cite later at 293.

2. Don Martindale, "Prefatory Remarks: The Theory of the City" in Max Weber, *The City*, translated and edited by Don Martindale and Gertrude Neuwirth (New York: The Free Press, 1958), 9-10.

3. John Sirjamaki, *The Sociology of Cities* (New York: Random House, 1964), 115.

4. Jean Gottman, *Megalopolis* (New York: Twentieth Century Fund, 1961), 234.

5. U.S. Census of Population, 1960, *Final Report PC(3)-10*, and *Current Population Reports, Series P-20, No. 163* (March 27, 1967).

Although they are compelling enough, census statistics may actually underestimate the magnitude of suburban migration. A core city may grow both in territory and in population by absorbing the suburbs that hug its borders. After annexation, any population increase in the newly enclosed suburb is spuriously credited to the central city. Newer cities bordered by unincorporated settlements have greater opportunities for annexation than the older cities, which are surrounded by incorporated municipalities. In a painstaking analysis which explicitly allowed for the distortions caused by annexation, Leo F. Schnore has demonstrated that suburban "rings grew over forty times as fast as the cities . . . bounded in 1950, and that they captured over 97 per cent of the total metropolitan increase." *The Urban Scene: Human Ecology and Demography* (New York: The Free Press, 1965), 119.

6. Harry Sharp and Leo F. Schnore, "The Changing Color Composition of Metropolitan Areas," *Land Economics*, 38 (1962), 171.

7. By the Census Bureau's definition, a city must have at least 50,000 population to be considered as the core city of a SMSA. This decision pitches Detroit and Manchester, New Hampshire, into the same bin. Most people would agree that Detroit can lay greater claim to the status of a metropolitan center than Manchester.

In a thoughtful essay, Daniel J. Elazar has traced some other strange consequences that flow from official census definitions. For example, the Census Bureau establishes 2,500 people as the lower limit of an "urban place." This definition has been exploited to show that we are a "nation of cities" because over 70 per cent of the population lives in urban places. To produce this result, Bolivar, Tennessee (1960 population: 3,338) is considered an "urban place." So is Boston. That many more Americans know of Boston than Bolivar says a great deal about the inadequacy of the definition. See "Are We A Nation of Cities?" in Robert A. Goldwin (ed.), *A Nation of Cities: Essays on America's Urban Problems* (Chicago: Rand McNally, 1966), 89-114.

8. Patricia Leavy Hodge and Philip M. Hauser, *The Challenge of America's Population Outlook—1960 to 1985* (Washington, D.C.: Research Report No. 3, National Commission on Urban Problems, 1968), 7.

9. Raymond Vernon, "Urban Change and Public Opinion," in Michael N. Danielson (ed.), *Metropolitan Politics* (Boston and Toronto: Little, Brown, 1966), 28-29.

Robert A. Gordon, in elaborating some of these trends, argues that the prosperity of the twenties in great measure was a function of the motor car. Its effects rippled widely through many diverse sectors of private and public enterprise. It stimulated investment and employment in steel, oil refining, tires and rubber, cement and asphalt, and building materials. On the public side, it encouraged rapid expansion in highways, bridges and tunnels, benefiting the large contractors who built them. See his "Cyclical Experience in the Interwar Period: The Investment Boom of the Twenties," *Conference on Business Cycles* (New York: National Bureau of Economic Research, 1951), 190.

10. Vernon, op. cit., 31.

11. Developers bypassed land just outside the settled areas for a number of reasons, which varied from case to case. In some instances, title to this land was clouded; in others, the topography was unsuitable. Sometimes, it was impossible to assemble enough land because one unwilling seller could hold up an entire project indefinitely. See Edgar M. Hoover and Raymond Vernon, *Anatomy of a Metropolis* (Garden City, New York: Anchor Books, 1962), 128. In recent years there has emerged a new factor. As limited access express ways have carried a greater share of commuter traffic, suburban developers are under a compulsion to locate their subdivisions near widely separated interchanges.

12. Ibid., 110-20.

13. James D. Tarver has measured the extent of the shift in the immediate postwar period. The percentage increase in dollar value of retail sales was greater in the suburbs than in core city. See his "Suburbanization of Retail Trade in the

Standard Metropolitan Areas of the United States, 1948-1954," *American Sociological Review*, 22 (August, 1957), 429-33.

14. Hoover and Vernon, op. cit., 32-40.

15. Vernon, op. cit., 32.

16. The industrial suburb, as we pointed out in chapter 1, is not new. It was first examined in 1915 by Graham R. Taylor, *Satellite Cities* (New York: Appleton, 1915), while in 1925, Harlan Paul Douglass differentiated between "the suburb of consumption," which imports goods and exports labor services, and the "suburb of production," the industrial suburb in which the export-import flows are reversed. See his *The Suburban Trend* (New York: Century, 1925), 84-85. Chauncey D. Harris, in a pair of articles published seven years later, made the same distinction. See his "Suburbs," *American Journal of Sociology*, 49 (1943), 1-13 and "A Functional Classification of Cities in the United States," *Geographical Review*, (1943), 88-89. Based on the 1958 Census of Business and Manufacturing, Victor Jones, Richard L. Forstall, and Andrew Collver concluded that manufacturing is the dominant form of business activity in almost half of all American suburban municipalities over 10,000 in population. Doubtless, including suburbs with less than 10,000 people would depress this percentage somewhat, but the figure would still be astonishingly high for those brought up on the notion that suburbs are middle-class compounds. See *National Municipal Yearbook, 1963* (Chicago: International City Managers' Association, 1963), 87-92 and table on 97.

17. Herbert Gans, "The White Exodus to Suburbia Steps Up," *The New York Times Magazine*, January 7, 1968.

Notes to Chapter 3

1. Jeffrey K. Hadden and Edgar F. Borgatta, *American Cities: Their Social Characteristics* (Chicago: Rand McNally, 1965), 107-10. It should be noted that they rest their comparisons on 227 suburbs with a 1960 population of 25,000 or more. They omitted suburban municipalities of fewer than 25,000 people as well as rural portions of SMSAs. In the aggregate, these exclusions would probably tend to cancel one another. Even if we concede that residents of smaller suburban communities are somewhat better educated and paid than those in the suburbs tallied by Hadden and Borgatta, income, education, and occupational standing all fall off in the semi-rural zone between outer margins of the urbanized area and the county line that marks boundaries of the SMSA. Income levels in bigger metropolitan areas run higher in urbanized areas outside central cities and then fall off sharply as population thins out in the outer ring. See Otis Dudley Duncan and Albert J. Reiss, Jr., *Social Characteristics of Urban and Rural Communities, 1950* (New York: John Wiley, 1956), 129-30 and 118-19.

2. Leo Schnore, "The Socio-Economic Status of Cities and Suburbs,"

American Sociological Review, 28 (1963), 76-85. In his introduction, Schnore made the telling point that aggregating data for all central cities and all suburbs gives disproportionate weight to the most populous metropolitan regions. Comparing each core city only with its adjacent suburbs is an efficient way of nullifying the overwhelming effects of sheer population size.

3. Schnore has presented data for central cities containing more than 100,000 inhabitants which show that North Central cities lagged behind those in the Northeast in decentralizing their populations. See "The Timing of Metropolitan Decentralization: A Contribution to the Debate," *The Journal of the American Institute of Planners*, 25 (1959), 203

4. Some indeterminate part of the difference is spurious. Core cities in the South and West have expanded territorially by annexing outlying areas, whether incorporated or not. For a number of reasons, those in the Northeast and North Central states have found it especially difficult to annex adjacent territory. It is reasonable to suppose that prospects of adding lucrative sources of revenue to augment the city's taxable base would make core city politicians particularly anxious to absorb adjacent territory inhabited by people who are relatively well off. Schnore's data show that those cities which have added the largest increments to their population by annexation also have proportionately more people living in the urban core than in the urbanized portion of suburban rings. See his "Urban Structure and Suburban Selectivity," *Demography*, 1 (1964), 172-73. For data showing how much of the reported suburban growth is actually due to annexation, see his "Annexations and Growth of Metropolitan Suburbs," *The American Journal of Sociology*, 67 (1962), 410.

5. The relevant data are found in ACIR, op. cit., 171-74.

6. Schnore, "Urban Structure and Suburban Selectivity," loc. cit., 164-76. Schnore's subtle index allows more refined discriminations than is possible by a simple comparison of adults completing some years of formal schooling. His index makes it possible to differentiate among four major patterns. They are:

1. a heavy concentration of lowest educational classes in the city,
2. a heavy concentration of highest educational classes in the city,
3. a heavy concentration of both highest and lowest educational classes in the city, and
4. a heavy concentration of both highest and lowest educational classes in suburbs.

Conventional measures resemble the first two categories but fail to take the remaining two possibilities into account.

Although we are chiefly interested in noting major differentials, Schnore found southern urbanized areas were fairly evenly divided among the first three, while those in the western region fell predominantly in the first and third. Overall, 90 urbanized areas (45 percent of the total) were characterized by the first pattern; of these, a full third were in the Northeast, with most of the remainder in North Central states. As might be expected, largest and oldest areas accounted for the largest share of all areas fitting the first pattern.

7. They have been elaborated in extensive detail by ACIR, loc. cit. Of particular interest are the data on housing, which conform to the regional status differences we have traced. For example, the really wretched, owner-occupied housing is found in the suburbs in the South and West, and in the city in the Northeast and North Central states, as is shown in the table at 185.

8. Robert L. Lineberry and Edmund P. Fowler have made the same criticism. Looking at regional variations alone may be useful as a first approximation, but it cannot substitute for more detailed analyses. The dominant reason is that all sorts of important *within-region* variations are suppressed once the decision is made to penetrate no further. Atlanta and Birmingham are both in the South. Apart from their common locations, they resemble one another as much as chalk does cheese. See "Reformism and Public Policies in American Cities," *American Political Science Review*, 61 (1967), 706-07.

9. Leo F. Schnore, "The Socio-Economic Status of Cities and Suburbs," loc. cit., 83-85.

10. Metropolitan Life Insurance Company, "Socio-Economic Patterns in Large Metropolitan Areas," *Statistical Bulletin*, 45 (1964), 1-3.

11. "The Social and Economic Characteristics of American Suburbs," in *The Urban Scene* (New York: The Free Press, 1965), 169-83.

12. A good if impressionistic account of these exurban communities is given by A.C. Spectorsky, *The Exurbanites* (Philadelphia: J.P. Lippincott, 1955).

13. Much the same finding results with more sophisticated analytic techniques, such as factor analysis, can be found in Benjamin Walter and Frederick M. Wirt, "Social and Political Dimensions of American Suburbs," in Brian J.L. Berry (ed.), *Classification of Cities: New Methods and Alternative Uses* (New York: Wiley, 1972).

Notes to Chapter 4

1. Data on the following Los Angeles suburbs are drawn from John J. Kirlin, "The Migration of Racial Minorities to Los Angeles Suburbs and Their Impact on Municipal Expenditures, 1960-1970," mimeo ms., August, 1971.

2. Patricia L. Hodge and Philip M. Hauser, *The Challenge of America's Population Outlook—1960 to 1985* (Washington, D.C.: National Commission on Urban Problems, 1968), Research Report No. 3, 26.

3. Morton Grodzins, *The Metropolitan Area as a Racial Problem* (Pittsburgh: University of Pittsburgh Press, 1958), 1-3.

4. Harry Sharp and Leo F. Schnore, "The Changing Color Composition of Metropolitan Areas," *Land Economics*, 38 (1962), 180-85. John M. Strange has noted that migration was the most important reason explaining black population increase in metropolitan areas during the forties, accounting for some 70 percent of the total. Although the urban black population continued to climb during the

fifties, the proportion attributable to migration tailed off to only 42 percent, natural growth accounting for the rest. The white exodus to the suburbs selected many couples in their child-bearing years; indeed, a good many went there because they thought it was a good place to rear their young. In many cities the median black age is ten years younger than the median white age. See his "Racial Segregation in the Metropolis," in Michael N. Danielson (ed.), *Metropolitan Politics: A Reader* (Boston: Little, Brown, 1966), 41-52.

5. John H. Kain and Joseph J. Persky, "Alternatives to the Gilded Ghetto," *The Public Interest* (Winter, 1969), 84.

6. See Reynolds Farley, "The Changing Distribution of Negroes within Metropolitan Areas: The Emergence of Black Suburbs," *American Journal of Sociology*, 75 (1970), 512-29.

7. Karl E. Taeuber, "The Effect of Income Redistribution on Racial Residential Segregation," *Urban Affairs Quarterly* (1968), 7-8. Further evidence of this segregation is found in Farley, loc. cit.

In line with our earlier note about misleading growth rates, it is interesting to note that, from 1910 to 1960, the black population in suburbs of Cleveland increased by 1200 percent. Over the same period, the white population increased ninefold. Yet the representation of blacks in the suburban population of Cleveland was no larger in 1960 than it had been in 1910.

8. Karl E. and Alma F. Taeuber, "White Migration and Socioeconomic Differences between City and Suburb," *American Sociological Review*, 29 (1964), 718-29. Fuller analyses of the situation by 1960 are found in the Taeubers' *Negroes in Cities* (Chicago: Aldine, 1965), and Leo Schnore, *The Urban Scene* (New York: The Free Press, 1965), chs. 13-16.

9. U.S. Bureau of the Census, *Social and Economic Characteristics of the Population in Metropolitan and Nonmetropolitan Areas: 1970 and 1960* (Washington, D.C.: Government Printing Office, 1971), Current Population Reports No. 37, Table D, at 7.

10. See the careful analysis for this finding in loc. cit. While not having 1970 census data available, Farley predicted the reversal for income measures; however, the 1970 census showed a city advantage for black education still to exist; see source in note 9 at 4. For a specialized study of this shift in New Haven, see David L. Birch, "Toward a Stage Theory of Urban Growth," *Journal of the American Institute of Planners*, 37 (1971), 78-87.

11. See source in note 9, Table C at 4. As this table shows, however, this surge has not yet worked its way through to college. While in all places more blacks have more college education, the increase over 1960 is quite small. The best is in non-SMSA areas, from 5.0 to 8.9 percent, 1960 to 1970; such areas had the largest proportion of college educated blacks in both censuses, while suburbs had the lowest (4.2 vs. 5.3 percent).

12. Farley, loc. cit.

13. Kirlin, loc. cit.

14. Kain and Persky, op. cit., 75-76.

15. Farley, op. cit., 525-26 briefly explores these explanations.

16. Lynn W. Eley and Thomas W. Casstevens (eds.), *The Politics of Fair-Housing Legislation: State and Local Case Studies* (San Francisco: Chandler, 1968), 15; this work includes two studies of suburbs where opposing actions occurred, in Berkeley and Ann Arbor. Note the poll evidence that the coming generation is far less prejudiced in this matter, a factor which, combined with giving of the vote to 18 year olds, may change referenda results around the country. For a Boston study, see Alan H. Schechter, "The Impact of Open Housing Laws on Suburban Realtors," paper presented to the American Political Science Association, 1971.

17. The federal law is Title VIII, Civil Rights Act of 1968, 82 *Stat* 81 (1968). For criticism of enforcement, see U.S. Commission on Civil Rights, *The Federal Civil Rights Enforcement Effort* (Washington, D.C.: Government Printing Office, 1970), note 4.

18. This theme is examined in many aspects in Frederick M. Wirt and Willis D. Hawley (eds.), *New Dimensions in Freedom in America* (San Francisco: Chandler, 1969).

19. Joseph D. Mooney, "Housing Segregation, Negro Employment and Metropolitan Decentralization," *Quarterly Journal of Economics* (1969), 299-311.

20. See Farley, op. cit., 517-18, 521-24.

21. Bernard J. Frieden, "Blacks in Suburbia: The Myth of Better Opportunities," paper presented at Conference on Metropolitan Governance, Resources for the Future, October, 1970. Frieden notes the wide variation in suburban school expenditures, which are lower where the black proportion is higher, thus, $522 in Baldwin Park vs. $975 in Beverly Hills. This reality underlies a decision by the California Supreme Court, August 31, 1971, declaring unconstitutional the local property tax because of its unequal effects upon educational opportunity.

22. See Theodore J. Lowi, *The End of Liberalism* (New York: Norton, 1969), ch. 3 on the efficacy of economic policy; for that of federal laws on voting and schooling, see Frederick M. Wirt, *Politics of Southern Equality: Law and Social Change in a Mississippi County* (Chicago: Aldine, 1970).

23. For explication, see Wirt, op. cit., chs. 14-15.

24. William M. Dobriner, *Class in Suburbia* (Englewood Cliffs, New Jersey: Prentice-Hall, 1963), 13.

25. Bennett M. Berger, "Suburbia and the American Dream," *The Public Interest* (Winter, 1966), 80-91.

26. Stanley Lieberson, "Suburbs and Ethnic Residential Patterns," *American Journal of Sociology*, 68 (1963), 673-81.

Notes to Chapter 5

1. *Time*, November 17, 1952, 24. As it happens, the Republican share of suburban Cook County ballots was actually *smaller* in 1952 than in 1920, 67 vs.

84 percent. However, absolute numbers rather than percentages count for victories in elections, and the suburban contribution to Eisenhower's plurality in 1952 was greater than it had been to Harding's three decades before.

2. See Edward C. Banfield, "The Changing Political Environment of Urban Planning," summarized in Robert C. Wood, *Suburbia: Its People and Their Politics* (Boston: Houghton Mifflin, 1959), 140.

3. Many readers think that this sketch falls halfway between caricature and parody. It does not. Consider Eugene Burdick's paradigmatic Joe Wilson of suburban Burlingame, who once was known in Pittsburgh as Jere Wilzewski. He becomes a white-collar worker, leaves for the suburb and, among other things, starts reading *Fortune* magazine instead of the funny papers. The new Wilsons "put a Dewey sticker on their car and eagerly said harsh things about Truman, and finally even began to reconstruct their memory of Roosevelt and remembered him as socialist, father of much-marrying children, fomenter of discontent, upsetter of the peace, and heard and believed that Eleanor had never loved him." See his *The Ninth Wave* (Boston: Houghton Mifflin, 1956), 286.

Much the same sort of satirical archetype of the New Suburban Man can be found in Louis Harris, *Is There a Republican Majority?: Political Trends, 1952-1956* (New York: Harper and Brothers, 1954), especially 118-39. In Harris' book, the grandson of an equally fictional Lladislaw Repulski becomes Jimmy Ripple, name-changing evidently being a very popular custom among new suburban residents. Note, however, that it is Joe and Jimmy, not Joseph and James. The émigrés strive for respectability without achieving it; both men fall between the slats, not quite Slav, not quite WASP. Also see William H. Whyte, *The Organization Man* (New York: Simon & Schuster, 1956) for an influential presentation proclaiming the pervasiveness of a bland but invincible suburban conformity.

4. As presented in op. cit., 141-49. The first variant of the theory is presented on pp. 141-42; the second, on pp. 142-49.

5. Samuel Lubell has proposed an ingenious and plausible variation. Those who attained middle-class status while Democrats were in power saw no compelling reason to shift parties. Another cohort of voters made the passage into the spreading middle class while Eisenhower was in the White House and looked to Republicans for stability and continued prosperity. With its political attachments intact, each group moved to a compatible suburb. See his *Revolt of the Moderates* (New York: Harper and Brothers, 1956), 62. Perhaps alone among commentators of the era, he recognized the importance of ethnically different suburbs, little more than big city enclaves placed in a country setting.

6. So far as we are able to tell, Wood was the first scholar to perceive the difference between two versions of the transplantation thesis. Noting the thin empirical support for either theory, Wood scrupulously avoids taking sides. The fragmentary evidence he brings to bear is, on the whole, more consistent with the second version of the transplantation thesis than the first. Op. cit., 146-49.

7. Even these figures may spuriously inflate the increase in the suburban

Republican vote. The comparisons are made between the core city and the remainder of the SMSA, rather than the core city and the urban fringe. As we noted in the first chapter, the SMSA takes entire counties in its sweep. It includes, therefore, more rural sectors of counties situated in the rim of the metropolitan region. Not only do they contain only a slight fraction of the entire suburban population, but they are also likely to be steadfastly Republican to begin with. In a study which uses a more restricted and demographically accurate definition of a "suburban residential belt," Bernard Lazerwitz had discovered that the suburban residential belt revealed both a smaller proportionate increase in Republican vote than *either* the core city or more rustic portions of the metropolitan region. In fact, Democrats held fast in suburbs between 1948 and 1956. As might be expected, Republicans did best in more thinly populated portions of the metropolitan region.

The significance of any comparison must be considered in light of the aggregating procedures. See Lazerwitz, "Suburban Voting Trends: 1948 to 1956," *Social Forces*, (1960), 29-36.

8. Jerome C. Manis and Leo C. Stine, "Suburban Residence and Political Behavior," *Public Opinion Quarterly* (Winter 1958-1959), 485-89. The inference in the portion we have quoted is not as sharp as one might wish. *All* party switchers might have come here before 1952, but evidently coding procedures did not permit this discrimination to be made.

9. Bennett M. Berger, *Working-Class Suburb: A Study of Auto Workers in Suburbia* (Berkeley and Los Angeles: University of California Press, 1960), 37. Also see Wood, op. cit., 152, for parallel findings from a survey of St. Louis voters.

10. Angus Campbell, Philip E. Converse, Warren E. Miller, and Donald E. Stokes, *The American Voter* (New York and London: John Wiley and Sons, 1960), 456-60. In recomputing data showing lack of association between social mobility and switching party identifications, we have omitted respondents who no longer acknowledged any identification with either party. Erstwhile Democrats were more likely to become Independents than former Republicans, whether they were traveling up or down the occupational status ladder.

11. Documentation for what follows is voluminous. For a convenient and penetrating summary of Survey Research Center studies of the American electorate, see Angus Campbell, "A Classification of American Elections," in Angus Campbell, Philip E. Converse, Warren E. Miller, and Donald E. Stokes, *Elections and the Political Order* (New York: John Wiley and Sons, 1966), 63-77.

12. *The American Voter*, 463.

13. For a fuller exposition based on these assumptions, see Kevin Phillips, *The Emerging Republican Majority* (New York: Arlington House, 1969).

14. David Apter, "Ideology and Discontent," in Apter (ed.), *Ideology and Discontent* (Glencoe, Ill.: The Free Press, 1964), 15-43; Walter Dean Burnham, *Critical Elections and the Mainsprings of American Politics* (New York: W.W. Norton and Company, 1970), 140-43.

15. In a brief analysis of the voting behavior of Philadelphia suburbs in Delaware county, Burnham shows this clearly. Blue-collar suburbs in the industrial belt along the Delaware River went heavily for Kennedy in 1960 but drifted towards Wallace in 1968. White-collar municipalities further inland voted for Nixon in 1960 and contributed very few votes to Wallace eight years later. Op. cit., 145-53.

Notes to Chapter 6

1. "Ecological Correlations and the Behavior of Individuals," *American Sociological Review*, 15 (1950), 351-57. For an interesting bypass of the problem, however, see W. Phillips Shively, " 'Ecological' Inference: The Use of Aggregate Data to Study Individuals," *American Political Science Review*, 63 (1969), 1183-96.

2. *Municipal Year Book 1963* (Chicago: International City Managers Association, 1963), 97.

3. Augus Campbell, Gerald E. Gurin, and Warren E. Miller, *The Voter Decides* (Evanston, Illinois: Row, Peterson and Company, 1954), 74.

4. Ibid,, 70-72.

5. Ibid.

6. For the 407 suburbs appearing in the 1960 Census, the correlation between median family income and the proportion of all families earning more than $10,000 a year came to .93. The correlation between median annual family income and the proportion of poor families reached $-.61$, and the correlation between proportions of rich and poor households came to $-.55$.

7. Choice of occupational status as the single criterion of status polarity may seem arbitrary. But, as Campbell et al., note, occupational differences were so highly correlated with income and educational measures that it made very little difference which objective measure of status polarization was finally used as the independent variable. See ibid., 344-5.

8. Angus Campbell, "A Classification of Elections," in Campbell, Philip E. Converse, Warren E. Miller, and Donald E. Stokes, *Elections and the Political Order* (New York: Wiley, 1966), 64-69.

9. Walter Dean Burnham, *Critical Elections and the Mainsprings of American Politics* (New York: W.W. Norton and Company, 1970), 146-7.

10. Explanation and development of this methodology are found in Benjamin Walter and Frederick M. Wirt, "Social and Political Dimensions of American Suburbs," in Brian J.L. Berry (ed.), *Classification of Cities: New Methods and Alternative Uses* (New York: Wiley, 1972), 97-123.

11. As further evidence, we may note that Republicans migrating to the Democratic Far West in the fifties remained Republican in their political allegiances. Again, new environments did not appreciably alter old convictions. See Campbell et al., *The American Voter*, 447-8.

Notes to Chapter 7

1. Charles Edson, "The Suburban Vote," senior honors thesis, Harvard University, May, 1955. Summarized in Robert C. Wood, *Suburbia: Its People and Their Politics* (New York: Houghton Mifflin, 1958), 144-5.

2. G. Edward Janosik, "The New Suburbia," *Current History* (1956), 91-95.

3. Louis Harris, *Is There A Republican Majority?: Political Trends, 1952-1956* (New York: Harper and Brothers, 1954), 122.

4. David Wallace, "Shifts in One Suburb's Voting Patterns," *Public Opinion Quarterly*, 26 (1962), 486-7.

5. Ralph A. Straetz and Frank J. Munger, *New York Politics* (New York: New York University Press, 1960), 41-45.

6. Op. cit., 146-9.

7. Philip E. Converse, "Information Flow and the Stability of Partisan Attitudes," 26 *Public Opinion Quarterly* (1962). As Donald E. Stokes and Gudmund R. Iversen have shown, the movement of the presidential vote since the Civil War has persistently been more volatile than the movement of the congressional vote. See their "On the Existence of Forces Restoring Party Competition," ibid., 26 (1962), 159-71.

8. At one time, political theorists tended to assume that the "popular will" or the "will of the majority" could be ascertained directly through elections or by counting votes in a representative assembly. No permanent organization intervened between individual citizen and decision-making body. For a sample of theorists who recognize the importance of regular party competition for maximizing political equality and responsiveness, see A.D. Lindsay, *The Modern Democratic State* (London: Oxford Press, 1943); Robert M. MacIver, *The Web of Government* (New York: Macmillan Co., 1947); Joseph A. Schumpeter, *Capitalism, Socialism and Democracy* (New York: Harper and Brothers, 1942); and Anthony Downs, *An Economic Theory of Democracy* (New York: Harper and Brothers, 1957).

9. Joseph Schlesinger, "A Two-Dimensional Scheme for Classifying the States According to Degree of Inter-Party Competition," *American Political Science Review*, 49 (1955), 1120-28.

10. "Inter-Party Competition, Economic Variables, and Welfare Policies in the American States," *The Journal of Politics*, 25 (1963), 273.

11. Ibid., 271.

12. *Political Parties in the American System* (Boston: Little, Brown, 1964), 16.

13. "The American Party Systems," *American Political Science Review*, 68 (1954), 477-85.

14. Schlesinger, op. cit., 112.

15. The authors wish to express their thanks to Virginia C. Kennedy who worked on the development of a similar method. See her Master's thesis, "The

Concept and Measurement of Inter-Party Competition in the American Party System," Vanderbilt University, January, 1967. Our discussion owes much to her insight and perseverance.

16. Op. cit., 16-17.

17. Writings in the late fifties on the "dominant life style" of suburban communities are more interesting as problems in the sociology of knowledge than they are as sociology. Together, they form a sort of Veblenesque criticism of a way of life found repellent by the critics. In addition to the obsessive concern shown by suburban fathers in clipping shrubbery and manicuring lawns, other sins cataloged by critics include a sort of marshmallow Protestant religion, with sleek preachers talking inoffensively and ecumenically about the latest Book-of-the-Month; a neurotic fascination with child-feeding; and a frenetic involvement in all sorts of community activities, hospital linen drives being particularly noxious exhibitions of bad taste. For a brilliant critique of this literature, see Scott Donaldson, *The Suburban Myth* (New York: Columbia University Press, 1969). Donaldson claims that liberal commentators looking for a scapegoat to explain away Stevenson's two defeats landed on the suburbs, already known to be intolerable on cultural and esthetic grounds.

Notes to Chapter 8

1. Joseph Zikmund, "A Comparison of Political Attitudes and Activity Patterns in Central Cities and Suburbs," *Public Opinion Quarterly*, 31 (1967), 69-75.

2. Amos H. Hawley and Basil G. Zimmer, *The Metropolitan Community: Its People and Government*, (Beverly Hills, California: Sage, 1970).

3. John Orbell, "The Impact of Metropolitan Residence on Social and Political Orientations," *Social Science Quarterly*, 51 (1970), 634-48.

4. John Orbell and Kenneth Sherrill, "Racial Attitudes and the Metropolitan Context: A Structural Analysis," *Public Opinion Quarterly*, 33 (1969), 46-54.

5. For an over-view of the methodological literature on contextual analysis, see Tapani Valkonen, "Individual and Structural Effects in Ecological Research," in Mattei Dogan and Stein Rokkan, eds., *Quantitative Ecological Analysis in the Social Sciences*, (Cambridge, Massachusetts: The M.I.T. Press, 1969).

6. See Arnold S. Tannenbaum and Jerald G. Bachman, "Structural versus Individual Effects," *American Journal of Sociology*, 69 (1964), 585-95.

7. See Angus Campbell, Philip E. Converse, Warren E. Miller, and Donald E. Stockes, *The American Voter*, (New York: Wiley, 1960).

8. Jack Rosenthal et al., "The Outer City," *New York Times*, May 30-June 1971.

9. Individuals with a consistent pattern of opposition to the expansion of

federal power in areas other than employment, education, and housing were defined as conservatives. For a description of the derivation of this dimension from the 1968 survey data see Carl P. Hensler, "The Structure of Orientations Toward Government," Ph.D. dissertation, Massachusetts Institute of Technology, 1971.

10. Angus Campbell and Howard Schuman, *Racial Attitudes in Fifteen American Cities*, (Ann Arbor, Mich.: Institute for Social Research, 1970), 38.

11. Harlan Hahn, "Northern Referenda on Fair Housing: The Response of White Voters," *Western Political Quarterly*, 21 (1968), 483-95.

12. It is not uncommon to find that little attitudinal variance is explained by such independent variables. Schuman and Gruenberg were also able to explain very little variance in racial attitudes with individual social background variables and city of residence. They suggest that at least half of the attitudinal variance measured by a single item may be due to random error—miscoding, respondent inability to understand questions, etc.—and that if one assumes that almost all of the "explained variance" is free of random error then the proportion of variance explained may be double that which is actually obtained. Howard Schuman and Barry Gruenberg, "The Impact of City on Racial Attitudes," *American Journal of Sociology*, 76 (1970), 226.

13. Hahn, op. cit., 490.

Notes to Chapter 9

1. John Orbell and Kenneth Sherrill, "Racial Attitudes and the Metropolitan Context: A Structural Analysis," *Public Opinion Quarterly*, 33 (1969), 46-54.

2. Oliver P. Williams, Harold Herman, Charles S. Liebman, and Thomas R. Dye, *Suburban Differences and Metropolitan Policies* (Philadelphia: University of Pennsylvania Press, 1965).

3. The theoretical sampling design used in 1970 is described in Raymond Jessen, "Probability Sampling with Marginal Constraints," *Journal of American Statistics Association*, 65 (1970). The five regions used in this analysis are an aggregation of ten geographical strata used in the Fall, 1971, LAMAS sample; these strata are in turn built on Census Civil Divisions within the county. Strata boundaries correspond to political jurisdictions; those outside the central city include independent municipalities and some county unincorporated areas. The line dividing east and west portions of the city core was derived after consideration of local planning area maps, consultation with the UCLA School of Architecture and Planning, and analysis of 1970 racial distribution. Figures are based on 1970 First Count Census data. Income estimates are derived from median housing value/median monthly rent data, since median income is not available. The housing value variable was trichotomized to yield rough estimates of relative income: "low" ($15,000 or $75/month median), "median" ($22,000 or

$115/month median), "high" ($30,000 or $150/month median). 1970 statistics indicate a highly segregated housing pattern; "white" tracts in this sample are all more than 95 percent white, while "black" tracts are at least two-thirds black. Spanish-surname counts are not yet available, but tracts designated as Mexican-Americans have highly visible concentrations of this ethnic group.

4. Robert C. Wood, *Suburbia: Its People and Their Politics*, (Boston: Houghton Mifflin, 1959).

5. Ibid.

6. Amos H. Hawley and Basil G. Zimmer, *The Metropolitan Community: Its People and Government* (Beverly Hills, Sage Publications, 1970); Williams et al., op. cit.

7. James Q. Wilson, "The Urban Unease: Community vs. City," *The Public Interest* (1968), 25-39.

8. Carl Hensler, "The Structure of Orientations Toward Government," Ph.D. dissertation, Massachusetts Institute of Technology, 1971.

9. Howard Schuman and Barry Gruenberg, "The Impact of City on Racial Attitudes," *American Journal of Sociology*, 76 (1970), 213-61; John Orbell, "The Impact of Metropolitan Residence on Social and Political Orientations," *Social Science Quarterly*, 51 (1970), 634-48.

10. Schuman and Gruenberg, op. cit.

11. Basil G. Zimmer and Amos H. Hawley, "Opinions on School District Re-organization in Metropolitan Areas: A Comparative Analysis of the Views of Citizens and Officials in Central City and Suburban Areas," in Charles M. Bonjean, Terry N. Clark, and Robert L. Lineberry (eds.), *Community Politics: A Behavioral Approach* (New York: Free Press, 1971).

12. See Kevin P. Phillips, *The Emerging Republican Majority*, (Garden City, New York: Doubleday, 1970).

Notes to Chapter 10

1. U.S. Bureau of the Census, *City Government Finances in 1966-1967* (Washington: Government Printing Office, 1968), 1.

2. U.S. Bureau of the Census, *City Government Finances in 1968-1969* (Washington: Government Printing Office, 1970), 5. Other tax sources include income taxes, sales taxes, and license fees. Cities also raise money through the sale of electricity and water to their inhabitants and to the residents of nearby communities. Intergovernmental transfers, primarily in the form of grants-in-aid, also add to gross revenues.

3. Idem. Real estate taxes have a particularly stern effect on renters. Landlords shift the property tax forward in the form of increased rents, but the tenants may not deduct the increase from their federal tax liability.

4. Robert Wood, *Suburbia: Its People and Their Politics* (Boston: Houghton

Mifflin, 1959), 213-17. Also see Anthony Downs, "Home Ownership and American Free Enterprise," in *Urban Problems and Prospects* (Chicago: Markham, 1970), 156-64. Also note that property taxes tend to discourage low- and moderate-income families from improving their property. If the tax assessor is on his toes, any new amenity that adds to the property owner's comfort also raises his taxes. It also makes it more difficult for him to find a buyer for his home if he decides to move. Less concerned with incremental increases in his property tax, the wealthier man is not likely to think twice before installing a tennis court.

5. Evidence may be found in Robert C. Wood, *1400 Governments* (Garden City, N.Y.: Doubleday Anchor, 1964). Wood's factor analysis of municipal expenditure levels convincingly shows that industrialization was exceeded only by sheer population size in accounting for budgetary variation.

6. Seymour Sacks and William P. Hellmuth, *Financing Government in a Metropolitan Area* (New York: The Free Press, 1961), 84-100.

7. Ibid., 189 and the charts and tables following.

8. As Sacks and Hellmuth put it, "It is the *demand* for government services, rather than the tax base, that determines the level of expenditure, although the required tax base must be in existence." Ibid., 115. The emphasis is ours.

9. Eugene S. Uyeki, "Patterns of Voting in a Metropolitan Area, 1938-1962," *Urban Affairs Quarterly* (1966), 77. The Shevky-Bell index forms an ordered measure of social class.

10. James A. Norton, "Referenda Voting in a Metropolitan Area," *Western Political Quarterly*, 16 (1963), 109. His conclusions are further substantiated by Richard A. Watson and John H. Romani, "Metropolitan Government in Metropolitan Cleveland: An Analysis of the Voting Record," *Midwest Journal of Political Science*, 5 (1961), 365-90.

11. Their fears were not entirely misplaced. In a penetrating analysis of the same group of referendum elections, Edward C. Banfield and James Q. Wilson discovered that suburban voters were decidedly cool about financing welfare payments through an increased tax levy. Within the city itself, upper-income voters were more likely to favor welfare expenditures than their suburban counterparts. Upper-income Jews and Protestants, Banfield and Wilson argued, are motivated by a code of *noblesse oblige* which prompts them to redistribute income from rich to poor. As Mayor Carl Stokes has discovered, ethnic populations deriving from Southern and Central Europe do not abide by this ethos. See their "Voting Behavior on Municipal Expenditures: A Study in Rationality and Self-Interest," in Julius Margolis (ed.), *The Public Economy of Urban Communities* (Washington: Resources for the Future, 1965), 74-91.

Their conclusions have been disputed, however. They have been supported by Robert L. Lineberry and Edmund P. Fowler, "Reformism and Public Policies in American Cities," *American Political Science Review*, 61 (1967), 701-16. They have been challenged in Raymond Wolfinger and John O. Field,

"Political Ethos and the Structure of City Government," Ibid., 60 (1966), 306-26, and Roger E. Durand, "Ethnicity, Political Culture, and Urban Conflict," paper read at the 1970 meeting of the American Political Science Association.

12. Oliver P. Williams, Harold Herman, Charles S. Liebman, and Thomas R. Dye, *Suburban Differences and Metropolitan Policies: A Philadelphia Story* (Philadelphia: University of Pennsylvania Press, 1965).

13. Ibid., 72.

14. Ibid., 112-13.

15. Ibid., 161-62 and 178-79. It should be noted that the state's formula provided an incentive for neighboring communities of *similar social rank* to join together and form a school district. Since the size of the state subsidy was partially determined by the market value of property in all the jurisdictions making up the school district, low value suburbs would lose by combining with more affluent municipalities. So long as communities had roughly equal social ranks, it would pay them to consolidate because the cash value of the subsidy was pegged to the number of enrollments.

Equalization experience in these Philadelphia suburbs should not be taken as a national norm. James B. Guthrie and his colleagues have shown that in Michigan the state thrust reinforced existing inequalities; see their *Schools and Inequality* (Cambridge: MIT Press, 1971).

16. Ibid., 211-21. It is not entirely clear what is meant by maintaining the "quality" of residents. The authors' attempt to distinguish between "excluding undesirables" and "maintaining quality" is not completely convincing.

17. For another example, see Wood, *1400 Governments*, loc. cit.

18. In each state, subsidies are parcelled out more or less mechanically according to a settled procedure stipulated by the state legislature. But interstate variations are immense. California, for example, allocates money proportional to municipal population, a formula that works to the benefit of Los Angeles. Massachusetts hands out less than 1 percent of its subsidies on the same basis. It prefers to distribute the bulk of its subsidies to local communities according to their tax effort in reserving money for "meritorious" programs, making the state legislature a voting member of every local council. In California, the same type of subsidy accounts for just a bit more than a fifth of the total. See Ira Sharkansky, *Public Administration* (Chicago: Markham, 1970), 254.

19. For a review of some research to this effect, see Ibid., passim.

20. See Aaron Wildavsky, *The Politics of the Budgetary Process* (Boston: Little, Brown, 1964); John P. Crecine, *Governmental Problem-Solving* (Skokie, Illinois: Rand McNally, 1969); and Ira Sharkansky, *The Routines of Politics* (New York: Van Nostrand Reinhold, 1970).

Thus, Lineberry and Fowler, op. cit., in arriving at their conclusions, fail to discriminate among various objects of expenditure, do not adjust both taxes and expenditures to account for (or "control for") transfer payments from other levels of government, and, more seriously, divide taxes by a "city's aggregate personal income" to generate a measure of tax effort. This index is distorted because the greater bulk of municipal taxes derives from property wealth, not from the salary and wages which form personal income. The distortion is particularly severe in jurisdictions which combine high property values with low personal incomes. In older cities, as we have shown in chapter 2, high-income households choose to live in suburbs; and, as Williams and his colleagues have shown, residents of industrial suburbs have low incomes.

21. Leo F. Schnore and Robert R. Alford have calculated that almost 85 percent of all city manager suburbs have nonpartisan elections. See their "Forms of Government and Socio-economic Characteristics of Suburbs," *Administrative Science Quarterly*, 8 (1963), 9.

22. Wood, *Suburbia*, loc. cit., 184.

23. James Q. Wilson, "Problems in the Study of Local Politics," in Richard I. Hofferbert and Ira Sharkansky (eds.), *State and Urban Politics* (Boston: Little, Brown, 1970), 49. The emphasis is Wilson's. For a close study of over 80 San Francisco suburbs which emphasizes the political consequences and variations in the use of nonpartisan elections, cf. Willis D. Hawley, *Nonpartisan Urban Politics* (New York: John Wiley, 1972).

24. Wilson, Ibid., 48. Emphasis added. His concern echoes a plea Wood made over a decade before the detailed analysis: "By and large, no muckrakers have appeared on the scene to describe in chapter and verse the inner workings of suburban politics in the way that big city bosses and urban political-business alliances were detailed fifty years ago. This is not surprising; the number and variety of possible suburban political patterns make the documentation needed for sound generalizations an exceedingly formidable job. It is little wonder that we know most about our national, less about state, and least about local politics. The task of research expands geometrically as we go down the scale." Loc. cit., 177.

25. Richard A. Peterson, "Must the Quest After Variance End in History?" in Mayer N. Zald (ed.), *Power in Organizations* (Nashville: Vanderbilt University Press, 1970), 93.

Notes to Chapter 11

1. Bryan T. Downes, "Municipal Social Rank and the Characteristics of Local Political Leaders," *Midwest Journal of Political Science*, 12 (1968), 514-37. Also see his "Suburban Differentiation and Municipal Policy Choices: A Comparative Analysis of Suburban Political Systems," in Terry N. Clark (ed.), *Community Structure and Decision-Making: Comparative Analyses* (San Francisco: Chandler, 1968), 243-68.

2. Oliver Williams, et. al., *Suburban Differences and Municipal Policies* (Philadelphia: University of Pennsylvania Press, 1965), 228-29.

3. Bryan T. Downes, "Issue Conflict, Factionalism and Consensus in Suburban City Councils," *Urban Affairs Quarterly*, 4 (1969), 477-98.

4. Heinz Eulau, "The Informal Organization of Decisional Structures in Small Legislative Bodies," *Midwest Journal of Political Science*, 13 (1969), 341-66.

5. Kenneth Prewitt and Heinz Eulau, "Political Matrix and Political Representation: Prolegomenon to a New Departure from an Old Problem," *American Political Science Review*, 63 (1969), 427-41.

6. Ibid., 433.

7. John J. Kirlin, "Electoral Conflict in City Councilmanic Races of Los Angeles Suburbs," unpublished paper, University of California at Los Angeles, 1971. Kirlin argues that Prewitt and Eulau robbed their paper of its richness by failing to take into account the number of incumbent councilmen turned out of office in any single election. His point is that the simultaneous ousting of two or three councilmen represents a change in regime rather than the more or less random replacement of isolated office-holders.

A similar finding using Kirlin's approach, but treating school board turnovers, is John C. Walden, "School Board Changes and Superintendent Turnover," *Administrator's Notebook*, 15 (1967). This is a study of 117 school districts in southern California.

8. Lineberry and Fowler explicitly used two of these measures (percent native born of foreign or mixed parentage, and percent nonwhite) as measures of social cleavage, and strongly suggested the importance of a high incidence of poor families as another measure of social conflict. See their "Reformism and Public Policies in American Cities," *American Political Science Review*, 61 (1967), 706 and 711. The first is particularly suspect as a measure of potential social conflict, for it casually lumps together upper-class Scandinavians and lower-class Czechs, Germans and Hungarians, and so on. A community where nearly all those with this census label came from Northern and Western Europe is, we suspect, different from one split between Scandinavians and Mexican-Americans. The complement of this measure, the percentage of the population *not* derived from foreign stock, succumbs to the same ailment. It bunches together Arkies with Yankees and blacks with red-necks.

9. Charles R. Adrian, "A Typology of Nonpartisan Elections," *Western Political Quarterly*, 12 (1959), 449-58.

10. This account of politics in Gray View benefits from a paper by Julia Everitt. All proper names are pseudonymous.

11. This account draws on papers prepared by Julia Everitt, Diane Downs, and Barry Roseman.

12. This account draws on a paper by Karen Asselta.

13. Robert R. Alford and Eugene C. Lee have shown that turnout is consistently lower in nonpartisan elections. See their "Voter Turnout in American Cities," *American Political Science Review*, 62 (1968), 796-813.

14. Williams and Adrian argue that nonpartisanship boosts chances of minor-

ity party members in local elections. So long as they have accumulated a good record in laboring for worthwhile causes and publicly insist on the separation of local affairs from state and national politics, their partisan affiliations will not be held against them. See "The Insulation of Local Politics Under the Nonpartisan Ballot," *American Political Science Review*, 53 (1959), 1052-63. Republican leaders in Oaklawn feel that " . . . the intellectual approach of the younger Democrats is notable. They hold meetings without any political overtones, and the cultural lectures they have are impressing many people."

15. See Robert A. Dahl, *Who Governs?* (New Haven: Yale University Press, 1961), pp. 11-62.

16. Thomas Stege has supplied us with these data.

17. We are indebted to Richard L. Carson for this information drawn from his unpublished honors paper, "Three Council-Manager Villages Under Differing Political Systems," (Denison University, 1965).

Notes to Chapter 12

1. Robert C. Wood, *Suburbia* (Boston: Houghton Mifflin, 1959), 178-79. We agree with Wood that such idyllic suburbs probably are exceptional.

2. See Wendell Bell, "The City, the Suburb, and a Theory of Social Choice," in Scott Greer, Dennis L. McElrath, David W. Minar, and Peter Orleans (eds.), *The New Urbanization* (New York: St. Martin's Press, 1968), 132-68. In another connection, Seymour Martin Lipset has written "There is one particular aspect of American society that makes the academic community especially vulnerable, and that is the intense American concern for children. Many commentators have suggested that, as compared with other countries, the United States is a child-oriented society. The school system is, of course, the major non-familial institution concerned with the child. Consequently, charges that children are being 'corrupted' will meet a more attentive hearing than almost any others." See "The Fuss about Eggheads," *Encounter*, 8 (April, 1957), 21.

3. Alan K. Campbell and Seymour Sacks, *Metropolitan America: Fiscal Patterns and Governmental Systems* (New York: Free Press, 1967), 65.

4. Seymour Sacks and David C. Ranney, "Suburban Education: A Fiscal Analysis," *Urban Affairs Quarterly*, 2 (1966), 103-19. Fiscal patterns under new federal funds are analyzed in recent Ford study of six major states; see Joel S. Berke et al., *Federal Aid to Public Education: Who Benefits?* (Syracuse: Syracuse University Research Corporation, 1971), and a summary and supporting tables in *New York Times*, January 31, 1971.

5. Wood, op. cit., 219.

6. See Anthony Downs, *An Economic Theory of Democracy* (New York: Harper and Brothers, 1957), 170-74 for a lucid exposition. Actually, foundations for the merits of substituting compulsion for voluntary coordination ante-

date modern economic theory. In *A Treatise of Human Nature*, Hume wrote: "It is very difficult, and indeed impossible that a thousand persons should agree . . . while each seeks a pretext to free himself of the trouble and expense, and would lay the whole burden on others. Political society easily remedies both these inconveniences."

7. Benjamin Walter, "On Contrasts Between Private Firms and Governmental Bureaus," in Mayer N. Zald (ed.), *Power in Organizations* (Nashville: Vanderbilt University Press, 1970), 323.

8. William M. Dobriner, *Class in Suburbia* (Englewood Cliffs, N.J.: Prentice-Hall, 1963), 127-40.

9. Ibid., 137.

10. Ibid.

11. Ibid., 94-115.

12. David W. Minar, "The Community Basis of Conflict in School System Politics," *American Sociological Review*, 31 (1966), 822-35. A national survey attesting to this relationship is Richard F. Carter and John Sutthoff, *Voters and Their Schools* (Stanford: Stanford University Press, 1960).

13. This finding is somewhat unexpected. Studies of national elections have consistently shown that voting rates and political involvement are positive functions of social rank. However, Robert R. Alford and Eugene C. Lee, "Voter Turnout in American Cities," *American Political Science Review*, 62 (1968), 796-813, have convincingly demonstrated that turnout rates in local elections *decrease* when there are many well-educated people in the adult population. One likely explanation is that the caucus system of nomination reduces the number of options to one, hence there is no particular reason for anyone to cast a ballot.

14. Julia Everitt has supplied these data.

15. We have relied on an unpublished paper by Lauren Le Roy, Neil Naliboff, and Alan Greenwald, "Americana in Action: A Study of Government in La Piedra" (University of California, 1966).

16. We are indebted to Richard Carson. "Three Council-Manager Villages Under Differing Political Systems," undergraduate honors project, Denison University, 1955.

17. For an examination of the relationship between social prestige and access, see David B. Truman, *The Governmental Process* (New York: Alfred A. Knopf, 1951), 339-40.

18. For material on Shawnee Hills, we have relied on an unpublished paper by Donald E. Seymour.

19. Le Roy, et. al., op. cit.

20. Alexis de Tocqueville, *Democracy in America*, edited by Henry Steele Commager (New York and London: Oxford University Press, 1947), 109.

21. Roscoe C. Martin also emphasizes the episodic nature of suburban school conflict; see his *Government and the Suburban School* (Syracuse: Syracuse University Press, 1962). Similarly, a national survey of parental grievances with

schools find very few, of which only a small proportion take the form of collective action; see M. Kent Jennings, "Parental Grievances and School Politics," *Public Opinion Quarterly*, 32 (1968), 363-78.

For a full review of the nature of local school conflict, see Frederick M. Wirt and Michael Kirst, *The Political Web of American Schools* (Boston: Little, Brown, 1972), chs. 3-6.

22. Arthur J. Vidich and Joseph Bensman, *Small Town in Mass Society* (Garden City, New York: Doubleday-Anchor, 1960).

23. Op. cit., 139.

24. Robert A. Dahl, *Who Governs?* (New Haven: Yale University Press, 1961) and Herbert J. Gans, *The Levittowners* (New York: Vintage Books, Random House, 1969).

25. For a theoretical development of this process, see Laurence Iannaccone and Frank W. Lutz, *Politics, Power and Policy: The Governing of Local School Districts* (Columbus, Ohio: Merrill, 1970), and doctoral dissertations at Claremont Graduate School in 1966 under the direction of Iannaccone: Richard S. Kirkendall, "Discriminating Social, Economic and Political Characteristics of Changing versus Stable Policy-Making Systems in School Districts," and John C. Walden, "School Board Changes and Involuntary Superintendent Turnover."

26. Alvin D. Sokolow, *Governmental Response to Urbanization: Three Townships on the Rural-Urban Gradient*, U.S. Department of Agriculture, Economic Research Service, Dept. 132 (Washington: Government Printing Office, 1968), iv.

27. Scott Donaldson, *The Suburban Myth* (New York: Columbia University Press, 1969). "Political development" concepts have been applied in an exploratory study of the suburbs of Des Plaines, Elgin, and Highland Park, Illinois by John A. Rehfuss, "Political Development in Three Chicago Suburbs," paper presented at the American Political Science Association convention, 1971.

Notes to Chapter 13

1. John B. Orr and Patricia Nichelson, *The Radical Suburb* (Philadelphia: Westminster Press, 1960), 12-15.

2. From an address to the Association for the Advancement of Science reported in *Urban Research News*, 5 (March 29, 1971).

3. Martin Nolan, "HUD's Inheritance: A Belated Effort to Save Our Cities," *The Reporter Magazine, 37* (December 28, 1967), 18. Another set of estimates is provided by Nathan Glazer, "Housing Problems and Housing Policies," *The Public Interest* (Spring 1967), 21-51. In contrast to some 600,000 units of public housing built during the history of the program and 80,000 built under urban renewal, over five million units have been built under FHA home mortgage programs. Since FHA does not publish statistics by type of jurisdictions, but only

by size and construction type, we are here assuming most mortgage programs are in suburbs, while renewal and public housing are in the core cities. The assumption is supported by statements of the Kaiser Commission that "the main weakness of FHA from a social point of view has not been what it has done but in what it has failed to do—in its relative neglect of the inner cities and of the poor, and especially the Negro poor." The National Commission on Urban Problems, *Building the American City*, Report to the Congress and to the President of the U.S. (Washington: Government Printing Office, 1968), 100.

4. R. Solomon and A. Saltzman, "History of Transit and Innovative Systems," (Urban Systems Laboratory: MIT, 1970), #USS-TR-70-20).

5. See Alan A. Altshuler, "Transit Subsidies: By Whom, For Whom?" *Journal of the American Institute of Planners*, 35, (1969), Martin Wohl, "Income Circumstances of Public Transit Users," *Traffic Quarterly* (1970). Wohl points out that data usually apply to all commuters—including those working in central cities and also living there.

6. See Willard W. Brittain, "Metro: Rapid Transit for Suburban Washington," in D.M. Gordon (ed.), *Problems in Political Economy* (Lexington, Mass.: D.C. Heath, 1971), 439-42. Brittain notes that the District was the "victim of coalition politics by the suburban jurisdictions." The arena for this politicking is presumably congressional since the District does not have the power to raise bond issues itself.

7. E.g., see Ruby Martin and Phyllis McClure, *Title I of ESEA: Is It Helping Poor Children?* (Washington: Washington Research Project, 1969).

8. A Department of Rural and Suburban Government had been proposed to previous Congresses but received little attention. See U.S. House of Representatives, Report on Bill HR 6927, Committee on Government Operations, Washington, D.C., 1965.

9. Daniel Elazar argues, for example, that cities smaller than 50,000 do not develop a "citified" outlook in the political arena. See his "Urban Problems and the Federal Government," *Political Science Quarterly*, 82 (1967).

10. U.S. Bureau of the Census, *City Government Finances*, 1968-1969 (Washington: Government Printing Office, 1969). The two per capita figures are given because the municipalities over 50,000 are listed by six size groups and no aggregate per capita figure is given. Municipalities of 1,000,000 or more received $16.82 per capita: 500,000–1,000,000, $31.18; 300,000–500,000, $10.60; 200,000–300,000, $11.79; 100,000–200,000, $9.24; and 50,000–100,000, $7.27.

11. Lawrence Friedman, *Government and Slum Housing* (Chicago: Rand McNally, 1968).

12. *HUD Statistical Yearbook* (Washington: Government Printing Office, 1968), 247.

13. *City Government Finances*, op. cit.

14. Bernard Frieden and Jo Ann Newman, "Home Ownership for the Poor?" *Transaction*, 7 (October 1970), 52-53.

15. *HUD Yearbook*, 326.

16. A report on this analysis and its potential problems, is included in Francine F. Rabinovitz and John J. Kirlin, "The Recipients of HUD's Largesse: A Statistical Inquiry into Participation in HUD Development Programs," papers submitted to the Subcommittee on Housing, House Committee on Banking and Currency, U.S. House of Representatives (Washington: Government Printing Office, 1971), Part II.

17. See National Commission on Civil Disorders, *Report* (Washington: Government Printing Office, 1967); National Commission on Urban Problems, *Building the American City* (Washington: Government Printing Office, 1968), and The President's Committee on Urban Housing, *A Decent Home* (Washington: Government Printing Office, 1968), Three Volumes: The Report, Technical Studies, vols. I and II.

18. See, for example, Section 702 of the 1962 Housing Act. It states that a project cannot be funded unless it is consistent with criteria established by HUD for a unified or officially coordinated areawide water or sewer facility system that is part of the comprehensive planned development of the entire area. In 1965, an amendment sponsored by Senator Edmund Muskie authorized planning grants for organizations composed of elected public officials who are representative of jurisdictions within the metropolitan area. In 1966, the program was strengthened by section 204 of the Planned Metropolitan Development Act (Title II) which provided that all federally assisted projects with a metropolitan impact including airports, water supply, highways, law enforcement facilities, etc., must first be reviewed by an areawide agency. Companion Section 205 provided supplementary bonuses for projects made part of an areawide plan, but this section has never been funded. See Charles M. Haar, "Washington and Metropolis: A New Federalism," *Utah Law Review* (September, 1970), 511 ff.

19. "Suburban problems are deep and complex because suburb and city are no longer separable. Once upon a time the suburb was a distinct unit, standing downhill from the city, below its fortifications, outside its walls and beyond its law. It had been settled by exodus from the city of hardy colonists willing to forego the city's safety to escape its crowding, confusion and constraints. That was long ago. Now cities and their problems are no longer set apart from the suburbs by walls or even by political boundaries. The realities of civic life . . . no longer correspond to the inherited dividing lines . . . Any attempt, in today's circumstances, to solve suburban problems in isolation, as though they could still be solved separately from the general areas, is doomed to fail." Task Force on Suburban Problems, *Final Report: Summary* (December, 1968), unpublished, 10-11.

20. Charles M. Haar and Peter Lewis, "Where Shall the Money Come From?" *The Public Interest* 18 (Winter, 1970), 101-13, provides the chairman's public view of the task force. The source in note 19 provides the broader package of recommendations. There were some programs with distinctive appeal to wealth-

ier suburbs, including special transport systems for low density areas and noise abatement. Other programs were for suburban grey areas, such as an experiment to insure homeowners against losses due to racial integration and a series of investment conversion options for the elderly. But the cornerstone of task force concerns was URBANK.

21. Orr and Nichelson, op. cit., 14-15. These authors are in disagreement with this view.

22. See John Kain, "Postwar Changes in Land Use in the American City," in Daniel P. Moynihan (ed.), *Toward a National Urban Policy* (New York: Basic Books, 1969), and "Alternatives to the Guilded Ghetto," in James Q. Wilson (ed.), *The Metropolitan Enigma* (Cambridge: Harvard University Press, 1969).

23. Anthony Downs, "Alternative Future for the American Ghetto," *Daeda lus*, 97 (1968), 1331-78, provides an excellent description of the alternative strategies.

24. James V. Valtierra, 91 U.S. 1331 (1971).

25. Haar, op. cit., 24.

26. The Act directs the HUD Secretary to "administer the programs and activities relating to housing and urban development in a manner affirmatively to further the policies of this [fair housing] title." 42 U.S.C. 2601.

27. See Steven Erie, John J. Kirlin, and Francine F. Rabinovitz, "Can Something Be Done?: Propositions on Metropolitan Institutional Performance," in Haar (ed.), *The Governance of Metropolitan Areas* (Washington: Resources for the Future Monograph Series, forthcoming).

28. See *New York Times*, November 7, 1969.

29. Ibid., November 6, 1970.

30. This summary relies on William Lilley, "Housing Report: Romney Faces Political Perils with Plan to Integrate the Suburbs," *National Journal*, 2, (1970), 2251-63. Vice President Agnew's statement was actually drawn from Paul Davidoff, Linda Davidoff, and Neil N. Gold, "Suburban Action: Advocate Planning for an Open Society," *Journal of the American Institute of Planners*, 36 (1970), 13. See also *New York Times*, March 10, 1970.

31. An emerging alliance of large builders and civil liberties proponents in 1970 was pressing for action by courts and higher governmental jurisdictions against large-lot zoning. The technique is so much used in suburbia that 80 percent of land zoned for residence within fifty miles of Times Square required a half-acre lot per dwelling by 1960. Seventy percent of all land zoned residential by towns in Connecticut is also zoned to require one acre or more per house. This is obviously opposed by building interests.

A number of recent lower court decisions go in the direction of prohibiting ordinances which restrict access to the community. The constitutional argument rests on the notion that discrimination in housing violates rights of the poor to equal protection. See Lawrence Sager, "Tight Little Islands of Exclusionary Zoning," 21, *Stanford Law Review* 767 (1969). However, the waters are muddied by the recent Supreme Court decision cited earlier that citizens may block low-rent housing projects by referendum.

In addition, Massachusetts has passed a law which provides that communities set aside a portion of their zoned land for federal low- and middle-income housing, although no community is required to give up more than .3 percent of its residentially zoned land in any one year, and each locale sets its own health and safety provisions. (Mass. Session Laws, 1969, Ch. 774.) Also, Senator Abraham Ribicoff has introduced a bill to forbid a government agency or contractor from locating in any community unless enough low-cost housing is available there to accommodate employees. The object is to force communities to modify restrictive zoning laws or give up luring federally supported industries.

32. *Washington Post*, June 12, 1971, A6.

33. "Statement by the President on Federal Policies Relative to Equal Housing Opportunity," White House Press Release, June 11, 1971, 11, 13.

34. A critique of the weakness of this agreement is made by Robert Cassidy, "GSA Plays the Suburban Game," *City* 5, Fall, 1971, 12-14, 72.

35. See 1970 State of the Union Address of President Richard M. Nixon as one example of this thinking.

36. See Charles L. Edson, "From Capitol Hill: The Housing and Urban Development Act of 1970," *The Urban Lawyer* (1971), 3, 142-5, for a review of the provisions. A history of the wranglings which preceded floor defeat and a conference committee success, is provided in Report #6 of the New Towns Development Research Project, Center for Urban and Regional Studies, University of North Carolina at Chapel Hill, December 7, 1970. See also, *New York Times*, December 19, 1970 and January 2, 1971.

37. William Nicoson, Director of the Office of New Community Development described the public interest in such new towns:

The history of urban growth has been an appalling misuse of a major national resource, land, through piecemeal urban development. Individual decisions, often unrelated, have not led to rational development. It is a first priority of federal policy to make the inevitable process of urban development rational, and provide for a firm planning basis to assure preservation and efficient utilization of resources, including land, water, air and human resources.

Statement to New Towns Development Research Seminar, University of North Carolina, Chapel Hill, North Carolina, Nov. 2, 1970, (John G. Brandenburg, Reporter), 9.

38. Herbert Gans, "The White Exodus to Suburbia Steps Up," *The New York Times Magazine*, Jan. 17, 1968.

39. One commentator reports: "Among many Nixon appointees, particularly centered in the Office of Management and Budget (formerly the Bureau of the Budget) there is a strong desire and commitment to improve the federal system. Their reasons went beyond the more traditional opposition to strong central government and the belief that more efficient management reduced spending needs,

although these motives undoubtedly encouraged much Administration support. The most articulate advocates of the New Federalism pointed to the sheer untidiness of the system, the obvious merit of consolidating grant-in-aid programs and decentralizing the administrative burden in Washington." Judson L. James, "Federalism and the Model Cities Experiment," paper delivered at the 1970 Annual Meeting of the American Political Science Association, 13.

10. A. James Reichley, "The Political Containment of the Cities," in Alan K. Campbell (ed.), *The States and the Urban Crisis* (Englewood Cliffs, N.J.: Prentice Hall, Inc., 1970), 169-95.

Notes to Chapter 14

1. It is tantalizing to speculate on whether dispersal could have become official policy if the president (and the courts at a later stage) backed it. In 1970, the answer is probably that dispersal would be politically unfeasible even with presidential support. Huitt, writing about political feasibility, notes that "Low feasibility also must be attached to whatever is genuinely new or innovative; especially if it rubs an ideological nerve." Dispersal was labeled as new and clearly touched a currently raw issue in regard to the federal role on race. See Ralph Huitt, "Political Feasibility," in Ira Sharkansky (ed.), *Policy Analysis in Political Science* (Chicago: Markham, 1970), 411.

2. This progression tends to confirm the hypothesis put forward by Robert Salisbury and John Heinz that when it is costly to organize the coalition needed to support a policy on an issue, it is likely the policy outcome will be structural, not distributive. See their "A Theory of Policy Analysis and Some Preliminary Applications," in Sharkansky, Ibid, 39-60.

3. See Harold Wolman, *Politics of Housing* (New York: Dodd, Mead, 1971); Suzanne Farkas, *Urban Lobbying* (New York: New York University Press, 1971); and Frederick Cleveland (ed.), *Congress and Urban Problems* (Washington: The Brookings Institution, 1969).

4. Rabinovitz is grateful to Judson L. James for providing materials emphasizing this point. See his *The Single System: American Intergovernmental Relationships*, ms., August, 1971.

5. Andrew Hacker, *Congressional Districting: The Issue of Equal Representation* (Washington: The Brookings Institution, 1963) 111.

6. Michael Danielson, *Federal Metropolitan Politics and the Commuter Crisis* (New York: Columbia University Press, 1965).

7. Morley Segal and A. Lee Fritschler, "Emerging Patterns of Intergovernmental Relations," in *Municipal Year Book, 1970,* (Washington: International City Management Association, 1970), 13-38.

8. *Congressional Quarterly*, 24 (Dec. 23, 1966), 3054-55.

9. Ira Sharkansky, "Voting Behavior of Metropolitan Congressmen: Pros-

pects for Changes with Reapportionment," *Journal of Politics*, 28 (1966), 774-93.

10. Cleveland, Ibid., 138 and 371.

11. For a review and analysis which notes the conflicting findings from different states on this matter, concluding that constituency differences are related to legislative vote differences under some conditions, see Thomas Flinn, "Party Responsibility in the States: Some Causal Factors," *American Political Science Review*58 (1964), 60-71.

12. Richard Lehne, "Warming Up for 1972," *Trans-Action* September 1971; Gerald M. Pomper, "Census '70: Power to the Suburbs," *The Washington Monthly*, May 1970 pp. 20-25. Rabinovitz is grateful to Richard Lehne for discussions on this point.

13. Martin Nolan, "HUD's Inheritance: A Belated Effort to Save Our Cities," *Reporter Magazine*, 37 (December 28, 1967), 16, writes, for example, that "The FHA since 1935 issued more than $84 billion in mortgage insurance, creating suburbia and helping to entice middle income families from central cities without due compensation to the cities." See also Martin Anderson, *The Federal Bulldozer* (Cambridge, Mass.: MIT Press, 1964).

14. Herbert J. Savliner, Harold G. Halcorn, and Neil H. Jacoby, *Federal Lending and Loan Insurance* (Princeton: Princeton University Press, 1958), 344. Rabinovitz is grateful to Karen Orren for clarifying the impact of FHA policies.

15. See the discussion in Glenn Beyer, *Housing and Society* (New York: Macmillan, 1965), 361 ff.

16. *Los Angeles Times*, April 19, 1971. A more thorough critique is found in this Commission's *Civil Rights Enforcement Effort* (Washington: Government Printing Office, 1970).

17. See Steven Erie, John J. Kirlin, and Francine F. Rabinovitz, "Can Something Be Done: Propositions on Metropolitan Institutional Performance," Haar (ed.), *The Governance of Metropolitan Areas* (Washington, D.C.: Resources for the Future Monograph Series, forthcoming); and Office of Executive Management, Bureau of the Budget, "Section 204 of the Demonstration Cities and Metropolitan Development Act of 1966: Two Years Experience" (Washington: Government Printing Office, 1970).

18. Martha Derthick, "Defeat at Fort Lincoln: A Case Study of a Housing Fiasco," *The Public Interest*, 20 (Summer, 1970), 38.

19. The Ralph Nader Study Group Report, *Land and Power in California* provides some illustrations.

20. Richard F. Babcock and Fred T. Bosselman, "The Contest for Public Control over Land Development," UCLA Institute of Government and Public Affairs MR-149 (Los Angeles: April 16, 1970).

21. "The City As It Is and As It Might Be," *Building the American City* report by National Commission on Urban Problems, 1968, reprinted in Louis K. Lowenstein (ed.), *Urban Studies* (New York: Free Press, 1971), 85-86.

22. See Bernard J. Frieden, "Blacks in Suburbia: The Myth of Better Opportunities," in Haar (ed.), *The Governance of Metropolitan Areas*, op. cit.; Leonard Blumberg and Michael Lalli, "Little Ghettoes: A Study of Negroes in the Suburbs," *Phylon*, 27 (1966), 117-31, and, for 1970 data, see this volume, chapter 4, 70 ff.

23. *New York Times*, Nov. 11, 1969, cited in Frieden, ibid.

24. For the substance of such proposals, see Adam Yarmolinsky, "Reassuring the Small Homeowner," *The Public Interest*, 22 (Winter, 1971), 106-10, and Anthony Downs, "Alternative Futures for the American Ghetto," *Urban Problems and Prospects* (Chicago: Markham, 1971), 27-74.

25. It is quite possible that the aftermath of any effort by courts to attack snob zoning would be as agonized as that which followed the 1954 school deseg regation decisions. See P.B. Kurland, "Educational Opportunity," *University of Chicago Law Review*, 35 (1968), 583 ff., for an analysis of the reasons for the courts' difficulties on such issues.

26. James C. Johnson, "Small Cities in the Metropolitan Sea: The Relationship between Black and White," Institute of Government and Public Affairs, MR; Reynolds Farley, "The Changing Distribution of Negroes within Metropolitan Areas," *American Journal of Sociology*, 75 (1970), 512-29; Ozzie Edwards, "Residential Segregation within the Metropolitan Ghetto," *Demography*, 7 (1970), 185-93.

27. *New York Times*, March 9, 1970, 22.

28. Ibid., May 31, 1971.

29. A comprehensive discussion of this question from the viewpoint of the economist appears in Marion Clawson, *Suburban Land Conversion in the United States* (Baltimore: Johns Hopkins Press, 1971), ch. 17.

30. The Nixon Administration's 1970 housing proposals were premised on this notion. They simplified the subsidy system, for example, into rental and home ownership programs for privately owned, FHA-insured housing and a revised public housing program. See Donald D. Kummerfeld, "The Housing Subsidy System," *Papers Submitted to Subcommittee on Housing Panels*, Part 2 (Washington: Government Printing Office, 1971).

31. Oliver Williams, for example, says: "There may be an implication that this (book) is written to advocate metropolitan government. In a way that impression is correct. But by metropolitan government we cannot simply mean the consolidation of city and suburbs. The urban form is becoming too extensive, complex, amorphous and centerless for that. Instead it is suggested that urban polities needs to be politicized, and once the urban process becomes more political, it will probably lead to the creation of large-scale administrative units." See *Metropolitan Political Analysis: A Social Access Approach* (New York: Free Press, 1971), 110. It is important to note that Williams makes this suggestion in full awareness of reasons why metropolitan reform arrangements have been rejected in the U.S. in the past. See for example his "Life Style Values and Political Decentralization in Metropolitan Areas," *Southwestern Social Science Quarterly*, 48 (1967), 299-310.

32. Committee for Economic Development, *Reshaping Government in Metropolitan Areas* (New York: CED, 1970).

33. Such a proposal is made by Lester C. Thurow, "Goals of a Housing Program," and in a somewhat different form by William C. Wheaton, et. al., "Housing Needs and Urban Development," Papers Submitted to Subcommittee on Housing Panels, op. cit. The Subcommittee recommended a system of housing bloc grants to state and metropolitan housing agencies to restructure housing assistance programs on an areal basis. See H.R. 9688, 92nd Congress, lst Session, July 8, 1971.

34. Rabinovitz is indebted to William L.C. Wheaton for discussion on this point.

35. H.R. 9688, 92nd Congress, lst Session, House of Representatives, July 8, 1971. Introduced by Rep. Wright Patman (D-Texas).

36. Strong arguments both for eliminating the bureaucratic layer and backing revenue sharing are made by Edward Banfield. See his *The Unheavenly City* (Boston: Little Brown, 1971) and "Revenue Sharing in Theory and Practice," *The Public Interest*, 23 (Spring, 1971), 33-45.

37. Serrano v. Priest, 89 Cal. Rptr. 345.

Author Index

Unitalicized numbers refer to pages; italicized numbers in a set refer to footnotes, the first being the chapter and the second and successive the footnote numbers.

243

Subject Index

Advisory Commission on Intergovernmental Relations, 28

affluence, and development of suburbs, 20, 21

Agnew, Spiro, 187

"agrarianism in reverse", 179–183

air pollution, attitudes towards, 126; control, future support for, 197

Akron, Ohio, 12

Albuquerque, New Mexico, 29

Aliquippa, Pennsylvania, 12, 35

Allegheny, Pennsylvania, 9

Alton, Illinois, 12

Ambridge, Pennsylvania, 12

American Society of Planning Officials, and metropolitan planning, 192

The American Voter, 73

annexation, 137, 217, *n3/4*

Baldwin Park, California: school expenditure in, 209

Barberton, Ohio, 12

Bay Area Rapid Transit (BART) and suburbs, 179

Beacon Hill (Boston), 11

Berkeley, California, 45

Beverly Hills, California, and school expenditure, 209

black: capitalism, alternatives to, 184; enclaves, 47; homeownership, suburb-city compared, 43; population, suburban, 203; power and dispersal policy, 187; suburb, analysis of, 35–48; suburbanization, constraints on, 43–46; suburbs, movement to post-WW II, 35, 203; SEE ALSO discrimination; dispersal; housing; integration; industrial suburbs; migration, black; Negroes; segregation; socioeconomic status; suburbs, black, housing of in certain suburbs, 39; racial distinction among, 41; and home-workplace relationship, 44–45; and federal home loan programs, 181

Blackjack, Missouri, and public housing, 186

Boston: and immigration, 16; population movement and voting patterns, 82; suburbs: history of, 5, 6, 8–12; presidential voting in (1950's), 83; attitudes in (case study), 117–125

Boston Area Survey Project, 118

Brookline, Massachusetts, 11, 35

Brooklyn, New York, 8, 12

Bucks County, Pennsylvania, 81

budgetary analysis and civic pluralism, 142–144; decisions and political judgments, 141; and community factors, 142

Burlingame, California, 11

business, dispersion to suburbs: SEE industrial suburbs; job opportunities; suburbs and dispersion of industry

businessmen and zoning politics, 168

California Supreme Court and school financing (Serrano v. Priest), 209, *n14/37*

Cambridge, Massachusetts, 8

Carnegie, Andrew, 12

Catholics, status of and local conflict (case study), 164

caucus system in local politics, 150–156, 165, 170, *n12/13*

Census Bureau SEE United States Bureau of the Census

Charlestown, Massachusetts, 8

Chestnut Hill, Pennsylvania, 11

Chevy Chase, Maryland, 6

Chicago: and immigration, 16; blacks in, 39–40; suburbs: history of, 9–12; political behavior in (1952), 51

Cincinnati suburban population (19th cent.), 9

cities: SEE ALSO suburbs-core city comparison; suburb-core city relationship; urban fringe, population, 7; history, 7–8, 15–17; as suburbs (20th cent.), 18; legal restraints and freedoms of, 133

city: definition of, 3, 104; as port of entry, 47

civic associations and suburban elections, 143, 148, 170

civil rights: SEE ALSO blacks, and enforcement, *n4/17, 18*

Civil Rights Act of 1968, *n4/7*

Civil Rights Subcommittee of President Nixon's Domestic Affairs Council, 187

class SEE socioeconomic status

Cleveland: and immigration, 16; revenue-expenditure patterns in (case study), 137–139; voting patterns in, *n10/10, 11*

Cohoes, New York, and Model Cities program, 181

Columbia, Maryland, 188

Columbus, Ohio and immigration, 16; attitudes in suburbs of, 103, 117, 124

Compton, California: and Model Cities program, 181; blacks in, 203n

community attachment attitudes (case study) 121–122

community good SEE public interest

About the Authors

Frederick M. Wirt earned advanced degrees from Ohio State and he has taught at Denison University and University of California, Berkeley. At the latter he has been visiting professor in the Department of Political Science, research political scientist in the Institute of Governmental Studies, lecturer in the School of Education, and director of the Institute for Desegregation Problems. He has written articles in American politics and civil rights, edited anthologies on civil rights, community power, and research problems. He is author of *Politics of Southern Equality: Law and Social Change in a Mississippi County* (Aldine, 1970), which received honorable mention for the Woodrow Wilson award in his profession for 1970. He is co-author of the forthcoming book, *The Political Web of American Schools* (Little, Brown).

Benjamin Walter took his undergraduate work at Yale University, graduating with a degree in History in 1952. He took his master's degree at Syracuse University and his doctorate at Northwestern. Before going to Vanderbilt, he taught political science at the University of North Carolina at Chapel Hill.

Francine F. Rabinovitz is Associate Professor of Political Science at UCLA and also a member of the faculty of the School of Architecture and Urban Planning. Her previous books in the field of comparative urban politics include *City Politics and Planning*, and with co-authors, *Urban Government for Greater Stockholm* and *Latin American Urban Research* (co-editor).

Deborah Rosenfield Hensler was born in New York in 1942 and experienced the middle-class trip from city to suburb while growing up there. She attended Hunter College, where she was elected to Phi Beta Kappa, and graduated summa cum laude in 1963. Ms. Hensler was a doctoral student in political science at the Massachusetts Institute of Technology from 1963 to 1968 and is currently attempting to complete her doctoral dissertation on the impact of suburban residence on political attitudes. Since 1970 she has been Assistant Director of the UCLA Survey Research Center, where she is coordinator of technical operations and director of the community research program. She has two children, Benjamin, age 4, and Rebecca, age 3, and an extremely liberated husband, Carl Peter Hensler, who is also a political scientist and her favorite colleague.